Praise for this

The late Pope John Paul II once referred to the Jewish people as "our elder brothers in the faith of Abraham." This insightful, probing, and very creative collection of essays on Jewish spirituality, edited by Rabbi Howard Addison, examines the many nuances of the Jewish understanding of redemption from a variety of perspectives and, in doing so, offers a fundamental backdrop against which Catholics and other Christians can examine their own understanding of the concept. For this reason, it is an invaluable tool for deepening our understanding of the roots our Christian heritage, challenging it, enriching it, and transforming it, so that we may enter into dialogue with our Jewish sisters and brothers and, indeed, with all who look to Abraham as their father in faith.

Dennis J. Billy, C.Ss.R, ThD, STD, DMin
John Cardinal Krol Chair of Moral Theology (2008-16)
St. Charles Borromeo Seminary
Author, *Conscience and Prayer: The Spirit of Catholic Moral Theology*

Rabbi Mordecai Kaplan, the founder of Judaism's Reconstructionist movement, taught that divine redemption is manifest in the human commitment to creativity and our efforts to achieve freedom. That understanding of salvation is exemplified in this fascinating volume. It explores spiritual direction, dance, art, liturgical innovation and social activism as practices for twenty-first-century spiritual renewal. In turn it connects them to Process Theology, beliefs in reincarnation and liberation theology in thought-provoking ways. It is important reading, especially for all who want insights into avenues for reinvigorating Jewish life.

Rabbi David A. Teutsch, PhD, DHL, DD
Wiener Professor Emeritus, Reconstructionist Rabbinical College
Editor in Chief, *Kol Haneshamah* Prayer Book Series

Seeking Redemption in an Unredeemed World offers fresh and diverse Jewish perspectives on the concept of redemption in Jewish life. I am delighted by its exciting new additions to the growing literature on Judaism and Spirituality, particularly in the area of Social Justice and Faith. There is no more important issue in our time, and this book is a wonderful resource, especially to all pursuers of justice. May our holy work be blessed!

Rabbi Amy Eilberg, DMin
Coordinator, Jewish Community Engagement, Faith in Action Bay Area
Author, *From Enemy to Friend: Jewish Wisdom and the Pursuit of Peace*

Seeking Redemption in an Unredeemed World is . . . a rich trove of Jewish historical interpretations of and approaches to the concept of redemption . . . Rabbi Addison's book is equally a message and a challenge to Muslims and Christians. Surely, the concept of redemption, in all of its expressions, is a constant theme in their theologies. Which Christian, which Muslim, would argue with the notion: "All life is interdependent. All life is interconnected?"

Shaykh Ibrahim Abdul-Malik, EdD, PhD
Ecumenical Studies, Fairleigh-Dickinson University
Co-editor, *Learning to Lead: Lessons in Leadership for People of Faith*

SEEKING REDEMPTION
IN AN UNREDEEMED WORLD

Essays in Jewish Spirituality

Edited by

Howard Avruhm Addison

GTF Books

Mishawaka

Seeking Redemption in an Unredeemed World:
Essays in Jewish Spirituality

by Howard Avruhm Addison

Published by GTF Books
Graduate Theological Foundation
Mishawaka, Indiana 46544 USA

Cover image: Copyright Elyssa Wortzman © 2018

ISBN (paperback) 978-1-7327134-0-6 / (ebook) 978-1-7327134-1-3

Printed in the United States of America on recycled paper.

Table of Contents

Foreword

When I first approached Rabbi Addison's *Seeking Redemption in an Unredeemed World*, I was prepared for a "universal" exploration of ways of finding redemption in places where the concept of being saved from sin or evil is not much in evidence. What I found instead was a rich trove of Jewish historical interpretations of and approaches to the concept of redemption. As a consequence, I quickly went from being a casual reader to being very personally invested in the unfolding themes and approaches.

One example that spoke powerfully to me is the fact that Judaism sees history as a spiral . . . cyclical, yet each cycle advances the arc of history from Creation toward the End of Days. As a Muslim, I resonate deeply with that concept.

Clearly, Creation, Revelation and Redemption are the three themes/events that have been central to Judaism throughout its long history. But there is no gainsaying that Redemption is the preeminent one. And beyond the many Hebrew words (and their definitions) that explain "redemption," the writers certainly confirm how these multiple explanations and approaches have reflected the great diversity in Jewish thought.

Yet I would be remiss if I did not also express how Rabbi Addison's book is equally a message and a challenge to Muslims and Christians, who recognize the times, places and figures of Judaism. Surely, the concept of redemption, in all its expressions, is a constant theme in their theologies. Which Christian, which Muslim would argue with the notion: "All life is interdependent. All life is interconnected?"

The unremitting fact is that while we often use the same words in our dialogue, when we are faced with truly challenging situations that demand *grace, humility, patience, and generosity*, more often than not, we come up short.

How do we deal with new/different concepts? In Barbara Breitman's article, "The Arc of Becoming: Process Theology and Jewish Spiritual Direction," she offers an interesting possibility—to consider God, not as a "Being," but as a "Process." Are we too stuck on the former to entertain the possibility of the latter?

At the beginning of the article, Dr. Breitman quotes Rabbi Toba Spitzer:

> God's reality does not stand at an untouchable remove from the created world, but . . . **is in process with it** *[my emphasis]*. Our godly task here on earth is to be partners in the process of becoming.

Yes, according to Qur'anic teaching, the idea of associating partners with God is entirely forbidden. But what about the first sentence? Does it challenge us to re-examine (at minimal, reflect on) our concept of God? The author reminds us that "we need ways of thinking about God that are consistent with how we understand and experience reality." And surely our 2018 understanding and experience of reality are quite different from what our forebears understood and experienced centuries ago. Does our current concept of The Creator reflect the realities of our time?

Undoubtedly there are those who will reject, out of hand, any thinking that probes their static views and beliefs; but we cannot escape the reality that life itself is dynamic, **not static.** Even our universe is expanding. Or to use the words of Process Theology: all of reality is "in process;" all of life is becoming.

Challenge? To many, many.
Worthy of consideration? Absolutely.

Shaykh Ibrahim Abdul-Malik, EdD, PhD
Ecumenical Studies, Fairleigh-Dickinson University
Co-editor, *Learning to Lead: Lessons in Leadership for People of Faith*
New York, September 2018

Preface

When people from different faith traditions begin to talk together they quickly discover that they share a vocabulary: they speak of "salvation," of "Messiah/Saviour," of "redemption," of "sin" and "grace." But as the discussion proceeds the impression may form that these traditions are religions divided rather than united by a common vocabulary. They use the same words—but do they mean the same thing?

At the hard end, they certainly don't. If, for instance, a Muslim understands "salvation" as Allah's vindication of the righteous and the penitent at the end of time that they may enjoy Paradise everlasting, the Christian understands "salvation" as "rescue by Jesus from the consequences of Adam's sin" and a Jew understands "salvation"—as do several contributors to this volume—to mean something like "spiritual guidance beyond human words," they are not going to make much sense of each other without unravelling their respective vocabularies, and even then, may fail to see eye-to-eye on basic issues. But the reality is softer and more nuanced. Within Christianity, within Islam, and within Judaism, a range of meanings has been assigned to the basic terms. It is this broad and often overlapping range, rather than any conventionally defined theology, that allows communities to work together to adapt and thrive in a changing world and to work together for the common healing.

I warmly welcome the initiative of the editor, Rabbi Howard Avruhm Addison, PhD, and his talented team at the Graduate Theological Foundation, in exploring the possibilities for developing the foundational Jewish notions of "redemption/salvation" in a contemporary context.

Theology, liturgy, sociology and even politics are reinterpreted, drawing on a wide range of sources from Bible, Talmud, midrash, Kabbalah, and popular Jewish custom.

Imagination and the arts, including dance (I love Julie Leavitt's image of "spirituality and God [as] great dance partners."), are viewed as channels for spiritual growth, while the role of dreams in "the revitalization of religious practice and societal healing" is explored by Addison himself. Arthur Waskow ("The Shofar and the White House") and Mordechai Liebling ("Imagining a Theology of Jewish Liberation") address what some might regard as politically contentious issues. However, even those who cannot fully endorse their critiques of current American and Israeli policies must acknowledge that if "redemption" is to mean anything in the contemporary world it is that we have a sacred calling to responsible stewardship of the Earth and to support ("redeem") the disadvantaged and the oppressed, wherever and whoever they might be.

Thoughtful consideration is given to readers who find the traditional Judeo-Christian and Islamic concepts of God and of life after death problematic. How can their doubts, which several of the contributors evidently share, be accommodated within the proposed new understandings of "redemption?" Constructive suggestions are made.

The contributors are all Jewish. Charlotte Sutker, to whom the title "Jew by Choice" is personally significant, calls us to a new awareness of the varied paths that can lead adherents to Judaism. However, this is very much a book to be shared by people of all faiths. Each, in his or her own way, will be challenged to work out the implications for life and work today of the great tradition of God's deliverance in the past and of how we are called to carry forward that deliverance both within the societies in which we live and in our individual spiritual journeys

Rabbi Norman Solomon, PhD
Senior Associate, Oxford Centre for Hebrew
and Jewish Studies
Author of *Torah from Heaven: The Reconstruction of Faith*
Oxford, UK, August 2018

Editor's Note

on Transliteration, Abbreviation, Textual References...and Gratitude

As one might expect from an anthology devoted to Jewish Spirituality, the essays that follow contain a great many Hebrew terms, with some Yiddish, Aramaic and a smattering of other languages included for good measure. Their transliteration is based on the 2013 Mesorah Matrix Guidelines (New Paradigm Matrix Publishing, New York) and appear in *italics*. Ḥ will represent *Ḥet*, the eighth letter of the Hebrew *Aleph-Bet; kh will* signify *Khaf*, the eleventh. Exceptions to this format include: the proper names of persons and places publicly known by different transliteration schema (i.e. *Elat Chayyim* rather than *Eilat Ḥayim*, Retreat Center) and Hebraisms which have become part of the United States English lexicon (i.e. Hanukkah, Kabbalah, Hasidism). The letters of certain words have been bolded to show their relationship through shared or homonymous Hebrew roots. The tetragrammaton, God's ineffable four-letter name, will be transliterated as *YHWH*, and translated as the Eternal.

Rather than having the reader consult a glossary again and again, we have attempted to clarify potentially obscure terms and the names of unfamiliar persons and texts as they appear, either within the body of the article or in a longer explanatory note at the essay's end.

A word about the names, nature and nomenclature of rabbinic literature. The Talmud is the major corpus of classical Rabbinic law and lore; it is composed of two sections. The *Mishnah*, a Hebrew compilation of laws interspersed with some anecdotal and aphoristic material, was codified by Rabbi Judah the Prince in approximately 200 CE. The *Gemara* contains wide-ranging legal analyses and homiletical reflections on the issues raised in the *Mishnah*. The more inclusive and authoritative version, the Babylonian Talmud (*BT*), was redacted between 500-600 CE; the Jerusalem Talmud (*JT*) was redacted between 350-400 CE. Thus, standard Talmudic citations include the version abbreviation, tractate name, folio number and the side of the page being quoted (e.g. *BT Shabbat 25a*).

Other rabbinic works mentioned in this volume include: texts contemporaneous with but not included in the *Mishnah*, known collectively as *Braitot* (sing. *Braita*); collections of legal *midrash* (e.g. *Sifrei* on Numbers and Deuteronomy) and homiletical *midrash* (e.g. *Lamentations Rabbah* or *Pesikta de-Rav Kahana*) often organized by biblical book and verse or by holy day, and later legal compilations, such as Moses Maimonides' *Mishneh Torah* (lit. "The Reiteration of Torah"), compiled 1170-80 CE. Kabbalistic and hasidic works are explained as they appear throughout the anthology.

Finally, let me thank the administration and staff of the Graduate Theological Foundation, including its President, Kendra Clayton, President Emeritus, John Morgan, and its Director of Publications, Kyna Morgan. Their insight, encouragement and skill, from this project's inception on, have proved invaluable.

Thanks also go to Cantor Naomi Hirsch: your attentive copyediting and standardizing of Hebrew transliteration has added immeasurably to the quality of this volume. To paraphrase a Talmudic blessing, your efforts have allowed us to see that which we envisioned come to life in our world.

Howard Avruhm Addison,
Philadelphia, PA
September 2018

Introduction

Celebrating Partial Redemptions

Howard Avruhm Addison

Rava said: *When assessing one's life after departing this world, the Heavenly Tribunal will ask... did you glimpse redemption?*[1]

The German Jewish theologian, Franz Rosenzweig (d. 1929), asserted that the Jewish view of history rests on three pillars: Creation, Revelation and Redemption.[2] While each of these infuse and mutually effect the others (e.g. Creation redeems reality from chaos, Revelation creates anew the relationship between humans and the divine), one could argue that Judaism values Redemption as pre-eminent among the three. Unlike ancient mythological religions, which understood history as a continuing reenactment of patterns shaped by the gods before time began, Judaism, from antiquity on, has viewed history as a spiral. While the seasons cycle yearly, history's vector proceeds from Creation through God's initial salvific act; the Exodus from Egypt; the Revelation of Torah at Mount Sinai; and on towards ultimate fulfillment during the End of Days. While Kabbalah, the Jewish mystical tradition, asserts that the revealed Torah is one continuous name of God,[3] that same Torah bids one to remember Redemption, initiated by the Exodus, "all the days of your life" (Deut. 16:3).[4] Rosh Hashanah and Yom Kippur might be known as the High Holy Days (Yamim Noraim—lit. "Days of Awe") but Pesaḥ (Passover) and the Seder meal remain Judaism's core and most widely practiced observance even today.[5]

Redemption's signal role in classical Judaism is reflected by the sheer number of Hebrew words used to denote it, including: Yeshu•ah (ישועה), Hatzalah (הצלה), Pidyon (פדיון) and Ge•ulah (גאולה). Yeshu•ah,[6] Salvation, originally signified spaciousness and living with abundance. Based on a folk etymology, the Hebrew word for Egypt, Mitzra•im, scene of the Israelite's first enslavement, and later Judaism's bondage archetype, is derived from the root tzar, meaning narrow, confining. To be in trouble, tzarah, indicates that one is closed in on all sides by life circumstances without options or avenues of escape. When experienced as Moshi•ah, Savior, God is understood to help liberate us from both external and internal forces that constrain or imprison us. Extolling God's salvation, the Psalmist sang: from the straits (ha-meitzar) I called out, "Oh Eternal" (Yah);[7] I was answered with spacious freedom Divine (merḥav•Yah) (Psalms 118:5).

The primary meaning of Hatzalah, Deliverance, is to snatch or pluck away, to rescue people, creatures or objects from threatening situations. Thus, Zechariah 3:2 refers to Joshua, then High Priest, and the *Yishuv*, the Judean community recently returned from Babylonian exile, as . . . *a brand plucked (mutzal) from fire.* Metaphorically applied, God is viewed as *ha-Matzil*, the Deliverer, whose power can rescue us from physical danger, sin, and even from death.[8]

Pidyon, Ransom, refers to an exchange of goods or money to restore people, animals or items to their originally intended status. If one wished to restore a ritually dedicated item to its mundane use, one needed to offer the Temple a *pidyon*, usually at 120% the value of the redeemed item (Lev. 26:13). *Pidyon Shevu•im*, the communal ransoming of those taken captive, continues to be a primary Jewish responsibility. When acting as *ha-Podeh*, The Restorer, God, Master of All, need offer no tangible exchange when releasing mortals from encumbrances or danger, be they physical or spiritual. As expressed in Psalm 130: . . . loving devotion abides with the Eternal *(YHWH)*, with whom is bounteous release *(pidut)*; God will restore *(yiphdeh)* Israel from (the taint of) all its sins (Psalm 130: 7-8).

Finally, *Ge•ulah*, Redemption, is derived from the lexicon of familial relations and the responsibility of kin to maintain the integrity of the clan. Thus, a *go•el*, redeemer, would pay a relative's debts lest family property be forfeited to outsiders; avenge injuries, especially death, inflicted upon one's kin; and marry the childless widow of one's brother or even cousin (as in the case of Boaz and Ruth). In turn, their first child would be considered the offspring and heir of the deceased. Therefore, the original definition of a stranger, *ger*,[9] is one who has no redeeming kinsfolk among those with whom s/he lives. Since the Egyptians treated the Israelites as *gerim (pl.)*, strangers, with no human kin to champion their cause, God promises to act as the Hebrews' divine **Go•el**.

That these terms, abstracted from human activity, were but metaphorically applied to God offers us perspective on the Jewish view of redemption. There are streams among the world's wisdom traditions that define redemption as deliverance from history and the human condition. Galatians 1: 4 states: *Jesus gave his life for our sins, just as God our Father planned, in order to rescue us from this evil world in which we live.* The Eastern traditions of Hinduism, Jainism and Buddhism offer diverse paths to liberate humans from *samsara*, the cycle of birth and rebirth, referring to ultimate salvation as *mukti, moksha,* or *nirvana* respectively. In turn, Judaism seems to emphasize redemption within history, even when those redemptions are partial and fleeting. We annually celebrate Hanukkah though the Maccabean liberation of Jerusalem and its Holy Temple in 164 BCE lasted only until Rome extinguished Judean independence barely a century later, in the year 63. Although a minority opinion, the Babylonian sage Samuel of Nehardea (d. 254 CE) contended that there will be no difference between history and the Messianic Era except that Israel will be liberated from the domination of foreign powers.[10]

The essays in this volume offer diverse glimpses of how redemption might break through the fissures of our all-too-fractured world. If *Yeshu•ah,* Salvation, connotes expansion beyond previous confines, "The Arc of Becoming: Process Theology and Jewish Spiritual Direction" by Barbara Breitman opens fresh possibilities as we consider God not as a "Being" but as "Process" and spiritual guidance as discerning another's (or our own) "Arc of Becoming." Julie Leavitt demonstrates in "The Choreography of Presence," how somatic experience and our bodies' wisdom can provide founts of spiritual insight beyond mere spoken words. Elyssa Wortzman describes her approach to expanding our spiritual imagination in "Art, Imagination and Ritual as a Way to Build Conscious Community," an account of her innovative synthesis of art, liturgical reflection and group spiritual direction.

James Michaels' "Saying 'We Believe'—The Blessings of Local Interfaith Dialogue" reveals how people of good will can achieve *hatzalah,* deliverance, from the pitfalls of superficiality, inflation or intransigence that too often subvert relations among the people of God. In "New Psalms for a Jewish Paradigm Shift" Herbert Levine transposes prayer into a "Natural Spirituality" key, offering spiritual rescue to those no longer able to believe in a theistic God.

As stated above, *Pidyon,* Ransom, implies both release and restoration. My own essay, "You Heal Me through Dreams," seeks to restore the historical connection between Scriptural interpretation and Dreamwork practice, while exploring how its transposition into a contemporary key can provide us with avenues for spiritual renewal and release. In "Re-discovering

The Afterlife," Simcha Paull Raphael seeks to restore traditional Judaism's wisdom about post-mortem existence to our current generation. Continuing in that vein, Charlotte Sutker's "The Soul Lives On," explores the profound existential restoration felt by Jews by Choice who sense they were Jewish in a previous life.

Ge•ulah, Redemption, reminds us that all life is interconnected and each of us is called to act as redeeming kinfolk for our endangered planet and the most vulnerable among our human family. Arthur Waskow and Mordechai Liebling call us ritually and theologically to take up our rightful roles as redeemers, go•alim (pl.) in their respective essays "The Shofar and the White House" and "Imagining a Jewish Liberation Theology."

Leaving aside contemporary Jewish eschatological debate, Classical Judaism itself seems divided over its expectations for Messianic Redemption. Moses Maimonides (d. 1204) asserted: *Anyone who does not believe in him (the Messiah), or who does not await his arrival, does not merely deny other prophets, but also denies the Torah and Moses, our Teacher.*[11] Almost a thousand years earlier, however, the Judean sage, Rabbi Yoḥanan taught: *The son of David will come only in a generation that is either altogether righteous or altogether wicked.*[12] Alas (or not, depending on one's point of view) neither condition seems very likely to be fulfilled. Amid this ambivalence how should we proceed? Let me suggest that guidance can be found in the practices of the Passover Seder, Judaism's yearly celebration of the Exodus, the first divine act in time's unfolding redemptive drama

Twice during the Seder, it became customary to rise from the celebratory table and open a door leading to the street. The first, according to Don Yitzḥak Abarbanel,[13] is just prior to asking the Four Questions. The head of the household should stand at the doorway, proclaiming to all passersby: *Let all who physically hunger come and eat; let all who are in spiritual or social need come celebrate Pesach with us.*[14] The second opening follows *Birkat ha-Mazon,* the Grace after the Meal; in anticipation of future salvation, everyone rises, faces the door and sings welcome to Elijah, the Messianic Herald. From these practices we can learn two vital insights:

- Elijah will not enter to proclaim ultimate redemption unless we open the door; however,
- A prior "door opening" is required—our redemptive responses to that and those in need of physical liberation, personal deliverance, social restoration or spiritual release.

We hope that the essays in this volume will open multiple doors through which the spirit of redemption may be glimpsed, welcomed and then pursued.

ENDNOTES

1
BT Shabbat 31a

2
Franz Rosenzweig, *The Star of Redemption.* University of Notre Dame, 1985, first published in German in 1921.

3
Zohar Shemot 123b.

4
Simeon ben Zoma, 1st-2nd century CE rabbinic sage taught: *"all the days . . ."* *includes not only historical but Messianic times as well."* Thus, daily verbal acknowledgement of the redemption introduced by the Exodus will be recited even during redeemed time. *Mishnah Berakhot* 1:5.

5
As of 2013, 70% of all-American Jews attend some form of Seder compared to 57% who fast all or part of Yom Kippur. See Michael Lipka, "Attending a Seder is Common Practice for American Jews" Retrieved from http://www.pewresearch.org/facttank/2014/04/14/ attending-a-seder-is-common-practice-foramerican-jews/.

6
Yeshu•ah is the Hebrew word from which Moses' successor's name, *Yehoshua* (Joshua), and the Hebrew rendering of Jesus' name, *Yeshua,* are derived.

7
Yah is a condensed biblical form of the tetragrammaton, *YHWH, as in hallelu-yah*

8
Psalms 33:19: *To deliver their souls from death and preserve them amid famine.*

9
Contemporary uses of *ger* most often refer to Jews by Choice, those who have formally converted to Judaism

10
BT Shabbat 63a.

11
Maimonides. *Mishneh Torah, Hilkhot Melakhim (The Laws of Sovereigns)* Ch 11.

12

BT Sanhedrin 98a.

13

Don Yitzḥak Abarbanel (d. 1508), Portuguese Jewish statesman, philosopher and biblical commentator.

14

Retrieved from https://artscroll.files.wordpress.com/2014/03/the answer-is.pdf. The custom of opening the door during the recitation of this Aramaic declaration, *Ha Laḥma Anya* (*This is the bread of affliction...*) has been superseded in many if not most Jewish communities by extensive, pre-Passover food drives known as *Ma•ot Ḥittin* (lit. "Coins for Wheat"). Thus, everyone can receive needed provisions in advance, rather than having to rely on chance encounters and last-possible-moment invitations.

ישועה

YESHU·AH/SALVATION

The Arc of Becoming

Process Theology and Jewish Spiritual Direction

Barbara Eve Breitman

God's reality does not stand at an untouchable remove from the created world but... is in process with it.
.... our Godly task here on earth is to be partners in the process of becoming.[1]

Traditional models of Jewish spiritual guidance have functioned within religious communities that envision an authoritative God and believe that *halakhah* (Jewish Law) is the primary, if not exclusive path for walking with God. Modeled on a hierarchical template of relationship, such belief and practice remain foundational for Orthodox Jews. Post-modern, liberal Jews, however, are not comfortable in that paradigm. Many contemporary Jews continue to study, perform *mitzvot* (lit. "commandments"), observe rituals, holidays and other practices, but they do so without a sense of being commanded by an authoritative God.

As many have observed, the modernist, scientific worldview challenged not only traditional theologies, but spirituality of all kinds. This has been particularly true for post-Holocaust Jews.[2] Still, contemporary Jews have spiritual longings: moments when we have direct experiences of the holy; times of suffering, when we need faith to sustain us; and faith that inspires us to pursue justice and shape ethical lives of meaning and purpose. We seek spiritual wisdom, guidance and companionship from many quarters and diverse traditions. We are increasingly aware of the complex interconnectedness of all life both in healing, lifegiving ways, and through the rapid devastation of Earth's ecological systems. We recognize that the modernist vision of our planet as senseless matter to be exploited for human use is deadly, and that we must recapture a vision of the earth as sacred and alive, as indigenous people have always known it to be. We need ways of thinking about God that are consistent with how we understand and experience reality.

Over the last many decades, scholars and theorists from diverse disciplines have turned to Process Theology as they've pondered life's ultimate or divine dimensions. Their goal—to reinvigorate religious understanding, tradition and faith for people who can no longer whole-heartedly believe in a theistic God. Feminists have been especially attracted to Process Theology because its metaphysics shares our foundational assumptions: that God's power is persuasive rather than authoritative, exercising "power-with," rather than "power over," and that the nature of reality is inherently relational, indeed, ontologically interdependent. A variety of Jewish thinkers have begun to re-envision God, Torah, *Mitzvot,* Covenant and Ethics from a Process theological perspective.[3] The hope and purpose of this essay is to explore how the contemporary practice of Jewish spiritual direction can be enriched by an encounter with Process thought, and perhaps to contribute to the ongoing development of Jewish Process Theology.

In recent years, more and more Jews have become interested in Spiritual Direction. A contemplative practice, it has enabled them to re-sacralize their lives and live with a deepened awareness of the sacred which underlies both the extraordinary and the everyday. I have been developing the ideas discussed below while serving others as a spiritual director and while teaching at rabbinical seminaries and in training programs these last twenty years. I've been moved to discover that both seekers and practitioners have found Process Theology generative for the practice of Jewish Spiritual Direction. I offer this essay as a further contribution to this emerging field.

A Small Bit of History

Process Philosophy and its attendant theology began with English philosopher Alfred North Whitehead (1861-1947), who taught at Harvard beginning in 1924, and his American followers, most notably Charles Hartshorne (1897-2000) and John Cobb, born in 1925 and still alive today. The insights of Albert Einstein and the then-new discoveries of quantum mechanics asserted that physical matter is not an enduring, unchanging substance; matter can become energy and energy can become matter. Thus, Whitehead and his followers created new categories to think about the universe, God and the nature of divinity, categories in alignment with contemporary scientific discoveries that would shift the long-held opposition between theology and science.

I write this essay not as an expert in Process Thought, but rather as a practitioner. As I have learned, there are "first-person" and "third-person" Whiteheadians. "Third-person Whiteheadians" hesitate to appropriate the metaphysical categories of Process Thought to describe everyday experience on the human level. "First-person Whiteheadians" are comfortable using such notions to illuminate subjective, conscious experience as it is lived by higher organisms. If I may deign to place myself in either of those categories, I fall among the "first-person" group.[4]

What Could it Possibly Mean for Post-modern Jews to "Hear God's Voice?"

At least one pastoral theologian, Carrie Doehring, proposes that we need a "trifocal lens" to understand and minister to contemporary seekers in need of pastoral care; we must look simultaneously through a lens which encompasses pre-modern, modern and post-modern approaches to knowledge.[5]

Doehring proposes that when we look through a pre-modern

lens, we focus on a person's religious and spiritual experiences of feeling connected to God. We explore how and what induces a sense of God's presence (or absence), noticing whether direct experiences of the sacred happen, for example: during worship, ritual, individual prayer, spiritual practice, or; through human relationships, in community, through activism or in solitude; through art and aesthetic experience or in nature. Looking through a modern lens, we recognize the times when a person's needs or suffering may be best addressed through medical or scientific means, and as pastoral caregivers we rely on and refer to physicians, psychologists or other specialists. Through a post-modern lens, we pay careful attention to a person's unique history and social identity, the complex intersections of gender, class, race, sexual orientation, and ability, and ponder the unique religious and broader life experiences that have shaped a person's faith. We also pay attention to our own social location and how each of us makes meaning at the intersections of our complex and multiple identities.

As I've been practicing and teaching both Pastoral Care and Spiritual Direction, I have come to understand Spiritual Direction as both an independent contemplative practice and a dimension of Pastoral Care. It is my sense that many contemporary liberal Jews move among and between the three positions described by Doehring. That is as true for pastoral caregivers and spiritual directors as for the people we companion.

Let me propose that a Process metaphysics enables us to move through all three dimensions with intellectual integrity, including our individual experiences of the mystery we call God. At its core, Process Thought has sought to reinterpret premodern concepts for contemporary people through the insights of modern science.[6] Thus Process Theology can enable spiritual directors to meet post-modern people "where we're at" amid our many layered perspectives, multiple identities and diverse spiritual journeys.

At the heart of Spiritual Direction is the practice of discernment, the "holy habit" of listening into our lives with awareness, with *kavannah,* the intention to hear how the Holy is calling. To do this, we need to develop sensitivity and attentiveness, to notice the sacred invitations present in the ordinary and extraordinary moments as well as over the longer arc of our lives. Through meditation, people cultivate the practice of mindfulness, which Jon Kabat-Zinn has famously described as "the awareness that emerges through paying attention, on purpose, in the present moment and non-judgmentally to the unfolding of experience moment to moment."[7] The awareness cultivated by mindfulness enables discernment, the practice of noticing how the Holy is calling us in and through those moments.

These calls come to us through our bodies and our inner lives, through other people, including strangers, friends and family, through work and play, through all kinds of relationships and varieties of experience. Calls can come from our tradition and our history, from our communities and current events in our nation and around the world, from the earth herself and from non-human creatures. As the heavenly retinue called one to another: ...*melo kol ha-aretz k'vodo* the whole world is infused with the Presence (Isaiah 6:3).

These calls and invitations come to all of us. The questions for discernment include... Are we listening? Do we notice the invitations? Do we have the patience and courage to take the time to attend, to discern how we are being called and toward what? Do we hear calls to service? How responsive and responsible are we to the calls we hear? And, in what ways might we resist these calls?

Process Thought gives us language and categories to imagine what "discernment" and "hearing God's voice" might mean to post-modern Jews, while enabling us to better communicate our experiences, evolve our consciousness and act ethically in the world. When I discovered Process Theology, I was able to ground what I had been doing intuitively as a spiritual director, in a conceptual universe that aligned with my understanding and experience of God as active in my life and the lives of those I companion.

Some Basic Principles of Process Theology

Let's look at some important concepts from Process meta-physics to see how they can contribute to the practice of discernment in spiritual direction. I will give brief explanations of these concepts and offer traditional language and metaphor to illustrate how they may be articulated in a Jewish idiom. In addition, I offer you, the reader, brief practice questions and illustrations from the lives of actual people, as they have been shared with me in individual spiritual direction, supervision or spiritual direction groups of various kinds.

As you read what follows, allow both your intuitive and your conceptualizing mind to work together. While keeping intellect online, listen with a poetic sensibility that resonates in the heart.

All of Life is Becoming

The foundational claim of Process Theology is that all of reality is "in process"; all reality is dynamic not static, becoming, perishing and becoming, always changing.[8] Or as C. Robert Mesle, who wrote an introduction to Whitehead's thought, says: "...the world is finally not made of 'things' at all, if a thing is something that exists over time without changing. The world is composed of events and processes."[9]

According to Rabbi Toba Spitzer, to whom I am indebted for her eloquent distillations of many of Whitehead's complex ideas, "Whitehead uses the word 'experience' to indicate that at all levels of existence, the world consists not of little units of matter, but of consequential moments of becoming--moments which combine elements of "choice" (that is different possible outcomes) with the influence of the past and the surrounding environment."[10]

Mordecai Kaplan, one of the most influential Jewish thinkers of the twentieth century whose teachings became the foundation of Reconstructionist Judaism, is sometimes considered a Process theologian. In an articulation of his theology in 1949, Kaplan asks:

> Does the awareness of God depend upon our conceiving God as a personal being, or may God be conceived in other ways and yet be the subject of our awareness, or the object of our worship?... Nothing would be lost if we substituted [for the notion of a personal being] the one of 'process', which, at least with the aid of science, most of us find quite understandable. Why, then, not conceive God as process rather than as some kind of identifiable entity?[11]

But we do not need to look only at twentieth century texts to imagine rooting Process Theology in Jewish tradition. The holiest name of God in Jewish tradition is the tetragrammaton, *YHWH* (the Eternal). This is the name that is sometimes transliterated into Jehovah or Yahweh. But this ineffable name is, in Hebrew, an impossible declension of the verb 'to be', collapsing past/present/future, being/becoming into one holy name. Perhaps the most well-known text in Torah, when God shares something directly with a human being about the nature of the divine essence, is the story of the Burning Bush. Moses asks for God's name and is told *Ehyeh asher Ehyeh—I will be that which I shall be (Exodus 3:14)*. The holiest name of God in Torah refers not to an entity, even a divine entity, but rather a process of becoming.

Although much of Jewish liturgy and ritual emphasize the importance of remembering, in Torah God often calls people into the future:

> **Most famously,** God says to Abraham: *Lekh L'kha. Go to the land that I will show you...I will make of you a great nation.* (Gen.12:1-2)

> **Later, God** assures the wary Patriarch: *Fear not, I am a shield to you, your reward shall be very great.* (Gen. 15:1)

> **In the desert** God's angel promises Hagar: *I will greatly increase your offspring; they shall be too many to count.* (Gen. 16:10)

> **Amid the Burning Bush,** God points Moses toward the coming Revelation at Sinai: *When you take the people out of Egypt, you will serve God on this mountain* (Exodus 3:12) The Hebrew word for "bush," *s'ne-h,* came to be seen, through the rabbinic imagination, as pointing Moses toward a future when the Ten Commandments would be proclaimed at *Si-n-ai.*

How can the idea of a God of process and becoming orient our holy listening as spiritual directors?

As we hear peoples' narratives, we are listening for **the arc of their becoming.** We may notice how they were shaped by the past and we need to attend to whether and how they are present in the moment; however, we also listen for how they are being called into the future, into becoming. This is one of the differences between Spiritual Direction and Psychotherapy. Most psychological systems, from Freud to the most recent theories influenced by contemporary neuroscience, are interested in how our "present" has been shaped by the past, often by trauma that has distorted our ability to perceive accurately what is unfolding now.

Ehyeh asher Ehyeh is how God "sounds" as the divine calls human beings toward becoming. Through the practice of Spiritual Direction, we want to encourage people to practice patience, to listen into their lives and into the world -- not to rush past or avoid the discomfort of unknowing. "To walk to the edge of what we know and sit awhile" listening.[12]

Practice: *Take a moment from your reading. Pause and listen into your life. Allow the words 'the arc of your becoming' to echo inside. Notice what arises. What are the edges of your becoming at this moment in your life? What is being born and what may be dying or coming to an end? What is emerging and what might you need to let go of? What may be pressing for expression, asking for attention, calling to you from beyond yourself? Perhaps, what risks, challenges, situations are presenting themselves that could be opportunities to grow or change in life-giving ways? How are you being called into the* *unknown, into service to follow what is holy?*

Creativity is of Ultimate Value

Conceiving of God as Process means conceiving of creation not as an event that happened thousands or even billions of years ago, but as ongoing and ever-unfolding. In Process Theology, God is understood to be present and active through creativity, which is the basic force in the world. Creativity is understood to be flowing constantly through us and all of Creation, ever bringing forth novelty. To be created in the image of God implies that our creative process flows out of and into the infinite process of divine creativity that sustains the universe. Humans may be unique in being able to participate in creative process with self-conscious awareness.

In a commentary on Genesis 1, the hasidic master, Rabbi Simcha Bunim of *Peshischa*[13] (1765-1827), offers an interpretation of Creation that is remarkably aligned with a Process metaphysic:

> The Lord created the world in a state of beginning. The universe is always in an uncomplicated state, in the form of its beginning. It is not like a vessel at which the master works to finish it; it requires continuous labor and renewal by creative forces. Should these cease for only a second, the universe would return to primeval chaos.[14]

Two additional examples, one from the traditional morning liturgy and the other from *Zohar*, the major corpus of thirteenth-century Spanish Kabbalah, further elucidate this point:

> **Ha-meḥadesh** *b'tuvo b'khol yom tamid ma·asei be·reishit...*renewing each day with constant goodness, Creation's work.[15]

> **A river issues** *from Eden to water the garden* (Gen. 2:10) ...That river flowing forth is called the world that is coming—coming constantly and never ceasing. This is delight to the righteous, to attain this world that is coming, constantly watering the garden and never ceasing.[16]

Melila Hellner-Eshed, a renowned Israeli scholar of *Zohar*, sees the river as a central metaphor, representing a dynamic eternal process issuing from Eden, the Creative Source that continually brings life. "The river symbolizes the divine flow of plenty within itself and from itself into different worlds."[17]

The idea of creativity as the ever-unfolding, basic divine force in the world has significant implications for how we might listen for God in a person's narrative. In Spiritual Direction, we can listen for how the creative process that is this unique person is being called to express itself. Here are some ways we can orient our listening:

Pay attention to the "invitations" in this person's narrative, to the moments and movements that call one to greater creativity, to action and greater aliveness in relationship with oneself and with others.

Listen for the opposite -- what is ending or dying, what does this person need to let go of or what is letting go of them. What does s/he need to leave behind to "Choose life!" to live with greater creative energy, freedom and vitality? What do they need to recreate or repair?

Listen for the opportunities through which one is being called into creative service, action or activism beyond their own needs, in service to local communities or larger movements for social justice?

Listen for how the Holy may be calling her or him through the Earth and her non-human creatures?

Pay attention to spontaneous experiences of the sacred, including what may emerge in prayer, dreams and spiritual practice. If you hear such moments in the narrative, take out your "cosmic highlighter pen." Bring directees back to dwell again in "this place," *ha-makom ha-zeh* (Gen. 28:16) and listen contemplatively for the wisdom that continues to echo within them.

Trust our own creativity. Spiritual Direction is a highly intuitive process unfolding between people amid the ever-creative and creating process we call God. Therefore, Process Thought encourages us to pay attention to intuition, to experiences and activity that is novel, adventurous, improvisational or playful. "The Primordial Nature of God is the goad toward novelty in the universe, stimulating us to realize new possibilities after the old ones no longer are sufficient to give zest to our enjoyment of being actual."[18]

Sally (a pseudonym), a white, cisgender, woman in her 40s is an ordained minister raised in a mainstream Protestant church. She experienced family trauma during childhood. While in her 20s she met and married a man and had two children. Sally became a successful minister in a mainstream church, but discerned, after years of service, that her calling could not be realized in that professional context nor in that marriage. With much courage, she stepped out of the conventional structures of her early adult life. The couple divorced. Sally left her position at the church to become a weaver and chaplain. Over time, she discerned she was queer and partnered again.

Sally is a talented person, brimming with ideas and passion. Like other creative people, she hears many internal "voices," different parts of her "self" vying for attention: voices from her past that can both ground and hold her back; invitations toward personal and social transformation; and strong callings to upset oppressive elements of institutional life that marginalize both people and ideas. Sally chose me, a Jewish director, because she wanted someone not subject to Christian denominational preferences and allegiances. Due in part to my social location, my listening during our sessions is not shaped by involvement or commitments to those communal or institutional worlds.

As Sally and I "listen into" her life for how she is being called, I support her to trust the strength of the creative flow as holy. At times she may hesitate when the river seems to be crashing against boulders of self-doubt or caught in swirls of limiting ideas from the past. As she has followed that creative flow, however, Sally has taken risks and faced many of the challenges in her life: she has changed religious communities, burst the seams of previous denominational boundaries, become more expressive in her artwork, challenged her abusers, asserted her queer identity and expressed a worldview that is uncomfortable in certain professional contexts. Her sense of freedom continues to expand. In the immediacy of the present, I often hear how past/present/future are mixed in a moment, in a drop of experience, as we discern how creativity is moving through each occasion.

As Sally was going through a challenging time, I invited her to pour out her heart to God. Sally emerged from silence saying she could not pray to that God anymore, but she could talk to (Mother) Mary. With my encouragement (not that she needed it!) Sally began a regular practice of talking with Mary and found her Presence in Sally's life to be a deeply comforting companionship. In subsequent months, Sally also decided to take anti-depressant medication to relieve unnecessary emotional distress.

As I reflect on the "arc of becoming" in Sally's life, I see the movement from her earlier years to the present towards ever greater freedom as she trusts the flow of creativity in and through her. I think we both understand that flow as the Holy in which she lives, moves and has her being.

It is possible to see how the elements of the tri-focal lens combine to form a rich context for spiritual guidance: the premodern experience of sensing Mary's companioning Presence; seeking a modern scientific-based mode of healing through medical psychiatry and the prescription of an anti-depressant; and the post-modern reality of a rich spiritual direction relationship formed through the connection of two people of different ages, faith traditions, cultural backgrounds and sexual orientations, (though of similar race and class backgrounds) each speaking in her unique voice from her own social location.

Practice: *Take a moment to listen into your life. Where do you notice the energy of creativity, the energy of life flowing? Where do you notice it is stopped up or stuck? What are your fears, hesitations or resistances to following the call of that creativity or taking the risks needed to do so? Are there, perhaps, revelatory moments when you are waking up to new insights, perspectives, awareness, being touched by the creativity of others or by the earth herself? In what ways is your own creativity moving in* *alignment with larger movements for social justice that support the emerging creativity and freedom of others, especially those whose creative energy has been distorted or squashed by oppressive forces?*

God's Power is Persuasive, not Coercive: The *Initial Aim*

Whitehead's conception of divine creativity centers around the idea that God provides each human being, indeed each created being, with an *initial aim*. God's persuasive power is felt within each created being as the *initial aim* to actualize the best possibility open to it, given its unique situation.[19] This may be discerned moment to moment, occasion to occasion, and over the longer arc of a lifetime as God "lures" or urges human beings toward that aim. Although God provides the *initial aim,* God does not have control as to whether it is fulfilled. That is left to the person, through discernment, choice and chance.

Three texts below articulate this idea in Jewish metaphor and idiom:

An ancient Rabbinic midrash teaches:

> **Rabbi Simon said:** You will not find a single blade of grass that does not have its *mazal* -- constellation of stars and/or angel -- in the heavens that says to it "Grow!"[20]

In 1949, Mordechai Kaplan wrote:

[Belief in God] is the faith that reality, the cosmos, or whatever constitutes for us the universe in which we move and have our being, is so constituted that it both urges us on and helps us to achieve our salvation, provided of course, we learn to know and understand enough about that reality to be able to conform to its demands.[21]

Rabbi Shalom Noaḥ Berezovsky (d. 2000), a contemporary hasidic master, known as the *Slonimer Rebbe,* expounded on a related theme at length:

> **In the holy book** *Yesod ha-Avodah, (lit. The Foundation of Sacred Service)* brought down in the name of the *Ari z'l,* "No day or hour that has ever existed from the beginning of time can be compared to any other day or hour. And in the same way, there is no comparing one human being to another since the creation of the first human onward and no one can do the repair work *(tikkun)* of his fellow human, which is determined by the season, the hour and the unique code of that person." These words become the important groundwork for finding our task in the world. Indeed, we need extreme clarity to discern *et asher Ha-Shem*[22] *Elohekha sho·eil mei·im'kha,* exactly what it is *Ha-Shem* is asking of us, and what path is ours. It is according to the unique root of our soul and our personal tendencies, combined with the specific era and situation in which we find ourselves that we will be able to draw near to *Ha-Shem.* For if we

lack personal responsibility for our world or lose touch with our task and purpose in life, we are like travelers who get lost on the way, unable to find our destination and never reaching our goal.

Before anything else, a person needs to meditate well and dig deeply into the knowledge of what his/her special task is in the world...We are given signs by which to discern it, and sometimes we know it because it is the most difficult thing we could ever undertake...But when we have this clarity about sh'lihuto alei admut, our special mission to earth through which we fulfill ourselves, we no longer get confused about the great work or equivocate about the amount of energy we must invest in it. Nor do we lose hope in life, because we know that our soul's purpose is fulfilled by means of it and no sacrifice is too precious to carry it out..."[23]

A pervasive metaphor in Jewish mysticism is that each soul[24] has roots in a specific dimension of God-self and has special tasks, tikkunim (pl., lit. "repairs"), to accomplish during this lifetime's journey. As directors we are, in a sense, always listening for the unique path of this soul. How does a specific opportunity or challenge express, reflect, redirect or detour the unfolding of that path? In Spiritual Direction, we encourage people to explore the possibilities inherent in all their lives' experiences. Looking through the eyes of discernment, we then propose these questions: Will you somehow materialize the possibility? Will you sense the wisdom for this moment?[25] Can you sense God's Presence, as support and perhaps even urging you on, "carrying you on eagle's wings" (Exodus 19:4)?

Practice: As you reflect on your life, what are the ways your unique creativity has been expressed? How have you materialized the possibilities? How has your creativity been gift to you, to others and to the world? How can you tell? How has that creativity been expressed through your strengths and how has it come through loss, challenge, suffering, or pain? At this moment in your life, in what ways do you sense you are living in alignment with that initial aim and how might you be off track? How might you resonate (or not) with the Slonimer's vision?

All Life is Interdependent--All Life is Interconnected.

Katherine Keller, a feminist process theologian, states that no theology has better embraced the truth of our radically relational interdependence than Process Theology, interdependence not as an ideal, but as an ontologically given reality.[26] Whitehead's Process Philosophy argues that "there is urgency in coming to see the world as a web of interrelated processes of which we are integral parts, so that all of our choices and actions have consequences for the world around us."[27]

In the thirteenth century, the *Zohar* observed: *God fills all worlds... binding and uniting one kind to another, upper with lower; even the four elements cohere through the Holy Blessed One, Who is within them.*[28] We now live at a time when science and Spirit are aligning to teach us again that everything is connected. Nothing in the universe can exist on its own. As we live into the effects of climate change, we are increasingly aware of the inescapable web of life on this planet and the consequences of damaging and violating that web. Covenantal partnership with God can be re-envisioned as responsible, creative action in relationship with other human beings and the Earth herself; we are ineluctably interconnected. Martin Luther King Jr. famously expressed this truth as a principle of social justice in his 1963 "Letter from a Birmingham Jail": "Injustice anywhere is a threat to justice everywhere. We are caught in an inescapable network of mutuality, tied in a single garment of destiny. Whatever affects one directly, affects all indirectly."[29]

Sandra Lubarsky, a contemporary Jewish Process theologian, re-envisions covenant as the "site for responsible creativity."[30] Or, as C. Robert Mesle writes, "...thinking of the world as deeply interwoven—as an ever-renewing relational process—can change the way we feel and act."[31]

One of the ways I understand **discernment is as a practice of cultivating aware participation in the sacred Web of Interconnectedness.** When we meet with a person in spiritual direction, we enter their unique web of relationships and can begin to perceive the calls coming to them from within that web. For some, the strongest calls come primarily through the most intimate connections of family or local community. For others, the calls emanate and echo most strongly down the generations. Still others, conscious of their location in history, sense a more expansive call, even a prophetic call to social transformation and justice. The nature, sense and magnitude of how one is being called not only differ among and between people, the call changes at different stages of life for the same person.

To perceive an individual's web, spiritual directors, like scientists who literally study spider webs, need to cultivate stillness and the "patience to notice": Who is the directee connected to? What are the visible and invisible lines of connection between that person and other people or beings, dead and alive? What are the ideas and influences within her/his thought field? Where is s/he located within the power dynamics of the greater society? What are the implications of those dynamics that might influence and shape that call? how are they being called from within their "small corner of the web" or through their unique location in history or society? How are they being called into service? How might you, as a spiritual director, support a directee to be attentive and open to the divine creativity moving through them, the small web of their own lives and the larger "macro" web of life in which they are embedded?

While these questions might seem overly intellectual rather than contemplative, I ask you to internalize the image of the Web of Life, the "inescapable network of mutuality." I invite you not only to see individual directees in front of you; but to perceive them also as interwoven within webs of relationship. Such an imaginal change in perspective can further reveal a Relational God of Process -- and help us to shift paradigms.

The following examples offer us tiny glimpses into how these questions might underlie the process of discernment as a practice of "cultivating aware participation in the web of interrelatedness," ranging from familial to generational to the societal and ecological.

*When she was a young woman, **Dianne** and her husband had difficulty conceiving. As a woman of Sephardi[32] descent, for whom passing down her family traditions is very important, the idea of not having children was deeply distressing. She and her husband decided to adopt Rose, a white child, likely from a non-Jewish background. From infancy, Rose had great difficulty forming an attachment to Dianne; she would literally arch away rather than mold to her mother's body. Later she had many behavioral, emotional, relational and educational problems. As educated, middle-class people, Dianne and her husband offered their daughter every opportunity they could, seeking out therapeutic, medical and educational support. Despite their best efforts, things continued to be extremely difficult for Rose. She and Dianne were not able to form a warm mother-daughter attachment. In contemporary times, Rose might be diagnosed and treated for a Reactive Attachment Disorder or perhaps Fetal Alcohol syndrome; however, during the years this family struggled, there was no such counsel or help available.*

Dianne felt challenged to make meaning out of this aspect of her life. Always a committed Jew, she became a more active spiritual seeker in her fifties, a path that included meditation and spiritual direction. Broken-hearted after years of therapy and the failure to form the relationship with her daughter she longed for, Dianne hit an existential and spiritual wall. She needed ways to "be" with the implacability of the situation, to encompass the truth of how things are, things she could not change.

As she listened to Dianne's narrative over several months, the spiritual director noticed that in the larger web of relationships in which Dianne was embedded, were two young women for whom Dianne was a beloved mentor and elder: one was an emerging community leader and the other had asked Dianne to be her daughter's godmother/Jewish grandmother because her own mother and mother-in law had died. The spiritual director noticed the joy and liveliness Dianne exuded when she spoke of these relationships. Gradually, Dianne began to see those relationships as the sacred opportunities they were, not only for personal fulfillment, but also as ways she was being called from a kinship web wider than immediate family, to make contributions to community and future generations. As Dianne integrated this shift of perspective, her sense of distress lightened, and she found some inner peace.

A year later, however, Dianne hit the wall again. Feeling hopeless and in terrible pain from her adult daughter's rejection and disconnection, Dianne decided to stop calling Rose or trying to reach out to her.

Knowing there are times when we are up against implacable realities we cannot change through our own effort or action, the spiritual director shared with Dianne that she thought this was one of those moments. "Feeling into" Dianne's experience, the spiritual director softened the edges around her separate self, opened her heart and encouraged Dianne to find a place inside herself from which she could cry out and ask God for help. Opening in vulnerability to the flow of life-giving creativity in the Universe, both Dianne and the spiritual director went into silent prayer.

As Dianne emerged from her prayer, she had tears in her eyes and was surprised that something had shifted inside. She wanted to make a phone call.

Sarah, a spiritual director in training, presents herself to her peer group for supervision. She was approached by Rachel, who is part of a shared network of friends and colleagues, to ask if she could meet with Sarah for spiritual direction. Members of the multi-faith peer group listen carefully, knowing that boundary issues in minority communities can be more complicated than in larger faith communities, and new directors can easily get entangled in challenging, over-lapping relationships.

The group learns that both Sarah and Rachel are children of Ashkenazi[33] Holocaust survivors and the two women have previously shared much personal history and life experience growing out of that common bond. Sarah is a liberal, observant Jew, while Rachel lives in an Orthodox world in which the roles she plays make it impossible for her to share her heart and doubts with anyone in that community. Rachel sees Sarah as one of the few people she can trust with her inner life, who also understands the worlds she comes from. In turn, Sarah's sense of self and calling has been shaped by the legacy of her parents' survival and the importance of companioning Jews whose lives have been damaged by the Holocaust. For this reason, Sarah feels called to companion Rachel even as she recognizes the potential challenges.

As Sarah deepens her reflection, the group can sense not only how hard it might be for Rachel to find the spiritual companionship she needs elsewhere, but also that there is a bashert (lit. "destined") quality to this match. Still, Sarah knows she needs the wisdom and support of the peer group as she begins to meet with Rachel in spiritual direction. Recognizing both the risks and opportunities, Sarah and the group covenant to keep a careful eye as this relationship unfolds over time, balancing the power of the call down the generations with the necessity to maintain ethical boundaries in the present.

Jacob is a child of Ashkenazi Holocaust survivors who grew up in a working-class, urban, racially diverse neighborhood with many immigrants from different countries. This context formed a rich foundation of experience and knowledge that informed Jacob's commitment to activism for most of his adult life. As a young man, Jacob was instrumental in creating an early version of a

"Children of Survivors" group, as people were beginning to identify the unique strengths and challenges faced by this population.

In mid-life, Jacob's ability to actualize his gifts as a community leader and social justice activist had to be put on a back burner; family members with significant illnesses and disabilities urgently needed his care over prolonged periods of time. In recent years, Jacob has been freed from these responsibilities, which he had lovingly fulfilled, to engage the fullness of his skill and gifts in pursuit of social and environmental justice. He has felt particularly called to join in transformative work around antisemitism and racism in spiritually-grounded social justice organizations, whose constituents include African-American Christians, Muslims, white Jews and Jews of Color. Jacob has a clear and compelling sense that, in part, this is the soul-work, the tikkunim, tasks of repair, that he is meant to engage in this lifetime. He recognizes both the compelling need of this historic moment and the unique social location of his birth, upbringing, finely honed skills and gifts. Members of the spirituality and action group to which Jacob belongs have witnessed, supported and themselves been inspired and transformed by Jacob's growth and spiritual development over the past decade, as he has heeded God's calls. Jacob has experienced the joy of purposefully actualizing "initial aim" of his life, while significantly elevating the ethical, empathic, and creative energies of expanding webs of diverse people and communities.

Practice: Again: take a moment. Thinking of discernment as *'cultivating aware participation in your unique corner of the web of life'*...allow yourself to see the season, your age and stage of life, notice your social location, the unique personal and social influences that have shaped your life, your unique skills, talents and gifts, reflect on the web of human relationships in which you are embedded, from family to larger networks, notice this moment in the history of your people and nation, the crucial moment in the life of our fragile planet. What are the calls, the invitations, opportunities, challenges, seeming road blocks? How might these be an expression of a larger sacred process that's unfolding? How might you be called into service because of your unique gifts, location and place in history? Is this a moment when you are primarily called by family, local community, your 'own people', by larger and more expansive needs and movements?

Notice there may be a demand here. *Though we use the language of 'invitation and lure', we can understand ourselves, as Jews, to be commanded through the inescapable, dynamic network of mutuality in which we are located.* ***Go forth!*** *(Gen.12:1)* ***Choose Life!*** *(Deut. 30:19)* ***Justice, justice you shall pursue!*** *(Deut. 16:20) As Jewish spiritual directors, we hear and honor these prophetic calls still emanating from Torah.*

God is in Process: God Changes and Evolves In, Through and With Us

Because God is active in God's creation in and through human beings, it is not only we who are in process; God is in process too, changing and evolving. Though communicated through narrative and metaphor rather than philosophical principle, this idea is woven throughout Torah and rabbinic literature. Indeed, it has been noted by scholars and rabbis, that the God of the Hebrew Bible is constantly learning, growing and changing through interaction with human beings, challenges by the Patriarchs, Moses, and the people Israel. Talmudic rabbis even celebrated God's capacity to change. For our purposes, a couple of examples must suffice:

> **In the story** of the Golden Calf, Moses argues with God and changes God's mind. Furious with the Israelites, God is ready to destroy them for building and worshiping a molten image as the one who brought them out of Egypt. Moses implores and cajoles until God renounces God's intention to punish the people with death (Exodus 32).

> **A beloved** Talmudic tale tells of a rabbinic dispute which ends with God calling out to validate the legal opinion of Rabbi Eliezer. Hearing God's voice, Rabbi Joshua, Eliezer's disputant, proclaims, "The Torah is not in Heaven! We take no notice of heavenly voices, since you, God, have already, at Sinai, written in the Torah to 'follow the majority.'" Subsequently, a Rabbi Nathan met Elijah the Prophet and asked him about God's response upon hearing Joshua's protest. Elijah declared, "God smiled, saying, 'My children have triumphed over Me!'"[34]

The notion that God is not only in active relationship with human beings, but that God needs people, so God may grow and evolve, is at the very heart of Jewish textual traditions: *So, you are My witnesses, says the Lord, and I am God"* (Isaiah 43.12). *Rabbi Simeon ben Yoḥai taught, "If you are 'my witnesses,' I am God, and if you are not my witnesses, I am not, as it were, God."[35]*

Continuing...

I often say (and you might too) that I would not be who I am were it not for the web of transformative relationships, of family, friends, colleagues, spiritually creative communities, progressive Jewish institutions and multi-faith organizations in which I have been and am embedded. Each context, in its own way, provides a "site for responsible creativity,"[36] which inevitably involves joy and struggle, as we strive toward whatever Covenantal partnership might look like among us as people and with God at this moment. As we are called into the future, we continue to change and be changed, change one another and can imagine a dynamic, creative God changing with us.

In that spirit of Becoming, I welcome those who find the ideas above engaging, challenging or troubling to join the conversation, with me, with others, and...

ENDNOTES

1

Spitzer, T. "Why We Need Process Theology," *CCAR Journal: The Reform Jewish Quarterly*. Winter, 2012. p. 89. and "The Blessing of Uncertainty: Kaplan, God and Process," *The Reconstructionist*. Fall, 2005. p. 62.

2

Lubarsky, S B. "Covenant and Responsible Creativity," in *Handbook of Process Theology*, Ed. McDaniel, J & Bowman, D. Chalice Press, 2006. pp. 274-285.

3

Lubarsky, S B. and Griffin, D R. (ed.) *Jewish Process Theology and Process Thought*. State University of New York Press, 1996.

Artson, B. *God of Becoming and Relationship*. Jewish Lights, 2013.

Both Spitzer articles also address these issues. See fn. 1.

4

Lubarsky. *Handbook of Process Theology*, Introduction, p. 2.

5

Doehring, C, *The Practice of Pastoral Care: A Postmodern Approach*. Westminster John Knox Press, 2006, 2015. pp. xxv-xxvii.

6

Internet Encyclopedia of Philosophy. "Process Philosophy." Retrieved from *iep.utm.edu*.

7

Jon Kabat-Zinn, see for example, http://mindfulnet.org/page2.htm.

8

Handbook of Process Theology, Introduction, p. 2.

9

Mesle, C R. *Process-Relational Philosophy: An Introduction to Alfred North Whitehead*. Templeton Press, 2008. p. 8.

10

Spitzer, *CCAR Journal*, 2012. p. 88.

11

Kaplan, M M. *The Future of the American Jew*. The Reconstructionist Press) 1981. p. 182-3. Retrieved from Spitzer, *The Reconstructionist*,

2005. p. 60.

[12]

See Kedar, K.D. *The Bridge to Forgiveness*. Jewish Lights, 2007. p. 90.

[13]

The Polish town Przysucha, vocalized in Yiddish as *peh·shis·ḥa*.

[14]

"Simcha Bunim of Przysucha." Retrieved from Lubarsky, *Handbook of Process Theology*, 2006. P. 280.

[15]

Siddur Kol HaNeshamah. Reconstructionist Press, 1998. p 268-9

[16]

Zohar 3:290b [Idra Zuta]; trans. Daniel Matt

[17]

Hellner-Eshed, M. *A River Flow s from Eden: The Language of Mystical Experience in the Zohar*. Trans. Wolski, N. Stanford University Press, 2009. pp. 230, 250

[18]

Cobb, J and Griffin, D. *Process Theology: An Introductory Exposition* Westminster Press, 1976. p. 59.

[19]

Cobb & Griffin, p. 53

[20]

Midrash Rabba Bereshit 10:6

[21]

Kaplan, M. *Future of the American Jew*. The Reconstructionist Press, 1981. P. 182
Retrieved from Spitzer, *The Reconstructionist*. P. 64.

[22]

Ha-Shem (lit. "The Name") is an appellation vocalized to indicate the ineffable *YHWH;* at times it may connote a quality of divine/human familiarity

[23]

Berezovsky, S N, *Netivot Shalom* (lit. "Pathways of Peace"), Introduction: Awareness, Ch. 6 "What Does YHWH your God ask of you" as translated by Rabbi Tirzah Firestone.

Yesod ha-Avodah, (lit. "The Foundation of Sacred Service") is a book reflecting the teachings of the First Grand Rabbi (Rebbe) of Slonim (Belarus), Rabbi Avraham Weinberg (d. 1883).

Ari *(The Holy Lion)* is the acronym by which Rabbi Isaac Luria (d. 1572), the innovative master of Safed Kabbalah, is commonly known. *z'l* is an acronym for *zikhrono(aḥ) liv'rakhah*: *m*ay his (her) memory be for blessing.

24

   "Soul" here is not referring to an entity, but to a process of divine unfolding

25

   Catherine Keller, *On the Mystery: Discerning Divinity in Process*. (Minneapolis: Fortress Press) 2008. P. 101

26

   Keller, p. 22.

27

   Mesle, p. 9.

28

   Zohar III: 225a

29

   Retrieved from *https://web.cn.edu/kwheeler/documents/Letter_Birmingham_Jail.pdf*

30

   Lubarsky. *Handbook of Process Theology*, p. 278.

31

   Mesle p. 3

32

   Sephardi Jews are those descended from the Jewish communities of the Iberian Peninsula that, following the Expulsions of 1492 and 1497, were scattered to Turkey, North Africa, the Middle East, the Netherlands and the Americas

33

   Ashkenazi Jews are those descended from Jews of Eastern, Central or Western European backgrounds

34

   BT Bava Metzia 59a-b.

35

   Midrash, *Pesikta de Rab Kahana 102b.*

36

   See fn. 29

Choreography of Presence

Julie Leavitt

A Dwelling Place for Holiness...

I sing the body electric! ...If anything is sacred, the human body is sacred.[1]

I am a dancer. I improvise with and without music. I choreograph and dance others' dances. I feel subtle and strong impulses, sensations in my collection of body parts that impel me to move from curiosity and from trust. This in turn led me to dance therapy, where the gift of listening empathically to sensation as bodily expressions of information and pathways to contemplation was the right fit.

In the early 1980s, I was studying for my Masters-in Dance/Movement Therapy and Expressive Therapies at Lesley University. A colleague named Miriam invited me to a Rosh Hashanah service at a congregation named *B'nai Or*, Hebrew for "People of Light." She said I would love it; she was right.

B'nai Or became a second family for me, a place to grow spiritually as a Jew that I had been seeking for a long time. The parallel streams of returning to Jewish life and studying Dance/ Movement Therapy wove together. Spirituality rose up in my dance studies and dance became a way to both know and seek God. (to connect Spirituality and God...Great dance partners!)

Let me offer you, the reader, some embodied ways of knowing in these next pages. Movement and body awareness are doorways to Jewish spirituality. They each ask for listening to the body with the faith... that is a dwelling place for holiness, like the *Mishkan*, the holy, temporary structure the Israelites used to carry with them through the desert. It would move with them to the next camp when God's protective daily cloud covering or nightly pillar of fire over the *Mishkan* disappeared. Today, we can listen for invisible, embodied signs which issue from our physical being to sense Divine guidance.

Three steps...

In the future the blessed Holy One, will be at the head of every dance troupe (ḥolah)...[2]

The choreography described in the *siddur*, the Jewish prayer book, is meant to unify us in prayer. Originally written down by poets and prayer leaders to codify prayers for their communities, they can offer ways into a deeper sense of personal and communal holiness. These words can also be taken for granted and lose their life force as portals to the

Sacred. Rabbi Zalman Schachter-Shalomi, z'l[3] (affectionately known as Reb Zalman) says, the *siddur* is a recipe book for prayer. Rarely does that recipe include an invitation to move and dance during the prayer service. I notice these words at the bottom of the page in small print, "For those who choose: Before reciting the *Tefilah*,[4] one takes three steps forward."[5]

Three steps backward, a bow. Then, three steps forward again. This is a waltz—certainly, a partner dance of the heart. In this dance, our partner is the Holy One of Blessing; we take three steps back and bow to find our own humility and make space for Presence. Then, the return; three steps forward allow us to enter the realm of the Beloved. To quote Rabbi Arthur Green: *Here the heart goes back to speaking its own language, offering those gifts that no prayer-book can prescribe.*[6]

Our bodies are where we live every single moment of this life. Reb Zalman first caught my attention when he paraphrased the great hasidic Master, Rabbi Nachman of Breslov (d.1810). "You can't have a spiritual experience without telling your body about it." As Dr. Jon Kabat-Zinn teaches, "Wherever you go, there you are."[7]

If embodiment offers such spiritual intimacy, why do we disconnect from our bodies? A continuum of traumatic to pleasurable memories is held in the body. These include family and societal judgements and criticisms that often become our own. When we are asked to dance or to feel anything in an embodied way, reactive inner voices often say, "No! I can't! I won't!" These can be learned self-protection to keep back a well of untold stories, unfelt feelings, and unprocessed sensations. We can also feel defensive and frightened when we feel emptiness or the vulnerability of not knowing.

I often ask directees to notice any sense of non-connection or absence. This invitation supports the possibility that they do not have to feel anything. Often, it is a step toward sensate awareness. Tools of breath and movement can return us to flow and presence, so that the present moment does not feel like a threat, but a return home.

As we are reminded each evening through the *Hashkiveinu* prayer[8]

U•f'ros Aleinu, sukkat shalom,
Spread over us wings of peace, shalom.
Draw water in joy from the living well,
Mayyim Ḥayyim, waters of life, shalom.

Or, in the words of an anonymous Sufi poet: *The body is the shore on the ocean of being.*

It is possible to feel we are "living wells" when we begin to embrace the "living well" of our bodies as spiritual vessels. Awareness of the body in prayer with the combination of silence and words, vitality and serenity can offer both structure and awakening of the felt sense in our lives.

Hineini–"Here I Am" (Gen. 22:1)

How do we draw on embodied listening as spiritual directors? We breathe deeply, feeling our heartbeats and connecting through our feet and legs to the ground (sacred ground). We are companions to fellow seekers, all attuning to the present moment. The sacred word from Torah, *Hineini,* was first spoken by Avraham, when he listened to God's call and responded.

Hineini, Here I am

My directee (spiritual direction client) is talking quickly, barely taking a breath. In a space between words, I gently say that I notice he is barely taking a breath. Would he like to stand and stretch? He stands and lifts his arms above his head, stretching. After a few moments, he drops his arms, and shakes from his shoulders allowing his arms and hands to follow. Bending his knees once, twice in a slight bounce, his body stands tall. He takes in a deep breath, letting it out slowly. He meets my eyes for the first time since he walked in the room. With a light smile, he says, "Thank you. I'm here now."

Hineini

A woman cries and curls into herself. I notice her left arm holding her right arm. Her left hand strokes her arm. "What does your left hand want for you?" "Kindness," she says, "kindness."

Hineini

She has a neurological disability that impairs her walking. She sits on a chair and speaks of her mother allowing her to choose her own religion while providing ample opportunities to experience many faith traditions. "Mother always told me that there is only one God." I ask her whether she wants to go into silence to feel the power of her story. She closes her eyes and after a few minutes, her right hand slowly rises, guided by her index finger She brings her left hand to her heart. She holds her pointed finger toward the sky as she slightly raises her head, eyes still closed.

Hineini

In my spiritual direction work, we work internally and externally, depending on what feels truest in the moment. I might suggest they listen for breath or notice where in their body they feel something they are talking about. Everything begins to slow, and it feels like another presence has entered. This reminds me of an image brought to us by former Spiritual Directors International executive director, Liz Budd Ellman. It is a photo of a field with three chairs in it. There is a chair for director, directee and, like the Passover practice of leaving the door open for Elijah the prophet beside a dedicated glass of wine, the third is a 'chair' for the Holy Blessed One.[9]

Please Enter Where You Already Are[10]

A young rabbinical student is scared of God's power. She has a longing for God's presence and at once, doesn't trust that God could truly support her. I ask her if she senses God's Presence here. She does and describes sensing this Presence over her right shoulder. She turns to face her right shoulder and begins to quietly cry. She is quiet for a long time. She opens her eyes, smiling, her eyes and cheeks still wet with tears. She has an impish, playful image of an invisible companion sitting on her right shoulder. It feels to her like a small, funny Divine Being with a sense of humor. No longer intimidated, she has a new friend and comedic consultant. This is right before Hanukkah. She sings, "Though the night is cold and dark, in our soul, there lies a spark ...."[11]

Rabbi Jay Michaelson calls *Neshamah,* the "breathing soul."[12] That is true for each level of soul we speak of, but for *Neshamah* there is a connection to emanation and radiance. He calls it the "air soul," as he equates the soul levels to the Elements. We can feel the inner soul and the Presence all around us as seamless. From the most inner to the most outer is a way we can connect to God through awareness of the breath and body. Psalm 150 sings, "The breath of every living thing praises the Eternal *(Yah)."* To quote Michael Fishbane: ... *God—the Source of all the vitalities that fill our lungs and bodies, along with every other living thing from sea to sky.*[13]

Between Us as Well as Within Us

Group prayer can lift and support the sense of God's Presence between us as well as within us. We offer both structure and also room for personal kinesthetic response. This is prayer that encourages expression of the body. Whatever word or image for Divine Presence feels most true is encouraged.

Modeh ani l'fanekha. I thank You (the Eternal—Adonai[14]) for returning my soul to my body.[15]

I offer the congregation a simple movement combination for anyone who wishes to move, in any way they are able to participate. We lift our arms in thanks, when almost reaching as high as we can; we circle our wrists, flicking away anything that would intrude in our waking gratitude, any distractions, and any judgements. We thank the source of life. I offer the image from a Jewish creation story that there are sparks of life in each of us, together becoming whole, from the One Source. We snap, creating a sound spark from side to side in rhythm with the melody of the sung prayer. There is a visceral opening to each other as we dance in gratitude for our awakening this morning. Singing together summons joy, dancing our prayer embodies it.

A group of Muslim and Jewish women meditate together as we near Hanukkah. We sit in stillness to experience the light inside, between us, and the light we collectively bring into the world. Afterward, we share what we need to help us remember this light with a movement. We weave the movements together to make a dance prayer and end with *Ameen, Amen.* We share an image of a web of light that we make together. An embodied prayer for peace. *Salaam, Shalom.*

Unscrolling the Torah of Body...

There's not a thing
I could say about God
That would be true.

And not a thing
I could say to God
That wouldn't be.

I only know
What happens when we
Meet.[16]

Every Day We Must Dance, if Only in Our Thoughts.[17]

She pulls in to her center. She speaks of turning inside. After a while, I ask if I can share an image that keeps coming up. She nods. I share my image of a Torah scroll, winding in on itself. I encourage her to stay spiraled for as long and as tightly as she needs. After a few minutes, her body releases a bit and she lies on her right side. Lengthening and softening, she breathes more fully. Her eyes are closed. After time in silence, she says, "I can feel my *Shabbos* soul.[18] I can rest here." She does this.

Slowly, her torso rises, weaving together her fingers, hands and arms. I see a bird with long limbs and beautiful plumage. She freely swings side to side. She ends her moving time in child's pose, her body curled over folded legs. Her head moves forward, nose almost touching the ground. Later, she tells me that her head was dipped in a pool of golden light, anointed. "My *Shabbos* soul took me from contraction and grief/a closed book, to freedom." I offer her an interpretive rendering of Psalm 30: "You have turned my mourning into dancing... You have taken me though darkness and shown me your face of light" (Psalm 30:12).

I share with you the wisdom of my friend, co-teacher and sister in dance, Rabbi Diane Elliott:

> Unscrolling the Torah of body, attending to ourselves with the same loving regard that our scholars have lavished for millennia upon each *pasuk* of our holy text, we learn a whole new language. *Sh'ma*: we can hear the pulsing of blood, the tension held in the pericardium when we're scared, the rush of adrenaline when we've got something to say, the churning of the intestines when our boundaries are violated, and we become angry. Developing a sensate vocabulary in ourselves and then sharing it with others, we create embodied community. We support each other in knowing the comfort of curling up and being held like a baby, the relief of lying on the floor and surrendering to gravity, the awkwardness of creeping and stumbling, the

exhilaration of leaping and spinning, the trust engendered by falling and being caught.[19]

We sit together. I invite Ellie to breathe and find some connection inside. If either of us has a prayer following the silence, we can offer it. We breathe together for a few minutes. She offers a prayer, "May we be with you, God." I then join her using a word for God that I recall her naming sometime earlier in the day, "Holy One, help us receive you in ways that are most healing for Ellie, for me, for all.

We meet eyes, Ellie speaks. She tells me that when we moved as a group earlier, she began to feel pain in her body. Pain is very familiar to her. She knows this as fibromyalgia and brushes away the diagnosis. "It's just pain and I want to hear what it is telling me."

"Where in your body wants your attention?" I ask. "My shoulders," she says, shrugging both shoulders up and down. She brings her left shoulder up by her ear and curves slightly toward it. "Your left shoulder?" I ask. She seems startled to be brought to a specific focus and nods. She describes the pain as coming up her scapula like a line up into the top of her left shoulder. I invite her to pause and feel this, offering the suggestion to breathe there. She does this and after a few minutes, I ask her what she notices. (I do not wait for her to initiate a dialogue with me, like I usually might, since I don't know yet if she is feeling a kinesthetic connection or is distracted by her thoughts). She isn't sure. I ask her if she'd be willing to express the feeling in her left shoulder with her right hand. She clenches the right hand into a fist with knuckles vertical and pushes out hard and then opens her palm suddenly with a strong hiss. We do this movement together a couple of times. I want to mirror her, so she feels empathically seen. She speaks of wanting to let go of the tightness and find freedom in her body, like she felt as a child. I ask her to check in with her left shoulder. It still hurts. Her right hand goes up to her left shoulder and touches it gently. She says it feels warm. I wonder out loud if her right hand is trying to help the left shoulder. "Yes." Can she let this happen? The warmth feels good, even though it still hurts. She wants to hear directly from her body, from the pain. I invite her to go back and forth between places in her body that feel good, and then back to the pain. As she does this, she says" I just want to let loose, I want to let loose!

I hear a prayer in these words and suggest we slow things down. Ellie is open this. "Let's begin with 'Let'." Softly, she says this a few times with her eyes closed. Then, I add, "Loose." I invite her to send these prayer words to her shoulder. We use the word as onomatopoeia-releasing the sound of the word with an exhalation "Loose!" Now let's put them together. "Let Loose." She begins to speak. "I've never given myself permission. I've always sought permission from others. "I say "Here you are giving yourself permission. Let...loose!" We joke "Let there be loose." She repeats this prayer with an exhalation to affirm giving herself permission for release.

We have only a few minutes left in the session. I suggest she might offer this prayer, this affirmation to any other parts of her body and being that need it. She is quiet. "I feel like my wings were cut off and now I am beginning to sense that they are here." I encourage her, in these last few minutes, to offer her wings this two-word prayer. She breathes deeply, moving her back in an exploratory way. Her face is full of color, her body moving with flexibility. I bless her new wings and her willingness to Let Loose as an embodied prayer.

...Dance is a Deeply Transformational Grammar.[20]

Carl Jung's practice of Active Imagination[21] can serve us well; when embodied, it can connect us to a co-creative sense of Presence. Where do the images in imagination come from? Where do words of prayer come from? We call on the Great Mystery as an act of faith to guide and transform our relationship with Life. Images that arise from within are gifts from the Unknown. Willingness to listen with our imaginations can deepen our interactive relationship with the present moment... Holy Presence. Through the deep listening of imagination, we listen for a midrash from the Torah of our bodies, the Torah of our lives. To quote Ruben Rais: *I believe there is some Torah that can only be found in our bodies, some teachings in our textual tradition that we may not fully understand unless we translate them into movement.[22]*

He tells me about a shift from our last time together. He feels more compassion toward himself. When he made an error at work, he now says "It's OK, I love you," rather than beating up on himself. Lately, he is anxious. He reports that it makes his prayer and meditation life more difficult to access. I ask him where he feels the anxiety in his body. He says he is talking about it, not feeling it. I understand that he is not connecting to his body in the present moment. Can he feel the compassion he has been working with? He brings his right hand to his solar plexus and breathes deeply. He says he feels a release, expansive. I ask him if he wants to savor this. His eyes fill with tears.

In the previous week, there had been the massacre of seventeen people at the Marjorie Stoneman High School in Parkland, Florida. He speaks slowly. "There is so much pain in the world." His tears continue to fall, his hand still at his heart. "It is hard to know what to do. There is so much pain."

Following some shared silence, he repeats, "This is my truth. This is my truth." "Though it is hard to allow sadness, it feels real and I am grateful for it." He ends with a spontaneous prayer, "May the pain of the world...."

Vayinafash: Restoring Rest

Because you are at work in what is, I rejoice
and the physical world your hands have made
Animates in my body your preciousness.[23]

A rabbinical student is overwhelmed with stress of school accentuated by where she is in the cycle of the month. She folds herself into the cushioned chair. There is a Japanese paper folding screen that I set up for her privacy. She just wants to be in bed.

She is so curled up, she is as close to bed as she can be! I say, "Let yourself be in bed...here!" She breathes out a full sigh and closes her eyes. She begins to cry quietly and after a few minutes, seems calmer.

When she imagines going back to the world/school, she becomes very anxious. I ask her if she would like to use the screen as a *mehitzah* (separation between men and women in an Orthodox synagogue.). She lifts her head, her eyes widen. I place the three-sectioned screen to block her view of the door. I hope she might feel some protection. Her breathing deepens as she rests. I put my sweater over her and call it my "*Shekhinah* sweater', referring to the feminine Divine Presence. We speak of wrapping her in the wings of *Shekhinah*. Still vulnerable at the end of our session, she feels grounded and at ease with her vulnerability.

In order to work, in order to be excited, in order to simply be, you have to be reborn to the instant. You have to permit yourself to feel, you have to permit yourself to be vulnerable...[24]

We brought in elements of Jewish life and the imagery of prayer to increase her sense of protection at a time of her female cycle.

This can be a time of increased vulnerability and sensitivity of woman. More internal time is often needed. This is not easy in the demanding life of a rabbinical student and still deeply needed. She was able to allow this retreat during the hour of our time together. This helped her align with her body and regain a sense of personal and spiritual connection. The deepening of her breathing and relaxing of her body, as well as her own words, confirmed this. As Martha Graham observes: *Movement never lies. It is a barometer telling the state of the soul's weather.*[25]

She offers an analogy of a machine that has been broken so long it cannot be repaired. The connections just can't be made in this machine. Currents can't flow through. Lots of parts are missing and probably no longer being made. We sit in silence for a few minutes with this image. For some reason, I think of Hanukkah (December). People were sent to get oil because there was just one more flask of oil found to light the *Menorah.*[26] This oil should have only lasted a day, instead it lasted for eight days, when the supply was replenished. Sharing this, I ask, "How did this precious flask last for eight days?" (I think to myself, what a terrible example of a miracle for her. And it is June, not December)! Surprisingly, she suddenly falls into the cushions to her right and cries deeply. We sit together. Suddenly, she says, "Isn't it funny that I had that reaction? That I fell into the pillows? Why did I do that?"

"Maybe you just let go," I say, "How did it feel?" "Comforting," she says, "so comforting, to hear that story, to remember a spiritual story when I feel so broken and impossible to repair."

I notice aloud that her hands are holding each other, as she rests in the pillows, with her cheek resting on the green velvet fabric. "How does this feel?" She didn't know and then says that it felt good. "Connected?" I ask. With tears in her eyes, she answers, "Yes, connected."

Places of Knowing, Sacred Scripture

It is necessary that we are each created for that one gesture that the world needs and that can come through only us.[27]

We must learn to listen to our bodies as places of knowing, sacred scripture. No matter how we have treated our bodies in the past, they readily return to us as a source of Presence. Just a few minutes will help us let go of distractions and stress, return us to more clarity. The word, Presence, has the word present in it. This moment has a gift for us, a present.
As Denise Levertov so eloquently states:

The vision
of river, of nectarine, is not mine only.
All humankind, women and men, hungry,
hungry beyond hunger, for food, for justice,
pick themselves up and stumble on,
for this: to transcend barriers, longing for absolution of each by
each luxurious unlearning of lies and fears; for joy, that throws

down the reins on the neck of the divine animal who carries us through the world.[28]

May the day come soon when we live together in a continual dance of peace, replenishing the planet with all the love that is needed through the rhythm of feet against the earth, dancing to the music of the One, that

...the feet of (t)his generation might heal the soul of those who listen and raise them to ever higher levels of faith.[29]

ENDNOTES

1
Whitman, Walt "I Sing the Body Electric," *Leaves of Grass*, 1855 #19.
2
This hasidic quote about the spirituality of dance and others found throughout this essay refer to original teachings on dance by the hasidic master, Rabbi Naḥman of Breslov (d. 1810). They appear throughout the anthology of his teachings, *Likutei Moharan,* including Section *II:4.* Among the sources from which I first gleaned these sayings was Michael Fishbane's *The Exegetical Imagination.* Harvard University Press, 1998.

For further information on Rabbi Nachman see Louis Jacobs, "Nachman of Breslov" retrieved from
https://www.myjewishlearning.com/article/nahman-of-bratslav/
3
Rabbi Zalman Schachter-Shalomi (d. 2014) was the founding spiritual

teacher of the Jewish Renewal movement. The abbreviation *z'l* stands for *zikhrono(a) livracha,* may his (her) memory be for blessing.

4

The rabbinic name for the *Amidah,* the standing prayer of devotion offered in lieu of the former Temple sacrifices, is *ha-Tefilah,* literally "The Prayer."

5

Mishkan Tefilah: A Reform Siddur. CCAR Press, 2007 p. 74.

6

Green, A. *Ehyeh, A Kabbalah for Tomorrow.* Jewish Lights, 2004 p. 165.

7

Jon Kabat-Zinn's bestseller, *Wherever You Go, There You Are,* was first published in 1994.

8

This interpretive rendering of the evening service's prayer *Hashkiveinu* ("Grant that we lie down in peace...") was composed by Rabbi Aryeh Hirschfield, "Wings of Peace" *(http://rebaryeh.com/music.html).* It appears in the prayer book edited by Rabbi David Zaslow, *Ivdu et Hashem B'Simcha.* 1997.

9

The image appears, among other places at http://www.sdiworld.org/topics/announcements?page=6

10

Marianne Williamson, from her *Illuminata: A Return to Prayer.* As quoted during a 2018 podcast interview with Oprah Winfrey. SuperSoul Conversations.

11

Chayim B. Alevsky, *"Banu ḥoshekh legaresh"* (We Have Come to Vanquish the Darkness) Retrieved from hebrewsongs.com/?song=banuchoshechlegaresh

12

Kabbalah posits three personal dimensions of soul: *Nefesh,* our instinctual, creaturely vitality, *Ru-aḥ,* our emotional, relational capacity and *Neshamah,* where intellect, intuition and reflective self-consciousness meet. See Michaelson, J. *God in Your Body.* Jewish Lights, 2007.

13

Fishbane, M. *Sacred Attunement.* University of Chicago Press, 2010.

14

Adonai: Literally "My Lord" The Hebrew appellation most vocalized to indicate the ineffable tetragrammaton, *YHWH.*

15

Recited daily upon waking, this is among the first prayers a Jewish child learns [*Modeh ani l'fanekha melekh ḥai v'kayam, she-heḥzarta bi nishmati b'ḥemla, rabbah emunatekha*—I give thanks before You, Living Eternal Sovereign, Who has graciously restored my soul to me. Great is Your Faithfulness] It initially appeared in its current 11-word form in *Seder Hayom,* (lit. "The Order of the Day") a mystical commentary on the *siddur* (prayer book) by *Moses Ibn Makhir* of Safed, Venice, 1599. Retrieved from http://alexandermassey.com/modeh-ani/

16

Rabbi Nancy Flam, "About God." Related by Cantor Lorel Zar-Kessler.

17

Rabbi Nachman of Breslov. See fn. 2 and http://dancingwiththemaggid.blogspot.com/

18

Jewish traditions reified the exhilaration felt on the Sabbath (Yiddish: *"Shabbos"*; Hebrew: *"Shabbat"*) by describing it as an additional portion of soul (*Neshamah Yeteirah)* each Jew receives on the Sabbath

19

Elliott, D. *Torah of the Body.* New Menorah. 2001.

20

Fishbane, M. *The Exegetical Imagination* on Rabbi Naḥman and Dance. See fn. 2.

21

For a short description of the Jungian practice of Active Imagination see *http://www.carl-jung.net/active_imagination.html*

22

Rais, R. *Torah of the Body-The Prayer of Dance.* jewschool.com. (2014).

23 Psalm 90 as translated by Roshi Norman Fisher in *Opening to you.* Viking Compass. (2002).

24

Graham, M. *An Athlete of God* as recorded in Allison, J. and

Geidman, D, ed. *This I Believe*. Macmillian Audio. (2006).
25

Ibid.
26

The seven-branched candelabrum kindled daily when the Holy Temples stood in Jerusalem. The eight-branched symbolic version which we light ritually on Hanukkah is more properly known as a *Hanukkiyah*.
27

Rabbi Pinḥas Shapiro of *Koretz* (d. 1791) as related by Rabbi Diane Elliott. For more on this hasidic master see David Leoni, "Rabbi Pinḥas of *Koretz*" retrieved from https://www.jewishgen.org/Yizkor/Korets/kor031.html
28

Levertov, D. *Life in the Forest*. New Directions. 1975.
29

Rabbi Nachman of *Breslov*. See fn.2.

For Further Reference

Elliot, D. *Torah of the Body*. New Menorah, 2001

Fischer, N. *Opening to you*. Viking Compass, 2002

Fishbane, M. *The Exegetical Imagination*. Harvard University Press, 1998

Fishbane, M. *Sacred Attunement*. The University of Chicago Press, 2008

Geshurei, M.S. *The Besht as Renewer of Dance. Ha-Tzofeh* 14, 1951

Graham, M. *An Athlete of God*. from *This I Believe*. ed. by Allison, J. and Geidman, D. Macmillian Audio, 2006

Green, A. *Ehyeh: A Kabbalah for Tomorrow*. Jewish Lights, 2003

LaMothe, K. *Why We Dance*. Columbia University Press, 2015

Levertov, D. *Life in the Forest*. New Directions, 1975

Levine, P. *In an Unspoken Voice*. North Atlantic Books, 2010

Michaelson, J. *God in Your Body.* Jewish Lights, 2007

Rais, R. *Torah of the Body-The Prayer of Dance. Jewschool.com,*
2014

Williamson, M. Podcast interview with Oprah Winfrey.
SuperSoul Conversations, 2018

Building "Conscious Community" Through Art, Imagination and Ritual

Elyssa Wortzman

Both art and religion make the individual an instrument of revelation, yet "it is no longer common in contemporary art for the two to intersect."[1] Art can be a powerful tool for initiation into the river of *shefa* (a kabbalistic term for divine emanation or flow of divine energy) that connects us to the ultimate Creative Source. As traditional prayer proves less relevant to today's Jewish community, in what way can art become a modality for finding God? We know that prayer becomes rote as early as pre-adolescence, primarily because it focuses on words. If prayer is truly the language of the heart then praying by seeking God's presence through art, shifts the focus from words and the intellect to images and the emotion, from the mind to the heart. The individual can then open her heart to become a co-creator with the Divine in creating sacred space and awareness. Where art and ritual meet, the individual can become an instrument of blessing, prayer, and intersubjectivity.

When the Israelites were wandering in the desert after the Exodus they were parched and thirsty, complaining about not being able to find water. Their awareness was constricted, and they could not perceive that water was right beneath their feet, merely inches below the surface of the land. Art, the language of color, form and line is a way "to forge a path to the river of soul that runs below everyday life, becoming more alive in the process."[2] For Allen, "(art) restores the connection to the soul...."[3] as we follow the flow of divine energy to "step in, become immersed, lose ourselves and emerge enlarged."[4]

For art making to consistently provide a doorway into the flow, it must be ritualized though "a process that is goal directed."[5] As a ritual artist and spiritual director, I work with groups to build conscious community through participatory, community-based art rituals like *22,* an arts-based, prayer circle described more fully below. It uses a methodology I have created called *Mindful, Art-Based Jewish Spiritual Direction* (MABJSD).[6] The experience of *22* seeks to attune participants to the "river of the soul." Through a process of quieting, silence and listening in, each individual is drawn to a particular image, color, line, form from a place of personal emotional responsiveness and momentary heightened awareness.

MABJSD, Spirituality and the *Eish Kodesh.*

MABJSD is based on the work of pioneering, spiritual art therapists, Pat B. Allen and Shawn McNiff. Adapted to a Jewish context, it draws inspiration from the teachings of the Grand hasidic Rabbi of Piaseczno, Poland, Kalonymus Kalman Shapira (d 1943, Trawniki Concentration Camp), known as the *"Eish Kodesh,"* or "Sacred Fire."[7] It is a multi-modality ritual process of opening, setting boundaries, intentionality, art making and witnessing.[8] It also embodies the principles of interconnection and evolution proposed by Process Theology, so that God is found both in and through the creative process.[9] By entering the ongoing process of Creation as creators ourselves, fashioned *b'tzelem Elohim*, in the Divine image, we automatically enter an intimate communication with the divine.

The *Eish Kodesh's* teachings provide a remarkable foundation for contemporary spiritual practice as many of his insights align with aspects of contemporary psychology, mindfulness and the expressive arts. Despite the Jewish history of an-iconism, the *Eish Kodesh*, like F. Kaplan and others, recognizes how the soul has an inherent "image-forming function" that has greater power than the word to reveal its depths.[10] Images, argues the *Eish Kodesh*, have the power to dissolve barriers to spiritual growth.[11] Visualizing the image arouses the soul: it brings wisdom and attracts Torah and experiences of the upper realm.[12] His spiritual exercises rely heavily on image visualization. Although externalizing the image, imagery functions in essentially the same way and for similar purposes in *22* as the *Eish Kodesh's* mental imagery and visualization techniques. In both cases, it is understood that God is not manifest in the material; rather it is human beings who require "a material image to help us reach outward ideas that are lofty and transcendent."[13]

While not Divine, the image does still act as messenger or angel, an "agenc[y] of transformation" that "guide[s] and enlarge[s] our lives."[14] In Biblical and later Jewish texts and imagination the angel carries similar duties. The Hebrew word for angel, *mal'akh,* means messenger. In the Torah, angels often appear as messengers of Divine will, for example to Hagar as she flees Sarah (Gen. 16:9-12) and to Abraham who offers hospitality to the three angels he originally perceives as human travelers (Gen. 18:9-16). McNiff, following Hillman, implores us to treat the image with hospitality[15] as did Abraham.

Like Hay and Nye's conception of spirituality as relational consciousness,[16] spirituality for the *Eish Kodesh* is also relational, the experience of connectedness "with the holiness of God, which permeates us and surrounds us." Each person has an inherent capacity to achieve spiritual greatness that extends beyond interconnectedness with God to relationships with and among the group. When individuals, desirous of drawing closer to God, intentionally unite their hearts through love and openness to all (even those outside their community), they heighten their awareness to the sacred in all things, and begin to create "Conscious Community."[17]

What is *22*?

22 is a participatory art experience of twenty-two canvases (8 x10 inches) on stands, where each canvas has a Hebrew letter on the back and an image on the front. Some sages interpret the rungs of Jacob's ladder (Gen. 28), as the twenty-two letters of the Hebrew *Aleph-Bet*. A surface reading of Genesis suggests that Jacob's ladder reflects a vertical image of spiritual growth—the angels go down towards the earth and go up to God in heaven. Yet, the repetition of ascent and descent throughout the night creates a circular motion that I imagine as a spiral of deepening meaning and awareness. We move constantly from one level of consciousness to another, although each time we come around the circuit our "place" has shifted slightly.

In *22,* the participants similarly experience such spiritual growth as they move around the circle of images to create a collective visual narrative. The transmutation of images into a visual narrative parallels a kabbalistic practice pioneered by Rabbi Abraham Abulafia (d. 1291). By meditating on the images of the Hebrew letters, their visual forms would transmute into other shapes serving as portals of divine meaning to "bring the spiritual abundance into the intellective soul ..." of the seeker.[18]

Each of the twenty-two canvas fronts contains imagery inspired by the earliest known Jewish mystical text, *Sefer Yetzirah, The Book of Formation*, which ascribes special meaning to the individual Hebrew letters. The corresponding Hebrew letter is on the canvas' reverse side with excerpts from the Torah and contemporary sources to provide context and meaning. As depicted by the cover images on the front and back of this volume, Fire is linked to the letter *Shin,* ש.

Participants are asked to pick up the twenty-two canvases,

arranged in a circle on stands, and move them around, transmuting them, to create visual messages that stir the soul on a deeper level. The visual message is constantly shifting as one person moves another's piece and participants become increasingly aware of their roles in creating a shared vision. Once the group is satisfied with the placement, each person is asked to take one canvas and contemplate it for a few moments. Then they are asked to contribute one to three words reflecting their experience of the letter, the image and the process. Linking these phrases together, I lead them in creating a shared blessing or prophecy. Prophecy is not a prediction of the future, but the transmission of divine wisdom in the present moment that comes through the image, acting as angel.

22 as a Process of Spiritual Development

Until modern times art making was a fundamental part of daily and ritual life, from basket weaving for food collection to cave wall drawings for hunt preparation, encoding it in our evolutionary biology. According to Ellen Dissanayake, art making is a human way of "making special."[19] Making or participating in art "satisfies something deep within us." While scientifically this something deep within is understood as an evolutionary impulse, in religious or spiritual terms, it is a longing to connect with the divine spark within and the larger source of all creation, the "Creative Source." Community-based artist Cinder Hypki, who uses ritual and art making to process grieving, argues that "spirituality is the basis of all art making, for art (including the art of ritual) is the means by which we both apprehend and experience transcendence."[20] Scholars like Kaplan and Dissanayake reveal the benefits of art making in a way that links directly to spirituality.[21] To more fully understand how the experience of *22* incubates spiritual growth, we will explore the experiences of two groups, one in Israel and one in San Francisco, who participated in this community, art-based ritual. This exploration based on the ritual phases of the MABJSD process, will reveal different aspects of *22*'s artmaking benefit.

The Participating Groups

In Jerusalem, I was invited to lead a group in *22* following Shabbat morning services and *kiddush* at Zion *minyan,* an egalitarian *Masorti/*Conservative congregation with a focus on joyful, participatory singing.[22] The group was comprised of about twenty self-selected participants varying in age from about 25 to 65. All the participants spoke Hebrew (although many were North American), and several were Jewish educators or Jewish professionals. Led by Rabbi Tamar Elad-Appelbaum and Yair Harel, the services already prepared the group to open their hearts through several hours of uplifting participatory prayer. People praying at Zion come for and with a desire to deeply engage the soul in their prayer. We began with a moment of silence leading into an explanation of what they were going to participate in (see "Setting Boundaries" below).

In San Francisco, the ritual was presented as the heart of a

Friday night *Kabbalat Shabbat* service I led at the egalitarian Conservative Congregation Beth Sholom. About sixteen men and women, aged approximately seventeen- to eighty-five-year-olds participated. None spoke Hebrew fluently, although many had a basic knowledge of Hebrew letters and words. None of the participants was aware that I would be leading the service in lieu of the Rabbi or that it would employ alternative modalities. This group had less Jewish knowledge than the group in Jerusalem, although at least eight of them were very regular attendees at prayer services. Four of the participants were non-Jewish teens there to observe the service as part of a comparative religious course at a local Catholic high school. These students were of Asian descent and appeared to speak English as a second language. We began with a short relaxation meditation followed by a selection of prayers from the traditional *Kabbalat Shabbat* service each proceeded by suggestions regarding how the prayer might relate to **22**'s goals of creativity, interconnectivity, and finding the flow.

The Jerusalem Saturday morning service provided a longer, more ecstatic lead up to the **22** exercise, whereas the Friday night Beth Sholom service was shorter and more contemplative. Given that Abulafia's "Kabbalah of Hebrew Letter Transmutation" was ecstatic, the Jerusalem prayer appears to have created a more efficacious preparation for participants to enter a deeper **22** experience. The similarity of both groups' verbal contributions to their respective blessings confirms that the impact of visual imagery does reduce the participants' need for prior knowledge of Hebrew language or Judaism. An essential purpose of any visualization practice is for the individual to access an inner authentic voice. Therefore, the depth of the experience is more dependent on any individuals' willingness to open up and express an inner truth than on any facility with the Hebrew language or Jewish tradition.

In both groups, the participants numbered less than twenty-two. When this occurs, participants are invited to select two canvases side by side for the blessing phase; those that want to do so quickly emerge. In the case of more than twenty-two people, I explain the importance of both participant and witness to the group and invite twenty-two people to participate with the remainder acting as witnesses. Such was the case during an earlier experience of *22* in lieu of a sermon at Shabbat morning services at Congregation Beth Sholom (San Francisco), where about 60 people were present. Interestingly, those that participated only as witnesses remained part of the primary experience. From them I received the following feedback: **(a)** that the next time they would want to participate; **(b)** that in witnessing the group moving together with awareness they were able to perceive the accumulation of sacred energy in the sanctuary; and **(c)** that they felt included in the blessing despite being outside the circle.

The Ritual Process

Opening: As with spiritual direction, the process begins with a few moments of quieting, allowing individuals to become aware of their surroundings, their bodies, their thoughts, and to begin focusing their attention in the present moment. This spurs the process of opening the heart and clearing a visual space to allow one to take in the twenty-two images. The choreography of the ritual, with participants facing each other in a circle around the canvases, requires them to acknowledge and see each other, thereby initiating the necessary process of opening to the other.

I observed that the ability of the group to immerse themselves in the process and their awareness and connection to each other was greater in Jerusalem, producing a deeper and more resonant prophecy. I attribute this partly to that group's prior participation in two hours of engaged, spiritually moving prayer. Additionally, the San Francisco group had a larger percentage of visitors new to the community and Judaism than did the Jerusalem group. Future experimentation is warranted to determine whether the depth of the experience of *22* is directly related to the engagement, depth and length of the opening process. Participants may also benefit from a contemplative process of "emptying" any retained visual imagery from their day or week to create space for the images in *22.*

Setting Boundaries: To create a sense of safety for our spiritual exploration, the next phase involves setting boundaries by explaining the process and the goal of the ritual: to create the opportunity for transcendent experience and meaning making through interconnectivity. This is particularly important in the context of a religious service where this type of innovative prayer is unfamiliar. I explain that we will work together to create a blessing or prophetic prayer based upon visual images related to the twenty-two letters of the Hebrew *Aleph-Bet* and the spiritual transformation of Jacob's ladder. I further describe the practice of transmuting the letters to connect to the divine and invite them to engage their senses to create a narrative of images. I ask them to allow themselves to be drawn to a succession of images that "speak" to them on a soul level and begin to transmute those images by arranging them in an order that resonates intuitively. I remind them that since others will be going through the same process, they need to be aware of the group activity and accept that images once placed may be shifted by another, until everyone in the group silently acknowledges that the visual narrative has been composed in a way that resonates.

Intention/*Kavannah*: Since "art directs the heart,"[23] art is an ideal modality for aligning the mind and body with the heart's direction. This attunement is known in Judaism as *kavannah*, a devotional tool for consciousness-raising. It is understood here in both the literal sense of focusing attention or aiming and in the hasidic sense of directing the heart. It requires a listening in to discern the heart's desire, and a subsequent external projection of that desire (here in the arranging of images) as the *Eish Kodesh* advises, "[l]isten and you will hear how far your gaze reaches."[24]

By employing the senses, art making brings us into the present moment and heightens awareness allowing us to focus our attention towards something[25] in the same was as creating *kavannah.* While the participants in **22** may have the individual intentions of praying, communicating with God, or engaging in a new experience, the process of engaging with art in a sacred context becomes the group *kavannah.* This is evident from the enthusiasm and attention (after some initial trepidation) I observe from the participants in both groups from the start of the session, who expectantly make eye contact with their co-creators. Knowing that they are all in this together creates a sense of community and interconnectivity.

Art Making: Guiding another into the flow we call *shefa* is central to the process of Spiritual Direction. Rabbi Dov Baer of Mezeritch (d. 1772), Hasidim's second teacher, described this process as one of God moving through us.[26] According to the *Zohar (The Book of Splendor),* the major corpus of thirteenth century Spanish Kabbalah, *shefa is a river of Divine creativity that runs through all of life and every particle of the universe at all times.*[27] This immersion in *shefa* corresponds to the first of Kaplan's benefits of art making as "optimal human experience" giving meaning and joy to life, while supporting spiritual growth.[28] Leading practitioner of mindfulness art therapy, Dr. Laury Rappaport, agrees that inherent within the creative process are mindful awareness and presence. She describes the art making process as an immersion in a "flow," in which the mind quiets, one steps outside of linear time, and one experiences a sense of oneness.[29]

In **22,** the process of transmuting the letters to create a group visual narrative becomes the art making. As the group begins there is a period of stasis as each individual silently observes each of the images, sometimes walking around the outside of the circle, listening for the call to the soul. Prior to each transmutation, there is a process of aesthetic meditation on the image. There is an ongoing process of witnessing each other as images are picked up, placed and moved again. They have to work cooperatively and pay attention to the way others are relating to the images and the narrative order, which is constantly shifting. Participants become more engaged because, unlike most museum experiences, they get to touch, feel and manipulate art works; this sensory process engenders an embodied experience.

Making art in community strengthens interpersonal bonds, an aspect of relational consciousness that defines spirituality.[30] As each participant's image is rearranged by another, her experience of *shefa* becomes inextricably intermingled with the others. As this happens over and over again within the group, the participants become aware of an energy that is greater than the individual that is directing the transmutation process and creating invisible bonds between them. These phenomen along with the process of transmuting the images into a visual narrative, allow the group to enter the flow. Removing the barrier between the individual and the art also creates a sense of trust and responsibility that engages the group.

Rosemary describes her experience of *22,* in San Francisco as creating community and heightening the power of her prayer:

I keep having two thoughts: community and visual prayer or prayer made visual...community is crucial because the energy of solo praying can be powerful, but uniting (in **22**), which includes our 'collective *nefesh* (soul),' gives it a power surge...in many ways it validates our individual prayers. My companions that night agreed: **22,** allowed a free and original picture of what it is to pray as a group, as a *minyan.*

22, therefore has the power to not only intensify prayer and create community but to revive the personal connection of the individual to the tradition of praying in a *minyan*, a group of ten adult Jews.

Making art also promotes problem solving and creativity, which help the spiritual seeker navigate life's challenges and develop strategies that can be applied to other situations.[31] Some of the participants in the Jerusalem group were particularly aware of this, as the post-exercise discussion revolved around what they could learn about themselves and others from the group dynamic and their individual participation in the process. Some saw how they held back at first in selecting an image as a reflection of how they held back parts of themselves from sharing in or helping with community. Others noticed how their eagerness to rearrange another's image might reflect a need to cultivate respectful listening. By taking the time to reflect on the group dynamic, the "collaborative, creative experience serves as a door leading to the co-creating of new meaning, understanding and resolve"[32] that may provide insight into the individual and her conception of community.

Ritual both builds and presupposes community; its symbols have the ability to bring the members of the group together in a shared experience.[33] Yet, those symbols, if they cannot be decoded, limit participation. Rosemary tells me "it was a totally non-threatening experience. It was easy to participate." Art making is an opportunity for non-verbal expression, which means a lower barrier for entry and reduced anxiety/selfconsciousness.[34] In the San Francisco group, this was particularly apparent with the participation of the four non-Jewish students from the local Catholic school. Generally, when such students attend Jewish services, they are relegated to the role of bystanders who may observe but, due to language and liturgical barriers, leave without knowing the experience. In this case, two female and two male students (whose first language was not English) did not hesitate to form part of the circle and become essential contributors to the blessing. The universal language of imagery, as exemplified in *22,* has the capacity to build community beyond denominational or religious divides.

Discerning the Message: After the period of silent reorganization, which usually takes about twenty to thirty minutes, people stop moving the images and a final order is established. Participants acknowledge silently that their work, and the group ordering of the images, is done. I ask them to take a few moments to look at the visual narrative and allow themselves to be drawn to a particular image that evokes something in their soul. Each person is asked to stand behind that image, and then hold the image, taking ownership and responsibility for that portion of the message. Once everyone has selected their piece, I tell the group that it is time to discern the message and that we will begin with one person and work our way around the circle with each person contributing one to three words to the message. The words are to be based upon their aesthetic meditation with the image and the Hebrew letter on the reverse side. Rearranging the images itself can help to develop language skills, which for spiritual seekers means a greater capacity to communicate.[35]

Slowly, as we move around the circle the message is revealed. After each person speaks, I hold the sacred space by echoing back to the group the entire message revealed so far. With the intense focus required to continually repeat the message, joining each person's contributions together, I am silently inviting God's presence into the words. Like the call and response of a song, the repetition allows the message to resonate on a deeper level and further strengthens the bonds of community as everyone bears witness to the others' experiences through deep listening to their verbal contributions to the message. When everyone's contribution to the message has been evoked, they are encouraged to join in the last repetition with one voice. This is followed by a moment of silence, to allow the group to take in their discovery/uncovering.

In both the San Francisco and Jerusalem groups, I noticed that the words offered, although coming from the soul, did not situate the individual within the blessing. In the Jerusalem group, for example, I was standing half way in the circle and used my words to place myself within the blessing. A subtle awakening of awareness within the group resulted as they recognized the potential of making prayer personal; my words had grounded the prophecy in a reality that directly engaged them and some of the following offerings also situated the group within the blessing.

Reflections

Prayer, says the *Eish Kodesh*, is not about the specific words, but about the process itself.[36] Making devotion come alive, and expressing the "deep emotional affect of your soul" cannot be done through "simple thought" but only through "holy thought" that derives when you "multiply visualizations and become immersed in the imaginal realm." The image attaches "to the holiness beyond itself...draw(ing) holiness from beyond that is unimaginable."[37] Connecting with the image expands relational consciousness as the awareness of self is heightened and the 'self' expands and merges with the object observed.[38] Based on the biblical verse, I set *(shiviti)* the Eternal *(YHWH)* before me always (Psalms 16:8), an artistically designed image of the tetragrammaton called a *"Shiviti"* was used to focus and deepen prayer.[39] Similarly, in **22,** through the modified *Shiviti* practice, the image becomes the focus of attention. Participants are encouraged to commune with the image by opening their senses and their hearts to its aesthetic call.

At the beginning of his prophetic career, Ezekiel beholds, within a cloud of flashing fire, the *Merkavah,* God's Chariot Throne, supported by four angelic Living Beings known as the *Hayot* (Ezekiel 1:1-5). Amid the fire and the *Hayot* is the radiant *Hashmal,* gleaming golden or amber, which according to tradition symbolizes the contemplative's ability to hear the "still small voice," the "meditative quietness of the mind out of which the Divine speech comes."[40] The Talmud asserts that prophecy itself comes from such meditative quiet. Thus, Ezekiel contemplated the *Hashmal,* and thereafter was able to prophesy. The Talmud also explains *Hashmal* as a mnemonic for *Hayyot Eish Memal•lelot,* "Living Fiery Angels Speaking."[4] In the case of MABJSD, when images are "seen" through aesthetic meditation, *Hayyot,* "living angels," are being created, intimating divine speech, evoking echoes of the "still small voice."

Another symbolic form that brings the group together is that of the circle in which the images and the participants are arrayed. The sacred circle is a part of many aboriginal traditions, symbolizing harmony and patterns of life[42] and may have a universal symbolic meaning. In the Talmud, Honi the Circle Maker drew a circle and prayed within it until God sent rain to end a serious drought.[43] The circle he drew in the sand became a sacred symbol. While every individual may not be capable of prophetic intercessory prayer,[44] in **22** the group synergy elevates and broadens the individual aspiration so that the message revealed by the group may approach prophetic blessing.

The form of the circle is also symbolic of our inward facing, never ending relationship to each other and to God. One participant in the Jerusalem group literally took the form of the circle a step further. Like the Biblical Naḥson ben Aminadav, the first to enter the Red Sea before it split[45] she took a first step by carrying her image about a foot further into the center of the circle. Inspired by her initiative the other participants also moved their images inward until the group was standing shoulder to shoulder. Their physical intimacy was but an outer manifestation of shared *d'veikut* (lit. "cleaving"), their willing adherence through spiritual experience to one another and the Divine. After the ritual, many described forming this inner circle as a profound moment of connection.

In a previous study, I discussed how spiritual art making as prayer results in measurable spiritual development with youth.[46] In Jerusalem and San Francisco, multi-generational groups were able to grow individually and together through the practice of **22** evoking the divine flow of *shefa*. They co-created an imaginal narrative whose order comes from the group and whose message emanated from the divine within and without.

Witnessing

Words spoken intentionally from a place of attunement with the heart have the power to influence and transform the speaker's soul and the soul of the listener.[47] Here, as they create the blessing, people's faces are glowing, they are all acutely present, they look around at each other meeting each other's eyes, their hearts are open and the soundless resonance of their awareness of the divine in that moment embraces each of them in this shared mystical experience. There is a deep recognition that the nature of the experience depends upon our interconnectivity. We saw during the art making phase, how the image acts as messenger or angel calling out to the viewer with its divine message. Here too, the imagination "plays a crucial role in the mechanics of prophecy...as the angelic intermediary that bridges spirit and matter, intellect and body."[48]

In Jerusalem, this message emerged just as Abulafia described, as the connection between the imagination and the image both engendered and was engendered by the overflow of the spirit of (shefa):

> The stars are among us with the fragrance of awareness that is as essential to us as *mayim*, water; with the realization that this place could divide us like the sky is divided from the earth

> I cry out and I am lost yet, the healing fire that burns within us and spreads among us is compassion and loving kindness...

> transmitted through the mouth and grounded in the earth through many channels and subterranean spaces that are primordial and existed before us and all their components

So that when we fall, we are raised up by the grace of this community with sparks and dreams that join us together. [48]

22 has the power to be an "initial revelation" as one's soul is revealed to a person and she is "ready to become a vehicle" or an instrument" for elevated consciousness. [49] As leader, the role of "instrument" is even more critical, bringing one's full presence and training as a spiritual director to bear in creating a vessel for transformation. I was humbled when Rabbi Tamar Elad- Appelbaum commented that my "acting as an instrument of blessing" and "gentle, attentive, joyful leadership" opened for her Jerusalem community "a moment of beautiful preparation to the possibility to turn every moment into deep prayer." While inspiring the individual soul, **22**'s strength lies in its ability to create sacred community through shared spiritual experience. It is a "weaving of one prayer out of many people," says Rabbi Elad-Appelbaum, that "creates one blessing made of many paintings and hearts."

After closing **22** with a *niggun*, a wordless, devotional melody, participants generally stay to share their reactions to the experience with others. There is a palpable sense of community and benevolence. In Jerusalem, Melanie, a trained Jewish prayer leader, with considerable experience with embodied prayer and meditation, shared her delight in being "able to operate in a different language...dropping into (her) experience and then creating a communal prayer and blessing through stringing together all the connections of everyone" in a way that was "nourishing and inspiring." Together with her fellow participants, she experienced "a vibration of holiness" that brought forth each person's "deep gifts and treasures" to "create a greater story from our singular stories." For Shira, an American Jewish educator, participating "was a powerful process." Because it was unfamiliar the spiritual experience took place when we were about half into the participants sharing. There was palpable building of trust. "Elyssa's call and our response as we built upon each other's blessings was powerful."

The San Francisco group also shared a powerful experience of connectivity. In Irene's words, their group "simply and magically created, in collaboration with each other, a magnificent, spiritual poem, a prayer to sanctify the beauty, the calm and the compassion of Shabbat. We left with a sense of communal bliss."

Participants in both groups reflected on how their **22** experience helped them transcend the loneliness they often feel during formal services. Robert relates that during traditional prayer in San Francisco he feels isolated: "it is me and everyone else is separate." With **22**, on the other hand, he felt a "profound" human connection:

> the experience was very powerful through the connection it provided with the other participants. When individuals assigned a feeling to the image it opened a window into that person that we could peep

into making it very intimate. Rearranging the pictures then connected us all as a group. We were all very accepting of each other's preferences, probably more than we would have been in a different setting and without the progressive experience. There was no 'ownership.'

Shira shared a similar experience of interconnectivity in Jerusalem, commenting how unlike traditional prayer, which "is much more inward, personal, and private," *22* "was more relational and communal." Shira learned a key element of being in a spiritual relationship with community or God—how to hold in tandem the paradoxical activities of choosing what one desires and surrendering to a larger power—as she selected a painting she was drawn to while relinquishing her preferred ordering of the canvases. She became aware of how much we communicate non-verbally with others and how working together in silence can help us notice this.

The artist, activist and ritual designer Andrew Boyd states:

> 'If it takes us outside of ourselves, then it manifests community. Lots of lip service is paid to "[creating] community," but it is hard to really experience it. When everyone [involved in a ritual] takes that risk together and moves out of their comfort zone, it's ...powerful, we...feel lifted, transcendent; we feel ourselves part of "a wider circle of connection, a larger circle of concern."[50]

To be a part of a transformative experience is to connect the heart of each person, one to the other, with an impressionistic bond that emerges in between and beyond words.

Sacred art making is profoundly effective as a means of spiritual growth because it is such an intuitive, elemental human ritual—pre-figuring verbal communication—through which we may approach our inception as spiritual beings. It deepens experience, inspires transformational awareness and, through a shared spiritual experience, creates community. Participants in **22** immerse together in the divine flow of *shefa* like an imaginal ritual bath, a *mikvah,* and connect both to each other and the divine through this shared experience of oneness. As Irene expressed, they experience a "sense of timelessness, peace and open communication" with each other and the divine. This "conscious community," as the *Eish Kodesh* would call it, like the group in group spiritual direction, keeps us on track, grounds and supports us, and reinforces the importance of spiritual *avodah* (service) in a busy world.

The *kavannah,* intentionality, of interconnectivity and inter-dependence that emerges can be used to shape our spirit and the world around us. To find God within and to contribute positively to Jewish society, one must "[r]emember each day your purpose and your aim [as...] a person's actions follow his will."[51] Rabbi Tamar Elad-Appelbaum describes the process of intentional action in **22** as "an invitation to pray through choosing, to connect one choice to the other and witness the generosity (of the group) to connect them all." Accordingly, one possible area of future exploration could be using **22** to create connection and relatedness between individuals or communities in disharmony. Jewish educator, Shira, envisions **22** as a community building exercise, with study before and after the process, to foster awareness of our often forgotten "interdependence" as "part to whole relationships in a group dynamic." Participants have also suggested using **22** as a means of preparing the group for more traditional prayer, so, according to Robert, "the individual would feel extremely connected with the entire group while they prayed individually."

With **22**, both the experience and the message are always new, always open and un-fixed, therefore it has the power to reimagine prayer in our hearts and minds and reinvigorate Jewish prayer life today. "Community-based, arts-based ritual," argues Hypki,[52] "is at its most powerful when it emerges from or is designed to reflect the history, traditions, culture or struggles, goals and aspirations of specific groups of people." **22** draws on the *Eish Kodesh*'s struggles and practices to develop a system for spiritual development and his goal of developing conscious community. As a form of communal *hitbodedut*, **22** reflects the Jewish traditions of meditation and ecstatic Kabbalah, the *shiviti,* and the symbol of the circle in prayer. Despite its rootedness in Jewish exploration, by engaging the community in a participatory, ritualized art experience **22** also uses the ancient technology of art making to engage contemporary seekers whose cultural language, through the adoption of technology, is increasingly visual/image based.

With its overlapping of art making and witnessing phases, individuals constantly shift back and forth between the inner attunement required to be drawn to a particular image and the outer awareness of the other as they place the work within the visual narrative, supplanting another's chosen placement. With practice, this develops a kind of spiritual flexibility that should allow participants to shift more easily between spheres of relational consciousness (the self, the group, the environment, the divine) in their daily lives.

ENDNOTES

1

Leibovitz, L. "Prayer as Art, Art as Prayer." *The New York Jewish Week*, Manhattan edition. 11 Feb 2005: 27. Print.

2

Allen, P B. *Art as a Way of Knowing*. Shambhala, 1995. P. xxi.

3

Ibid. p ix.

4

Allen, P. B. *Art Is a Spiritual Path*. Shambhala, 2005 p. 10.

5

Kaplan, F. *Art, Science and Art Therapy: Painting the Picture*. Jessica Kingsley Publishers, 2000, p. 72.

6

Wortzman, E. *Creating Soul Connections: Art as a Means of Jewish Spiritual Direction with Youth*. Graduate Theological Foundation, unpublished dissertation, May 2017.

7

ibid.

8

ibid. For theological reflections on the process see Wortzman, E. "Process Theology, Aesthetics, Halacha and Spiritual Development Through Art." in Morgan, J.H. (Ed.), *Foundation Theology*,

GTF Books. Pp.141-157.

9

 Ibid.

10

 Shapira, K K. *Conscious Community: A Guide to Inner Work.* Trans. by Coehn-Kiener, A. Rowman & Littlefield Publishers, 1996. p. 31-3.

11

 Shapira, pp. 21-2.

12

 Shapira, pp. 31-3.

13

 Shapira, p. 24.

14

 McNiff, S. *Art Heals: How Creativity Cures the Soul.* Shambhala, 2004, p. 85.

15

 McNiff, p. 101.

16

 Hay, D. and Nye, R. *The Spirit of the Child.* Harper Collins, 1998.

17

 Shapira. *Conscious Community. p. 5.*

18

 Idel, M. *Hitbodedut as Concentration in Ecstatic Kabbalah.* Retrieved from *http://www.bahaistudies.net/asma/hitbodedut.pdf*

19

 Kaplan, p. 65-6.

20

 Hypki, C, et.al. *Memorial Ritual and Art: A Case Study and Exploration of the Potential for Healing. Retrieved from https://www.mica.edu/About_MICA/Deapartments_and_Services/The_C enter_*

21

 Kaplan, p. 65.

22

 The term *Kiddush* (lit. "Sanctification"), the blessing recited over wine on *Shabbat* and Holy Days, is also extended to the post-worship collation at which this ritual is enacted. *Minyan* (lit. "Number") is a quorum of 10 adult Jews required to conduct all aspects of a public worship service. By extension, *Minyan* can refer to an ongoing, regularly convened prayer fellowship.

23

Coleman, V. D. & Farris-Dufrene, P M. *Art Therapy and Psychotherapy: Blending Two Therapeutic Approaches.* Accelerated Development, 1996. p. 111.

24

Shapira, K. K. *A Student's Obligation: Advice from the Rebbe of the Warsaw Ghetto.* Trans. Odenbeimer, M. Rowman & Littlefield Publishers, Inc., 1991, p 22.

25

Kaplan, p.66

26

Kushner, L. *The Book of Miracles: A Young Person's Guide to Jewish Spiritual Awareness.* The UAHC Press, 1987. p. 71.

27

Zohar: 2:290b.

28

Csikszentmihaily quote retrieved from Kaplan, p.71.

29

Rappaport, L. *Focusing-Oriented Art Therapy.* Jessica Kingsley publishers, 2009. p. 32.

30

Kaplan, p.75-6.

31

Ibid.

32

Hypki.

33

Kollar quote retrieved from Hypki,

34

Kaplan, p.66

35

Kaplan, pp.75-6

36

Shapira. *A Student's Obligation.* p. 70.

37

Shapira. *Conscious Community.* p. 30.

38

McNiff, S. *Art Heals: How Creativity Cures the Soul.* Shambhala, 2004, p. 57.

39

For an overview of the *Shiviti* practice see *mussarinstitute.org/*

Yashar/2013-09/shiviti.php
40

Kaplan, A. *Inner Space*. Moznaim Publishing Corp., 1990. p. 165.
41

BT Hagigah 13b
42

Regnier, R. "The Sacred Circle: A Process Pedagogy of Healing" *Interchange*. 25.2 April 1994. p. 129.
43

BT Ta'anit 13a
44

Greenberg, M. *On the Refinement of the Conception of Prayer in Hebrew Scriptures*. Retrieved *http://www.jstor.org/stable/1486338?seq=1#page_scan_tab_contents*, accessed December 28, 2017.
45

Numbers Rabbah 13:9
46

Wortzman. *Creating Soul Connections.*
47

Shapira. *A Student's Obligation.* p. 128.
48

Wolfson, E. *Abraham ben Samuel Abulafia and the Prophetic Kabbalah p 80*
Retrieved from
*https://s3.amazonaws.com/academia.edu.documents/31143993/abulafi a_and_prophetic_kabbalah.pdf?AWSAccessKeyId=AKIAIWOWYYGZ2Y53 UL3A&Expires=1509577435&Signature=xpgTd0qKmO8YTC62De7kzRz c5yY%3D&response-contentdisposition=inline%3B%20filename %3DAbraham_ben_Samuel_Abulafi a_and_the_Prop.pd*f, accessed December 27, 2017.
49

Shapira, K. K. *Jewish Spiritual Growth: A Step-by-Step Guide by a Hasidic Master*. Yaacov David Shulman, 2016. P. 16
50

Andrew Boyd quote retrieved from Hypki, Cynder, et.al. *Memorial Ritual and Art op. cit.*
51

Shapira. *A Student's Obligation.,* p. 31 and p. 128.
52

Hypki, Cynder

For Further Reading

Allen, P. B. *Art Is a Spiritual Path*. Shambhala, 2005. Print.

Artson, B. "*Ba-derekh*: On the Way–A Presentation of Process Theology." *Spiritual Path*. Shambhala, 2005. Print.

McNiff, S. *Art Heals: How Creativity Cures the Soul*. Shambhala, 2004. Print.

Paintner, C. V. and Beckman, B. *Awakening the Creative Spirit: Bringing the Arts to Spiritual Direction*. Morehouse Publishing, 2010. Print.

Regnier, R. "The Sacred Circle: A Process Pedagogy of Healing" *Interchange*. 25.2 April (1994). Print.

Shapira, K. K. *Conscious Community: A Guide to Inner Work*. Trans. Cohen-Kiener, A. Rowman & Littlefield Publishers, 1996. Print.

Wortzman, E. *Creating Soul Connections: Art as a Means of Jewish Spiritual Direction with Youth*. Graduate Theological Foundation, unpublished dissertation, May 2017.

Wortzman, E. "Process Theology, Aesthetics, Halacha and Spiritual Development Through Art" in J. H. Morgan (Ed.), *Foundation Theology*. GTF Books, 2017. pp. 141-157.

הצלה

HATZALAH/DELIVERANCE

Saying "We Believe"

The Blessings of Local Interfaith Dialogue

James R. Michaels

The term *Interfaith Dialogue* has been popular for well over half a century. The concept resonates with large numbers of clergy and laity who are committed to building bridges between various faith communities. The impetus is to learn about neighbors without the desire to proselytize or to engage in polemics. Although it began during the liberal era of the 1960s, it seems that we need it more today as political and religious leaders seek to demonize "the other."

The work of interfaith dialogue has been ongoing, as documented by Dr. Leonard Swidler of Temple University, who has catalogued its principles as they have arisen over the decades.[1] Reading over the various lists Swidler cites, one might wonder whether they were developed in somewhat cloistered circumstances. While acknowledging the excellent credentials of their various authors, it may be asked how effectively these principles have been culled from and transmitted to clergy and laity in local communities. That is, with all the efforts to bring people together, why are we more polarized today than we were fifty years ago?

As a congregational rabbi and chaplain for more than forty years, I suggest we need to pay more attention and put more energy into dialogue at the local level. Instead of a "top-to-bottom" approach, let me propose a "grass roots" model for interfaith dialogue and cooperation. That is, I believe true progress can and should be made at the local level, seasoned with generous helpings of patience and grace. In the twilight of my rabbinic career, I would like to offer the following personal recollections and insights to illustrate these three pillars of interfaith cooperation.

Personal History

I became a rabbi in 1974 but, in a real sense, have participated in interfaith work all my life. Growing up in Auburn, New York, a city of 35,000 people, I knew that I was in a religious minority. To be sure, there were other Jews in town; in my grade school class, for example, there were three other Jewish kids. But I was acutely aware that most of my neighbors were Christian; the prevalence of Christmas lights and trees in every house on our block made that clear. We also put decorations in our windows—for Hanukkah—but they didn't attract much attention. To be honest, I always liked others' lights because they were much more creative and pretty.

When I was eleven years old, I was surprised when I went to Sunday school on a snowy day in February and learned that I would not be required to be in the classroom that morning. Instead, students in our class and those who were older would attend a service in a church across the street. "It's Brotherhood Week," said the rabbi, "I'm giving the sermon."

It was probably the first time I had been in a church. It was exciting to walk in, nod and smile to a couple of kids I knew from school, and listen to the choir sing "All Praise the Living God." My teacher pointed to the upper right hand corner of the hymnal page; "Adapted from *Yigdal*"[2] was printed there. I thought, Wow! They're even singing our songs!

The prayers were somewhat strange; in retrospect, I realize the minister made a point of not mentioning the Trinity. Then our rabbi got up to speak. He gave great honor to the church, and especially the pastor who had become his friend. "I am his assistant minister," he said. "He is my assistant rabbi." We all left happy. And the following Friday evening, the minister spoke from the pulpit of the synagogue.

I can't say that I decided to become a rabbi at that moment, nor can I say that I made any solemn vows to focus on interfaith work in the future. I can say, however, that it made an impression.

I also became aware that I could sometimes be called upon to serve as an ambassador for Judaism. I didn't need to tell anyone I was a Jew. It seemed that everyone knew that the Michaels, the Goldman, and the Schwartz families were Jewish. (Those names accounted for about 75% of the Jews in Auburn!) It was not unusual for a parent driving car pool to ask me questions about Judaism. If I was the last kid to be dropped off, I might be asked to continue the discussion while we sat in the car outside my house. I was also aware that I needed to give honest answers, even if I was not fully informed of all the facts.

Auburn was a heavily Catholic city; most of the people were descendants of Polish and Italian immigrants. When Pope John XXIII convened Vatican II, it was big news everywhere, especially among the faithful of Auburn. As the news came out of Rome about the changes swirling in the Church, it created quite a stir. Suddenly the priests in the pulpit were telling their parishioners that the ethnic and religious slurs spoken about Jews at home were no longer kosher. They announced that Jews weren't Christ-killers, and that Jesus was actually a Jew!

To celebrate, our rabbi called the local Catholic bishop and asked how he could invite the local priests and deacons to attend a service on a Friday night. The bishop arranged for all of Auburn's Catholic clergy to attend the service on the specified date. The synagogue was filled to capacity. Our soloist sang "One God," which begins: *Millions of Stars Placed in the Sky by One God.*[3] I especially liked the last line: *Your God and my God are one.* One of the priests spoke that evening and addressed the changes that we all were reading about in the newspapers and Life magazine.

The next morning, the rabbi said to me, "There are great things happening in the world. You can play a part in them." I had already been thinking of becoming a rabbi, so I knew what he meant.

The following fall, I went off to Cornell University. I quickly found my way to the Hillel office. It wasn't in a separate building, as would be the case on most campuses. It was one of many religious groups which were housed in Cornell United Religious Work (CURW). I was impressed that all the denominations were found in the same building and could easily talk to each other. Shortly after I arrived, a coffee house opened in the CURW building. It was intended as a place where people of all beliefs (or no belief) could exchange ideas and enjoy some good coffee.

It was the fall of 1964, so the presidential election was on everyone's mind. Liberals and independents had been thrilled that Lyndon Johnson had won, so we were dismayed a few months later when the president started escalating the Vietnam War. People started organizing demonstrations and teach-ins; they were all planned in CURW's coffee house. As the political activism of the mid-1960s grew in intensity, CURW was always the place where the latest events were discussed, and many of the protests were planned there.

In Auburn, if there was ever a Jewish event (political as well as religious) it was planned at the synagogue. So, to my mind, it seemed only seemed natural that religious activities would intertwine with social or political activism. I could attend Shabbat services in the chapel and then walk down the hall to help plan an upcoming rally with like-minded people who were Protestant or Catholic. I never saw any conflict, and I was able to broaden my horizons to meet Muslims, Evangelical Christians, and Catholic priests who were more comfortable wearing turtlenecks than they were in clerical collars. We all gathered, drank coffee, and found common cause. Working together, we felt we could eliminate racism and end the war. And when I applied to rabbinical school, I asked the Hillel rabbi and a Jesuit priest to write letters of recommendation.

As with many young Jewish men in 1968, one impetus for me to enter a rabbinical seminary was to avoid the draft. Although I had regularly communicated with HUC-JIR about my interest in attending rabbinical school, avoiding the draft was an added benefit. The foment of the decade entered the halls of sacred learning, and many of us insisted on bringing our studies to bear on the problems of day. It was not unusual for me to attend services on a Saturday morning, and then go to an antiwar demonstration in the afternoon. That was my way of observing Shabbat. I also became friendly with some members of VISTA and often assisted them in community organizing in one of the city's impoverished neighborhoods.

Six years of a person's life is a significant chunk of time, so it would not be right to say nothing happened while I was pursuing my rabbinical studies. Plenty happened, but for the purpose of this article, I'll focus on one year when I actually left school and worked as a rabbinic intern at a congregation in St Paul, Minnesota. I had spent the previous summer there, and decided I needed a break from school. One of my responsibilities was to participate in interfaith activities. The senior rabbi said, "My heart's in it, but I don't have the time."

I was already friendly with a Presbyterian minister who invited me to participate on a panel of interfaith clergy. The event went well, and afterward my friend encouraged me to do as much of this as possible. "You never know who will be affected by your presence," he said, "There are people who live within a mile of your synagogue who have never met a Jewish person." That was a revelation, so I made a point of accepting as many invitations as I could to address churches and church groups. This was a commitment which I brought wherever I have served after ordination. If I was invited, and if it was logistically possible, I always agreed to speak to non-Jewish groups.

Progress Comes from Acting Locally

My first congregation was in Whitestone, New York. Like most of New York City, there was a significant Jewish population, but the bulk of the community was not Jewish. Almost as soon as I arrived, I began reaching out to my Christian colleagues and participated in the local interfaith clergy association. As I had before, I found common ground and enjoyed the opportunity to get together socially with those who shared common experiences in various congregations. The neighborhood was religiously diverse, so I was able to meet and know people I hadn't previously encountered: Russian Orthodox, Greek Orthodox, Evangelical Christians, and I made a concerted effort to include Roman Catholic clergy from the local parish.

Having received attention in neighborhood newspapers, I was also known by local political leaders. I was honored, therefore, when our local City Council member asked me to help resolving an issue involving a group of Muslims. The group had established a mosque in a house in a residential neighborhood. Long-time residents were suspicious of the group and resented the newcomers setting up a place of worship. I was asked to convene a group of religious leaders who could provide a forum for the Muslims and their neighbors to discuss their feelings and begin a process of reconciliation. The meeting was successful, as the hard feelings began to dissipate.

A few weeks later, I was invited to meet a *Shaykh* who was the spiritual mentor of the Muslims I had helped. The man lived in Pakistan and was traveling through the United States. He had heard how I had helped the people in the mosque and wanted to thank me. I was impressed that he would take the time to meet me; in turn, I was also impressed with the palpable air of spirituality he possessed. His message to me was that Jews and Muslims historically had lived and worked together, and we could continue this effort despite the political and military tensions in the Middle East.

About a year later, after I had moved from Whitestone to Wilkes-Barre, Pennsylvania, I received a formal invitation to address a national gathering of the *Shaykh*'s sect. I was asked to be part of a panel which would speak on how faith could overcome fear and suspicion. The event would take place in New York City, so I arranged to attend and participate.

I chose to speak about the common father of Islam and Judaism, Abraham, as an exemplar of faith. During my remarks, I mentioned in passing how Abraham exhibited faith when he followed God's command to sacrifice Isaac. It was one sentence in a talk which lasted twenty minutes. When I finished, the moderator stood up, turned to me, and declared "It was Ishmael!" and never looked at me again. When the event concluded, a few people thanked me politely and walked away. Otherwise, I was ignored, and I left the gathering alone. I never heard from the sect or its Shaykh again.

As I drove back to my home in Wilkes-Barre, I thought about what had happened and why the good feelings could dissipate so quickly. Eventually I realized that two words were missing, and that made all the difference. Those words were "We believe." The Muslim moderator's stark declaration, "It was Ishmael" was a dogmatic, defensive statement, leaving no room for discussion. It left others in the audience with a dilemma. If they moved in my direction, they would betray their faith and risk animosity from others. On the other hand, had the moderator simply said, "We believe it was Ishmael," it would have left open room for dialogue and exploration of each other's beliefs. I also realized that I hadn't done my own homework; I didn't realize how one ill-timed sentence could defeat all of my good intentions. Essentially, I also offered no opportunity for dialogue. Had I said, "Jews believe"... it might have opened the subject for dialogue, either there or in subsequent forums. I resolved that I was going to learn from the experience and use it in my continuing commitment to interfaith cooperation.

Patience Leads to Lasting Achievements

My synagogue was one of several houses of worship in the center of Wilkes-Barre. By coincidence, the spiritual leaders of all them had arrived in 1988. There had been a long tradition of interfaith dialogue and our lay leaders encouraged us to continue that path. An opportunity quickly presented itself. November 8, 1988 would mark the fiftieth anniversary of *Kristallnacht*. My Lutheran colleague called and said, "What are we going to do about it?" He explained that the Lutheran Church of Germany had aided and abetted the beginnings of the Holocaust, not by commission, but by its silence in the face of the violence. He felt the need to atone. We quickly gathered the other newcomers and decided to organize a community event.

On the night of November 8, hundreds of people gathered at my synagogue and began a march through the center of the city, passing several churches along the way. We prayed at each building, and parishioners joined the group. The procession ended at the Public Square where a brief memorial was held. The climax came when I held a pane of glass in my hand and smashed it with a hammer; the shards fell harmlessly into a trash basket. Those who were able then recited the Mourner's *Kaddish*,[4] and all the clergy joined arms and led the song, "Let Peace Begin with Me." TV cameras recorded the event and broadcast excerpts at 11 p.m.

A few days later my colleagues and I got together again to discuss how we could build on the momentum of the event. We brainstormed for a while and came up with an idea to present a series of programs to introduce our religious beliefs and customs to each other and to the wider community. We agreed that to do this in depth, we would need to present more than just one program for each religious tradition. Instead, we would devote an entire year to one, and then another year to the next. The first year, we would focus on Judaism, the second on Islam, and the third on Russian Orthodox Christianity. My Protestant and Catholic colleagues said that all three were "hiding in plain sight." People knew who we were, yet they didn't know what we stood for or how we practiced our faith.

The year-long format provided lots of opportunity for in-depth discussion among the presenters and informal dialogue after each presentation. Six programs were devoted to each religious group. Local clergy and laity did most of the presentations, although some guest speakers were occasionally invited from New York or Philadelphia. The local news media were invited to attend, and the events received prominent attention in the newspapers and television.

During these presentations, the ability to say "we believe" was important because it allowed for courteous and reasoned dialogue, avoiding polemics and disagreement. The effect was quite dramatic. For example, for one of the presentations on Judaism, I persuaded my Orthodox and Reform Colleagues to join me on a panel where were would each present aspects of our particular "brand." I told the other rabbis not to hold back. We each presented our unique approaches to Jewish belief and observance, explaining frankly why these differences existed and why they weren't likely to dissipate. From my perspective, I believed we had succeeded. When the panel concluded, however, a Protestant minister had been asked to offer comments and observations. He said, "Isn't it remarkable how these three rabbis could demonstrate such unity!" The rabbis had presented religious differences; Christians saw none of our sectarian divisions which in some ways mirror what they have experienced since the Reformation.

The deep understanding and trust engendered by these programs had long lasting benefits within the community. Here are a couple examples:

- In the aftermath of the Operation Desert Storm in 1991, there was a lot of attention paid to the plight of the Kurds in northern Iraq. Together, the clergy organized a demonstration of support and prepared materials to educate our congregations and the community about the issue.

- A few years later, a self-proclaimed Nazi moved into town and started distributing literature. All the clergy spoke out against him and provided a counterweight to the attention he was receiving in the media. Ultimately, he couldn't generate much support and quietly left town.

I continued my involvement in interfaith projects throughout my career as a pulpit rabbi. When I was awarded an honorary doctorate by the Jewish Theological Seminary, the citation noted my commitment to working with religious leaders of all faiths. I even had a television show called Spiritual Spectrum on local cable TV. As the name implied, the program featured interviews with a wide variety of religious leaders, including Muslims, Buddhists, and even Christian Motorcycle Ministries.

Stressing Grace

The concept of grace as undeserved favor is common among all religions. While it's usually expressed as a divine attribute, people should be willing to extend grace to each other, even to those they don't know. I became more aware of this as I made a transition from pulpit rabbi to health care chaplain.

When I was in rabbinical school, the words "health care" and "chaplain" were never uttered in the same sentence. It was simply unheard of as a career option. However, as I served in various congregations, I also found employment as a part-time chaplain. I eventually realized it was an avenue of rabbinic service I needed to pursue. I obtained the required training and was fortunate to be selected as Director of Pastoral Care at the Hebrew Home of Greater Washington, DC. I've served in this capacity since 2003.

This career change did not mean I gave up my commitment to interfaith work. In fact, I have found more opportunities than ever. Even though the Hebrew Home's religious and cultural demeanor is Jewish, we provide spiritual care for all residents, regardless of religion. About 50% of the residents in our skilled nursing buildings aren't Jewish. I make sure there are Christian worship services on Sundays and major holidays. I also work closely with the local Catholic parish; the eucharistic ministers provide communion for Catholic residents, and the priests respond rapidly to provide anointment for Catholics who are near death.

Our Clinical Pastoral Education program offers chaplaincy training to all people. We've developed close relationships with several nearby seminaries. As their students learn pastoral skills, they learn more about Judaism and Jewish people. Here's an interesting story illustrating how this has worked:

"Sol" (a pseudonym), ninety-five years old, was brought to our skilled nursing building after living for many years in Florida. He had been religious all his life, and his daughter requested that we bring him to services every day and assist him to wear tefillin.[5] One summer, Sol was befriended by one of our CPE interns, a student studying for the ministry at

Virginia Theological Seminary in Alexandria, Virginia. This young man enjoyed sitting next to Sol at morning services; he was particularly interested in how he would wear the phylacteries. I eventually asked him if he would like to learn how to assist Sol. When he agreed, I showed him a book with explicit instructions. He quickly learned the technique and then helped Sol every day for the next five weeks. Toward the end of his training, I asked the student how he would use this experience in the future. He responded, "God only knows," which he meant in its literal sense. He couldn't predict how, but he knew that this lesson would one day be important in his ministry.

Sol and the young man were actually providing grace to each other. Each benefitted from the other's gifts which, in turn, would lead to favor extended to others in unforeseen ways. This is the potential and the promise of sincere interfaith dialogue and cooperation.

Conclusions: Where Do We Go from Here?

As I approach the end of my career, I can see how the lessons of my commitment to interfaith work can help heal a fractured world. I would like to suggest three areas where this is sorely needed.

Challenges to personal faith: In a recent article, David Rosen (a true hero of interfaith dialogue) writes that dialogue is becoming harder because "the participants are never talking the same language." He writes that in a post-modern world, people of differing traditions have increasing difficulty communicating with each other. This, in turn, leads to insecurity as believers feel that the lack of common ground will shake the faith of believers.[6]

In very recent years, this has been exhibited as some Christian groups have pressed conservative agendas under the guise of claiming religious liberty. To use one example, some people have claimed providing service for homosexuals is a violation of their rights. When the issue concerns a custom-made wedding cake, it seems almost trivial. However, if health care providers are allowed to withhold their care-giving skills to gay and lesbian couples, it becomes much more serious. (As I write these words, the current administration in Washington is pushing for exactly that).

This and similar issues (e.g. reproductive rights) present a challenge but also an opportunity for a new kind of dialogue. Religious people who are politically liberal should have the opportunity to say, "We believe..." to those who are conservative, and vice versa. Optimally, people can learn how their desire for religious liberty can deny it to other believers. And if both "sides" of the debate can extend grace to each other, perhaps they can begin to find common ground.

Conflicts in religious hot spots: The Middle East is a cauldron of tension and misunderstanding. Most people who watch or read the news come away with the feeling that there is no way

Muslims, Jews, and Christians can find opportunities for dialogue. To be sure, the media accentuate the areas of conflict, usually portraying the conflict as beyond resolution.

What goes unreported are the many on-going efforts to bring together people of different beliefs to find ways they can live together. In his recent book, *The Other Peace Process*,[7] Rabbi Ronald Kronish reviews his work of over twenty years as the founding director of the Interreligious Coordinating Council of Israel. He illustrates how grass-root efforts have created many examples of joint actions of peace building between the three major religious groups in Israel.[8]

"Warm fuzzies" are nice but not sufficient: As outlined above, single efforts for dialogue may produce a good feeling for a moment, or even for a day. To be sure, there are people who can execute initiatives which will have implications on a global scale.

I have found, however, that the most successful projects are those which create local networks and coalitions. (I have always remembered that my biggest failure was when I was addressing a national gathering.) Individuals and groups working together in local communities will be the most likely to create change. In the long run, these efforts can make a difference on a larger level.

While it's always good to organize programs that have immediate criteria for success, it's more important to build caring coalitions based on ongoing relationships. Trust may be the most important product of interfaith action. Based on my own experience, I feel lasting trust will lead to true understanding and continued cooperation across religious lines, embodying the words of the Psalmist: *Behold how pleasant it is for brothers and sisters to dwell together in unity* (Psalm 133:1).

ENDNOTES

1

Swidler, L. "Decalogue Commandments: Ground Rules for Interreligious, Inter-ideological Dialogue," *Journal of Ecumenical Studies* 20:1 (1984). Retrieved from *http://www.contemplative.net/interfaithdialogue-a-39.html*

2

Yigdal ("May He [the Living God] be magnified") is a hymn based on Maimonides' 13 Principles of Faith. For further information see *http://jewishencyclopedia.com/articles/15086-yigdal*

3

Rotheray, D & Heaton, P, "One God" lyrics © THE SONGWRITERS GUILD OF AMERICA, Universal Music Publishing Group   Retrieved from

www.lyricsfreak.com/b/barbra+streisand/one+god_20274179.html

4

For a full discussion of the *Kaddish* see *https://www.jewishvirtuallibrary.org/the-mourners-kaddish*

5

Known in English as "phylacteries," these are leather boxes which contain four passages from the Torah instructing Jews to: *bind them as a sign upon your hand, and they shall be a frontlet between your eyes* (Deut. 6:8). Handwritten on parchment, these passages are inserted in the boxes, which are worn on the upper arm and upper forehead, affixed by leather straps. Traditionally worn by men, today some women are also performing this commandment.

6
   Rosen, David, "The Challenges of Interfaith Dialogue," *Berkeley Center for Religion, Peace and World Affairs*, June 27, 2016.

7
   Kronish, R. *The Other Peace Process*. Hamilton Books, 2017.

8
   In chapter 5, Rabbi Kronish is very critical of conferences which issue statements, but don't produce any meaningful results for action on a local level. He urges people involved in this ongoing work to learn how to use the internet and social media. He says extremists have already mastered this, so peace-makers need to learn how to get their message out in equally effective ways.

New Psalms for a Jewish Paradigm Shift

Herbert J. Levine

When people of other religious backgrounds study Judaism, it is crucial that they remind themselves that Jews are a religious ethnicity rather than a creedal religious community, such as Christians and Muslims constitute. As an ethnicity, Jewish forms of worship are highly particularized with reference to the Jewish experience of peoplehood: Exodus, Torah, and a longed-for, but never quite arriving Final Redemption.

The promises made by the God of the Bible to the Hebrews (whose descendants are known as Jews) represent the first Jewish paradigm: a covenant focused on:1) loyalty to God and God's law, 2) arrival at a promised land, 3) exile from that land as punishment and 4) eventual return as proof that God remembers His covenant with Israel. The emergence of State of Israel in the mid-twentieth century is evidence to some believers that the covenant and the four-stage paradigm it represents are still valid.

There is another view, however, which posits a succession of paradigms within that larger historical arc. The biblical paradigm, focused on the holiness of place, was first disrupted by the Babylonian exile and then ended with the Roman destruction of the holy Temple and the sacking of Jerusalem. What followed was the rabbinic paradigm, which necessarily created a portable religion, focused on Torah in the synagogue and ceremonies in the home for Shabbat and holidays. This placeless paradigm selected among possible biblical images of God in order to emphasize a God who stressed mercy over strict justice. Rather than all agreeing to revere an all-powerful God responsible for every aspect of history, we begin to find rabbinic homilists, like the *midrashim* collected in *Lamentations Rabbah*, who portray an empathic God, weeping along with his people in the innermost chamber of God's heavenly palace, because of His inability to prevent the destruction of their Temple and capital, Jerusalem.[1] This radical (and admittedly minority) theological development corresponds to a stress on the anthropocentric in rabbinic teachings. These can best be summed up in the famous axiom of Hillel describing the essence of Torah: "What is hateful to you, do not unto your neighbor. The rest is commentary. Go and learn it."[2]

The rabbinic paradigm lasted for about 1800 years, until the European Enlightenment and corresponding political liberation gave Jews citizenship in the European countries in which they lived. For the first time, Jews could aspire to live out the universalism envisioned in the latter chapters of Isaiah. Beginning with the development of Reform Judaism, Jews sought ways to reconcile the particularity of their religious tradition with those universal aspirations.   Early reformers challenged the centrality to the Jews of peoplehood in their self-understanding by seeing themselves as a religious confession, like that of their Christian confreres. They were to be French or German men and women of the Mosaic persuasion.

The major Jewish denominations were all created in response to the tradition shattering assumptions of modernity, including even modern Orthodoxy, which manifested the most conservative tendency on this spectrum of reactions. Reform, Conservative, Reconstructionist—all took evolutionary, not revolutionary, positions with respect to Torah and liturgy. While leaving out or revising certain passages of the liturgy that may have offended a modern person's rational commitments—such as belief in the Resurrection of the Dead or a literal Messiah or God's Election of Israel – the most extreme of the changes—all created a recognizably theistic mode of worship. All these denominations taught that the Torah was at least partially the product of human agency and not solely verbal divine revelation. Rarely, however, did this revolutionary idea become manifest in a new liturgical approach to the centrality of Torah. The Holocaust marked the end of the modern Jewish paradigm -shattering for many Jews a belief in a God who made and keeps promises to his people. For the first time, there were Jewishly-trained theologians who proposed the "Death of God,"[3] which was excoriated by the Jewish establishment, but took practical hold among Jews who left their synagogues' pews. The rebirth of Hebrew as an everyday language of the Jewish people, the creation of the State of Israel, a rebirth coming after the death of one-third of the Jewish people, the ingathering of exiles to a Jewish homeland restored ethnicity to a central position in creating meaning for Jews not only in Israel, but around the world as well. For a generation, the religion of American Jews became what has been called civil religion, with its own rituals—Holocaust Remembrance Day, Israel Independence Day—and its own sacred spaces, including Holocaust memorials in numerous North American cities and Federation-sponsored pilgrimages to Israel. While many secular Jews continued their affiliation in synagogues, they attended mostly on the High Holy Days and when invited to family life passage events. Since religious affiliation seemed to be the only way, outside of immigration to Israel, to preserve Jewish identity, it could be indulged in a few times a year, keeping it within bounds deemed not to be fanatical.

The post-Holocaust period has given rise to a great deal of experimentation in all the Jewish denominations. Today one can find synagogues that offer eastern-influenced meditation sessions, Torah yoga, dance as a metaphoric analogy to verbal liturgy—practices that would have been unrecognizable as Jewish in any of the previous paradigms. (Even within Orthodoxy, feminism has made some inroads, giving rise to all female prayer communities and other experiments). Some of these experiments have clustered under the banner of "Jewish Renewal," the legacy of one of the most original Jewish thinkers and spiritual leaders of the twentieth century, Rabbi Zalman

Schachter-Shalomi. He was a *Lubavitch*[4] Hasid who immigrated to America in the late 1940s, met and embraced the Aquarian Age of the late 1960s, without ever dropping his commitment to the particularity of Judaism---now seen as only one of many legitimate paths for spiritual enlightenment.

In his 1985 book *Paradigm Shift*, Schachter-Shalomi brought into Jewish discourse the Gaia hypothesis, formulated by biologists in the 1970s, which posits that biological organisms and the inorganic world form a unified, self-regulating system that preserves the conditions for continued life on Earth. Expressing this in evolutionary terms, humans are the embodiment of the cosmos becoming self-conscious, and, in moral terms, are therefore responsible for the future of that evolution. Gaia, he told his followers, was the living God, and they were Gaia's vanguard.

With the human crisis on the planet (climate, population size, food resources) becoming ever more pressing, rabbi-theologians have been following his lead in describing various versions of God as Gaia—most recently, Arthur Green's *Radical Judaism* (2010) and Bradley Artson's *Renewing the Process of Creation* (2015). In the past two decades, we have seen God presented as a verb, as the verbal phrase is-was-will-be, as a transformative, liberating movement toward justice, as the interdependence of humans and plants—all formulations welcome, it seems except those that attribute to God unrestrained omnipotence, the power of being fully in charge, which most post-Holocaust Jews find difficult to accept.

This capsule summary of Jewish history and the evolution of its paradigms brings me to my recent projects of writing nontheistic psalms and blessings. My project of writing secular psalms was prompted by Shaul Magid's call in the 2015 Winter issue of *Tikkun* for forms of Jewish worship to embody Rabbi Schachter-Shalomi's paradigm-changing approach to Jewish theology. In an accompanying sidebar approving Magid's message, Schachter-Shalomi admitted he had not been ready to initiate such a change during his life but knew that its time was coming.

Marcia Falk's *Book of Blessings* and *The Days Between* opened the way for bi-lingual, non-theistic Jewish poems and prayers. Many Jewish poets have similarly offered prayerful poems with no God-term as contemporary psalms, including Karl Shapiro, Irving Feldman, Allen Ginsberg, Paul Celan, and Yehuda Amichai, among others. I think especially of the exemplary God-discourse of Yehuda Amichai in his final book, *Open Closed Open* (Mariner Books, 2006). There he claims that "change is god and death is its prophet," suggesting that our only bedrock is change itself, the mutability of the visible world to which lyric poetry has always been devoted. Amichai, in turn, was building on the committed secularism and Jewish allusiveness of Chaim Nachman Bialik, poet laureate of the Jewish people in the late nineteenth and early twentieth centuries.

These iconoclasts loom large as my paradigm-changing Jewish forebears, as I go about creating a devotional language for those who seek a new balance of the universal and the particularistic within a Jewish context:

O blessed world, you give us each day visions and problems to
solve and to praise.

These verses of a contemporary psalm came to me in Hebrew,
the Jewish language that I find best suited for enduring Jewish
continuity and creativity. I wrote most of the poems that appear
in this essay first in Hebrew and then translated them into
English. They offer alternatives to traditional forms of Jewish
prayer and psalmody that do not require a leap of faith. I invite
the reader to think of them as post-theistic—that is, their
author has been deeply imbued with theism, maintained a
lifelong quarrel with it, and emerged as an unconflicted
nontheist.

Just as the lad Abram put a hammer
in the hand of the biggest idol
in his father's workshop
and pointed to it as the one who shattered
all the rest, so our father Abraham
put that self-same hammer in our hands
so that we might destroy images of God, which since then have
screened us from seeing that there is nothing holier than the
world.

By adopting the familiar biblical model of the quarrel with God
and by playing, especially in Hebrew, with resonances from the
Bible and the prayer book, I understand my post-theistic poems

to speak a Jewish language for Jewish seekers. In Israel, for instance, there are seekers who have never before experienced Jewish prayer yet meet on *Shabbat* evenings in community centers and open spaces (a large group meets on the beach in Tel Aviv) to share both traditional prayers and spiritual poems in community. Here is one of my Israel-centered prayer-poems that both breaks with and embraces the past.

In the archives at Kibbutz Beit *Ha-Shita*
I discovered forgotten hand-written notes of a Passover Seder from 1927.
In the place of the holiday Kiddush was written
Barukh ata kibbutz, Blessed are you, Kibbutz. Now let's widen the blessing circle and say together, 'Blessed are you, world,' to praise your fragile, complex beauty.

Like that enthusiastic kibbutznik
who insisted on making his time new
let's make new what's old
and make holy what's new
and join what's called secular to what's called holy and what's material to what's called spiritual
until the gulf between them disappears.

The 2013 Pew Research study, "A Portrait of American Jews,"[5] found declining religious affiliations and a growing number that self-define as Jewish, not religious. Yet most of our synagogues and ḥavurot (lit. "fellowships") continue to perpetuate Judaism as intergenerational religious nostalgia. We teach our children the forms we knew as children because they offer us comfort and continuity even though we mostly don't believe in the God that we're teaching our children to worship. Our children pick up our doubts, so that by the time they reach bar and bat mitzvah age—if they are savvy—they are proud atheists who stand at a remove from Judaism. But when their own children reach school age, they will likely once again offer them the same comfortable, but ultimately alienating forms, which replicate themselves like genes, but with diminishing returns, in each Jewish generation.

I have written my contemporary psalms for this growing group of non-religious Jews who may become seekers. Spirituality begins in gratitude and awe. Gratitude—not an emotion, but an attitude—reminds us that we are not self-created, but limited beings dependent on many contingencies, especially other people, for our wellbeing. Awe is our response to powerful experiences—seeing snow-capped mountains, holding a newborn—that remind us of our finite nature in the face of what is grand and enduring. I often use autobiographical reminiscence like the following to explore paths to gratitude and awe.

> Every Rosh Hashanah during my childhood, my father
> Would ask my *Bubbe*,[6] 'Why are the corners
> of your prayer book's pages folded over?'
> Every year she answered him, 'This is where we cry.'

From her life of wanderings,
my *Bubbe* understood tears
and what follows from them: in no way
challenge fate by failing to mention
the One who watches over all,
but hope with 'the help of God' and be grateful with 'Praise
God,' and 'Thank God.'

I also want to express hopes and
give thanks for the good in my life and be amazed by the
wonders of the universe.
With the help of the world,
my tongue is getting used to new expressions.

In these poems, I believe I am contributing to the evolution of
Jewishness into a reality-based, cosmos-centered approach to
the world that is not limited by our traditional narratives and
rituals, but is nevertheless in an authentic relationship to them.
So my paradigm-shifting poems integrate science and spirit for
a world where Darwin and Einstein are what Moses once was,
prophets of ultimate truth. Here are two stanzas that bring
insights from biochemistry, evolutionary biology, geology,
chemistry, and astrophysics into what I hope is prayerful
speech.

My life and yours began through a crack
in the ocean floor, through which heat rose (and still rises) from
the core of the earth and catalyzed
the salty waters. The amino acids

were created, containing the history of life
in the sea, on land and in the air.
The psalmist sings, "with you is the source of life."
Every day, I too acknowledge the source of life
that still enlivens my breath.

From Einstein and his students I learned
that the elements in me were forged
in the same furnace as the stars.
From other great ones, I've learned
to sit, breathe, pay attention
with watchful eyes
to a world filled with glory and wonders
... like me, like you and like the stars.

The pillars of traditional Judaism are God, Torah, and Israel, or, expressed in temporal terms, creation, revelation and redemption. New Jewish prayer-poems inevitably create alternative ways for envisioning these categories. To reframe Torah for our time, I offer the following:

This is the Torah
that was written by humans
over many generations,
that Ezra put
before the people of Israel
in the name of Moses,
that Hillel the Elder summarized
hundreds of years after Ezra:[7]

What is hateful to you, don't do to your fellow.
The rest is commentary that's worth studying
and, afterwards, do what needs doing.

Re-envisioning Torah requires a language for commandments that does not include a commander. So, I turn *mitzvotav*, God's commandments, into *mitzvoteinu*, our practices for becoming more conscious of self and world, for taking responsibility for both self- and world-transformation. This is in line with the Torah's view that God chose Abram because he would teach his children to do what was right and good.

Our ancestors were right
when they said that one mitzvah leads to another, and, likewise,
a misdeed.
This I know from the mistakes of my life.
I don't believe in a commander, but the
language of 'Thou shalt" reminds me
that we inherited the *mitzvot*
in order to be refined,
like silver in the hands of the smith,
like gold separated from its dross.

The Torah concludes with the Promised Land always on the horizon, while the Tanakh completes the circle with Cyrus of Persia's declaration that the Jews should now return to the land. Whether authenticated by God or by an earthly emperor, the overarching narrative of Jewish scripture ensures that we will fail to see the other people in the land, even as our legal codes urgently reiterate the need to treat the strangers among us with compassion and justice, "for you were strangers in the land of Egypt" (Exodus 23:9, Deut. 10:19). With tragic consequences for ourselves and for our 'others,' we continue to live with this unsolved tension. Several of the Psalms retell the great stories of the Bible. In my revisionist versions of Bible, I reintegrate the stranger into the narrative of the family circle. Here is the opening of the poem, "All in the Family."

We sat, my brother and I, in the back
of the family car and quarreled unceasingly,
until our mother, may she rest in peace, would ask,
"How will there be peace in the world if
two brothers cannot live together in peace?" We knew from the
Bible stories she had taught us
that Cain killed his brother Abel out of jealousy,
that Ishmael beat up Isaac, even if it meant
his exile, that Jacob was ready to steal and Esau
to murder to receive what he could never get,
the one indivisible blessing.

Nowadays my brother and I meet for meals
on our birthdays, talk of our cholesterol levels and
sleep apnea, of the jobs that our children
have taken, and of the Israelis and Palestinians,
he, embarrassed like a Diaspora Jew, and I, shaken by this
quarrel of brothers
who rise from their graves
to deceive and to fight, to die and to kill, united

by their shared family plot, where they
pause for a moment to bury their dead.

As a committed diaspora Jew, I know that redemption will not be finished when the Palestinians have their own state or are even, as Martin Buber and Judah Magnes[8] envisioned, part of a bi-national state in the whole of the historic land of Israel. In a poem that juxtaposes the particular and the universal aspects of Judaism, I affirm that

I believe with perfect faith
that the Jews came out of Egypt to testify that there are narrow
straits in every place that all of us must pass through
to march toward a promised land
that we will not reach,
but which will never disappear.

A while back I visited the National Museum of the American Indian. Afterwards, I made note of a remark made by the father of one the artists, Calvin Hunt of the *Kwag'ul* band,[9] about the tradition of the *"Potlatch,"* the ceremony of mutual gift-giving and feasting between tribes: *If we did not carry on, our hearts would break.* For many years, this was my rationale for maintaining a traditional Jewish practice. We inherited this tradition from our forebears at great cost to them. Who was I to throw it aside? But increasingly, I've been saying to myself, "If I carry on in this way, my mind will break." I have written my bilingual, bi-cultural poems to bring heart and mind together.

Poems quoted in this essay are from *Words for Blessing the World: Poems in Hebrew and English (Ben Yehuda Press, 2017)*. A shorter version of this essay first appeared in *Tikkun v. 32, 1 (Winter, 2017)*.

ENDNOTES

---

[1]
Lamentations Rabbah, proem 24.

[2]
BT Shabbat 31a

[3]
Rubenstein, R. *After Auschwitz* (Indianapolis, IN; Bobbs-Merrill, 1966)

[4]
Lubavitch. The Yiddish pronunciation of *Lyubavichi*, a rural village in modern day Belarus, which became the seat of the Chabad Hasidism (lit. "Pietism") in approximately 1812. Today Chabad-Lubavitch is among the largest and best known hasidic movements, renowned for its Jewish outreach programs around the world

[5]
http://www.pewforum.org/2013/10/01/jewish-american-beliefs-attitudes-culture-survey/

[6]
Bubbe: Yiddish term of endearment which might best translate as "Nana" or "Grandma."

[7]
Hillel the Elder (d. 10 CE) Renowned early Talmudic sage, scholar and founder of a dynasty of sages who led Jewry in the Land of Israel until the fifth century CE.

Ezra the Scribe (d. 440 BCE) Reintroduced the Torah to the *Yishuv*, the Jewish community that returned from Babylonia to Judea.

8

Judah Leon Magnes (d. 1948) Reform rabbi in both the United States and Israel who advocated for a bi-national Jewish-Arab state in Mandate Palestine.

9

The *Kwag'ul* are a tribe of indigenous coastal peoples of the Canadian Pacific Northwest

פדיון

PIDYON/RELEASE AND RESTORATION

You Heal Me Through Dreams...

Howard Avruhm Addison

Rav Yehudah also said in the name of Rav: There are three things for which one should pray: good rulers, good years, and good dreams... as it is written; *You heal me through dreams and thereby cause me to live (Isaiah 38:16).*[1]

I. Regaining Contact

Beginning with the publication of Freud's *The Interpretation of Dreams* in 1900, the last century plus has seen a renewed interest in dreamwork. On the popular front, searches on Bing.com reveal ten general dream interpretation sites ... on its first page alone and virtual dream sharing groups ranging from *The Facebook Dreamer Group* to *Dreamdigging*, and *Awakening in the Dream*. More seriously, an early 2016 *New York Times* article highlighted the research of Buffalo, New York, hospice physician, Dr. Christopher Kerr, on the therapeutic role played by patients' end-of -life dreams and visions.[2] Ten months later dream work reappeared in a *Times* report on Kim Gillingham's use of Jungian dream practice to help actors emotionally deepen their performances while preparing for upcoming roles. Interviewed among Gillingham's more accomplished clients were Tony Award-winner Judith Light and Golden Globes recipient Sandra Oh.[3]

Given Western culture's preference for the practical and the scientific, we might ask why the current interest in dreams? Kelly Bulkeley, a leading authority on the topic of religion and dreams, points to the inability of contemporary rationalism, commercialism and individualism "to always lead to a fulfilling, meaningful life."[4] Calling upon the work of Carl Jung and later dream theorists, Bulkeley writes "that dreams are legitimate means of regaining contact with spiritual energies whose traditional outlets have been repressed by the scientific rationality of modern Western culture."[5] They do so, in part, by bringing us in contact with deeper aspects of ourselves which we're not aware of during waking life.

At times dreams can also generate intense, meaningful images whose narratives touch upon life's fundamental issues. These serve as "Root Metaphors," reshaping the dreamer's interpretation of reality, perception of the world and one's place within it.[6] Such dreams can have deep transformative effects, impelling the dreamer to action.[7] Perhaps Dreamwork's contemporary appeal, particularly among the growing numbers who consider themselves "spiritual but not religious,"[8] is its potential to offer inspiration and guidance without recourse to formal religious rituals, symbols or creeds.

Dreamwork also seems to be regaining a measure of acceptance within Western religious life. Durham University's Iain Edgar has observed that Islam, which honors posing dream questions through a rite known as *Istikhara,*[9] might well be the most extensive dream culture on the planet.[10] A 2010 New York Times article mentions that at least 200 church-based dream groups are now active across the United States.[11] Separate Bing.com searches reveal eleven specifically Christian and ten dedicated Muslim dream interpretation sites on their respective first pages. While Judaism has no comparable web presence, several books on Judaism and Dreams have appeared over these last few decades.[12]

The following observation by a seeker offers insight into the spiritual immediacy Dreamwork can offer believers, an immediacy not always found in formal communal worship and religious study

> *I find the dream world to be a 'thin place'[13] for encountering the Divine in all aspects of my life. Dream group experience is both intimately connecting with others and an important piece of my own personal work.[14]*

The goal of this essay is to explore how contemporary adaptations of traditional religious dream practices can deepen and re-sacralize our lives. We will consider some ways that spiritually inspired Dreamwork can help us redeem the often shallow "Flatland"[15] which both the secular and, due to the trap of rote observance, even the devout among us sometimes live.

II. Caution, Humility and Hope

Classical teachings within each of the Western traditions have affirmed dreams as legitimate sources of ongoing revelation. Tertullian of Carthage (d. 240 CE), an early Church Father, claimed the majority of humanity learns of God through dreams —not divinity in general but the One, True God.[16] A *Hadith*[17] reports that at the time of his death the prophet Muhammad proclaimed that naught shall remain of Prophecy's good tidings after his passing except for true dreams.[18] The *Zohar* (Book of Splendor), thirteenth century Spanish Kabbalah's major corpus, states:

> For nothing happens in the world but what is made known in advance either by means of a dream or a proclamation... when prophets were no more, their place was taken by the Sages, who, in a sense, even excelled the prophets; and in the absence of Sages things to come are revealed in dreams...[19]

However, the imagistic, nonlinear and sporadic nature of dreams has also rendered them institutionally unreliable as ongoing sources of Divine guidance. Dreams and dreamers can and have proven subversive to established religion, challenging both doctrine and authority based on personal visionary inspiration.[20] Western religious history contains real stories of how deluded self-inflation can taint even scripturally inspired dreams, bringing calamity in their wake: the false messianic dreams of a young *kabbalist,* Shabbetai Tzvi, in 1648[21;]; Nat Turner's dreams of being ordained to lead a violent slave uprising in 1831[22]; the importance of dreams in formulating the strategic plans of current day jihadis.[23] While these episodes visited slaughter and despair upon some whom the dreamers considered victimizers, they brought shame and/or death to the dreamers and, paradoxically, tragedy upon those the dreamers sought to deliver. Thus, it's not surprising that voices within each tradition have sought to minimize, marginalize and even demonize the spiritual nature of dreams.[24]

There are those who believe that dreams are literally messages from God, much in the way they're described in Scripture. However, many of us living in this Post-modern era, with its advances in Psychology and Neuroscience, have trouble understanding dreams in this way. Still, a sense of mystery can pervade our dreams when they offer us guidance from sources we know are outside our consciousness will. On the objective level, researchers continue to wonder while exploring the underlying dynamics of ESP which can occur in dream states, revealing things not currently known to the dreamer, information of the future and content suggestive of telepathy.[25]

Carl Jung perhaps best described the ageless yet subjective mystery of dreams, calling them:

> a little hidden door in the innermost and most secret recesses of the soul, opening into that cosmic night

which was psyche long before there was any ego consciousness, and which will remain psyche no matter how far our ego-consciousness extends.[26]

It is from this latter perspective that we will now consider the transposing of some traditional dream practices into a modern key. While not denying the pre-cognitive, non-local or telepathic nature of some dreams, this study hopes not to reclaim forms of divination but to help advance spiritual renewal. As part of this enterprise, I consider it important to underscore the historical connections among Scripture and its interpretation, traditional dream practices and contemporary dream work. Highlighting this continuity provides historical authenticity to our contemporary practices while offering familiar touchstones to the many who are far more comfortable encountering Scripture than their own dreams. And, as Joyce Rockwood Hudson, author of *Natural Spirituality,*[27] told me in a personal interview: "Scripture can provide the timeless and tested container through which we might better discern the contours of the timely flow of spirit, our dreams."[28]

III. Scripture as "Oracle"

Seeking God

Perhaps the primary link between Scriptural interpretation and dream work can be found in the phrase, *lidrosh et YHWH*, (lit. "to seek the Eternal,") which appears twice in the Hebrew Bible. The first occurrence portrays Mother Rebecca, alarmed by her twin sons' violent movements in her womb, proclaiming, "if this be so why do I exist?" The verse then states, "*va-teilekh lidrosh et YHWH*—she went to inquire of the Eternal."[29] Classical commentators understand this phrase as an idiom meaning "to consult a prophet or oracle," in Rebecca's case, her father-in-law Abraham.[30] The phrase's second appearance finds King Artaxerxes empowering Ezra the Scribe to move to Judea in 458 BCE and assume both religious and judicial authority over a Jewish society still tenuous despite having returned from Persia eight decades earlier. His qualifications? "For Ezra had prepared himself (lit. his heart) to inquire of the Eternal's Torah -- *l'drosh et Torat YHWH* -- to enact and teach statutes and judgments in Israel."[31]

The morphing of this phrase into "*l'drosh et Torat YHWH*" during the early Second Temple period heralded a major shift in Jewish religious history. Not only did the Bible "become the repository of past revelation; as interpreted by its scholars, it now took the place of prophecy as the source of guidance for the present and near future."[32] This had profound implications for the explication of Scripture through oracular and dream interpretation techniques. The Torah itself could actually be read as endorsing such practices. Numbers 12: 6-8 contrasts Moses' prophecy to that of other visionaries, including his brother, Aaron, and sister, Miriam: *When there is a prophet among you, I, the Eternal (YHWH), reveal myself in visions, I speak in dreams. But this is not true of my servant Moses; he is faithful in all my house. With him I speak face to face....* While God asserts the primacy of Moses' direct revelation (the Torah), dreams and visions are also described as God's disclosures, albeit of lesser rank. Therefore, in the absence of bona fide prophets, methods used to uncover underlying messages in dreams and visions could also be employed to disclose hidden levels of revelation embedded in the words of Scripture.[33]

It is significant that the same terms, **Pesher** (Aramaic: to remove, to solve) and **Patar** (Hebrew: textual translation, the magical transfer of harmful energy) were used to denote dream interpretation and an early form of scriptural exegesis found extensively in the Qumran texts.[34] While examples of dream interpretation styled *Pesher* are found in Classical Judaism[35] and Islam,[36] perhaps the best known is found in the first chapter of *Matthew's Gospel:*

> **The Lord's angel** spoke to Joseph in a dream: Joseph, son of David, don't fear taking Mary, your wife, into your home. This child was conceived within her through the Holy Spirit. You will name the son she bears Jesus (Joshua)—**because he will save his people (Sirach 46:1),** from their sins fulfilling the Lord's word through the prophet: **Behold, the virgin (*alma*—lit. maiden) shall be with child and bear a son, that will be named Emmanuel, God is with us (Isaiah 7:14).**[37]

Here the first century CE Gospel writer finds in ben Sirach's early second century BCE ode to Moses' successor Joshua, (lit. "He will save") a foreshadowing of Jesus,[38] who shares the name and the salvific mission it denotes. Isaiah's eighth-century prophecy is interpreted to reveal that Mary was the predicted maiden and Jesus the presaged child, who will embody *Emmanuel,* the Incarnate God Who is with and among us.

An opening section of *Midrash ha-Gadol* (lit. "The Great Midrash")[39] states:

> 'A dream carries much implication' (Ecclesiastes 5:2). Now... we reason: if the contents of dreams, which (empirically) neither help nor harm, may yield a multitude of interpretations, how much more, then, should the important contents of the Torah imply many interpretations in every verse.[40]

It goes on to list thirty-two hermeneutic techniques *(middot)* for interpreting Scriptural narratives. In 1950, Dr. Saul Lieberman noted that at least five of these methods were derived from ancient dream interpretation practice,[41] including: **Notarikon,** reading single words as acronyms or anagrams; **Remez,** finding allusions based on word plays, often derived from homonymous roots; **ATBaSH,** reading unknown terms as cryptograms to be decoded through letter substitution cyphers;[42] **Mashal,** symbolic or allegorical meanings;[43] and **Gematria,** deriving meaning from the numerical equivalents of the Hebrew letters comprising words or phrases.[44] This form of Scriptural interpretation using, among others, techniques that are still staples of contemporary dreamwork, is known as *Midrash.*[45] It has allowed Judaism, Christianity and Islam to elicit continuing revelations through exegesis, and, like dream interpretation, has opened many levels of meaning in response to ever changing conditions. By stimulating the growth of rich bodies of legal and homiletical exegesis, it has permitted text-centered religions to largely avoid the pitfalls of ossification.[46]

"Take It on as Your Dream"

Tawil,[47] the esoteric and allegorical interpretation of the Qur'an, has a long, continuing history which dates to the early centuries of Islam, as does the interpretation of Qur'anic symbols, Qur'anic acronyms (Haroof Muqqat•a•aat)[48] and the relationship between numbers and the words of the text.[49] However, the precept attributed to Muhammad, "Whoever says something in interpreting the Qur'an based on his own opinion should find his place in the Fire,"[50] certainly decreases the likelihood of individual Muslims interpreting the Qur'an as one would a personal dream.

Since neither liberal Judaism nor Christianity finds itself bound by such strictures, there are contemporary seekers who deepen their personal understanding of Scripture through the use of dreamwork techniques. Theresa, a hospital chaplain and spiritual director, has written of gaining new insights into aspects of herself and being empowered as a woman and as a seeker by applying dream analogies to the tale of Zelophehad's Daughters (Num. 27:1-11).[51] To briefly recap, Zelophehad, of the tribe Manasseh, died in the Sinai Wilderness leaving five daughters but no sons. Proscribed from inheriting their father's portion in Canaan, the five women appeal this injustice to their father's memory and themselves. After consulting God, Moses publicly vindicates the Daughters and announces a change in law, so that they and other women who have no brothers are acknowledged as their families' rightful heirs.

Theresa finds significance in the Daughters being members of the tribe Manasseh, son of Joseph the Dreamer, situated among the Israelite camp's westernmost tribes (Num. 2:18-24); the "West" represents the sunset's darkness, the place of dreams and the unknown, whence change can arise. In Jungian terms, "Four" is completion and "Five" represents "what's next," in this case five sisters, compassionate adventurers, persuasive, motivated, seeking justice and the welfare of family and tribe. In each of the sisters she sees projected aspects of herself: Mahlah,[52] the "Burden Bearer," accountable for her sisters' worries and concerns; Noa,[53] the "Courageous Crusader" confidently counseling her kin forward to do what's right, perhaps hiding her own inevitable fears; Hoglah,[54] the faithful "Honored Heiress," possibly first to marry a tribal cousin and thus insure her own and her sisters' inheritance (Num.36:1-12); Milkah,[55] a "Satisfied Soul" who carries out her duties and responsibilities, but might be too complacent, afraid to transgress boundaries, and Tirzah,[56] the lively "Joyful Jumper," big-hearted, hospitable, filled with creative energy, a favored dancer and musician during festivals.

Together these sisters seek the just transformation of a community through integration into its cultural consciousness. Perhaps some of the very same archetypes manifest by Moses, including visionary, advocate, pioneer, seeker, and guide, can be observed collectively in the Daughters. Moses, already a luminous image, encounters the Daughters who will "become of treasure to the tribe."[57] Facing their own doubts, as Moses did from the "Burning Bush" until then, they confront the "Shadow" energy of custom, law and those who would deny women their full humanity to strive, in their own way, for a more liberating, righteous social order. Moses speaks to the Eternal in the Tent of the Desert Tabernacle where God dwells. There no woman could enter, a condition that prevails in some traditions to this day. Perhaps the space where God quietly and gently enters into the lives of the Daughters also becomes holy, a locus for the collective emergence of the sacred feminine force.

Having taken Zelophehad's Daughters' tale as her own dream, the "deeper meaning of my complex Self" has been further revealed to Theresa. The Daughters have called her to reflect upon and further integrate their "many parallels in my psyche": faithfulness and worries of accountability to others; confident courage and hidden fears; advocacy for what's right and complacency; joyful creativity and a hesitancy to transgress boundaries. On the societal level she feels awakened to the liberating reality that, "created in God's image, we [as women] are called upon to realize the divine inheritance in ourselves."

To quote Joyce Rockwood Hudson on the application of dreamwork techniques to understanding Scripture:

once we've gone deep into dreamwork we can bring that depth into viewing Scripture ...since dreams and Scripture with its parables come from the same place of metaphor, they call us to the same place of deep understanding...bringing us into conversation with Wisdom...to teach us living with God.[58]

IV. ...and Explain It upon the Tablets[59]

If One sees...in a Dream

Given the foundational role that the sacred texts play in classical Judaism, Christianity and Islam it is little wonder that these provided the lenses through which those traditions historically viewed dreams. The Talmudic "Dream Book," *BT Berakhot* 55-7, invokes a host of biblical verses to elucidate dream practice and symbols. The dreams of early Christian martyrs like Perpetua of Carthage (d. 203 CE) are replete with images that mirror those found in the Hebrew Bible and the New Testament[60] and, since the *Qur'an* and good dreams both come from Allah, Muslims may use symbolism from the former to interpret images from the latter, based on authentic commentaries.[61]

The appearance of Scriptural figures, images and books all hold special import. Seeing the Prophet Muhammad in a dream is a sign of its veracity, for "whoever has seen me in a dream, has in fact seen the truth, for Satan does not appear in my form."[62]

Saturus, who was martyred with Perpetua[63] dreams of being born aloft with her by four angels (Ezekiel 1:5-25)[64] to a Pleasure Garden[65] where he hears a united angelic chorus chanting "Holy, Holy, Holy..."[66] as he stands before the Ancient of Days,[67] Whose younger face, perhaps alludes to a shared divinity with The Son, Jesus.[68] The Talmud teaches that seeing the Books of Ezekiel, Proverbs or Ecclesiastes in dreams are harbingers of wisdom. Psalms and Song of Songs foretell piety, while Jeremiah, Job and Lamentations may portend punishment.[69] Biblical verses and imagery were also used in formulae to help ameliorate bad or uncertain dreams;[70] one such prayer is still recited in traditional synagogues during the Priestly Benediction.[71]

Ever Reaching out to Us[72]

There are many ways by which contemporary seekers and spiritual guides elucidate dreams through Scripture. Fran, a Jewish seeker, was considering retirement and options for the next chapter of her life. One night she dreamed of diving into a deep body of water and retrieving a treasure. Although she postponed her retirement another six years, the dream stayed with her, as she recognized "water" as a Scriptural symbol for Torah[73] and a psychological symbol of the unconscious. Six weeks following her ultimate retirement, her synagogue announced the offering of an ongoing seminar on Judaism and Dreams. Having already begun to regularly attend services and weekly Torah study classes, Fran, a decades' long recorder of her own dreams, understood her "Water Dream's" call. She further "dove into the deep waters" of Torah and her unconscious, becoming active first as a dream seminar participant and then as a founding member of a monthly Jewish dream group.

Linda,[74] a Protestant spiritual director, drew insight and guidance through a nocturnal encounter with Biblical figure:

> I'm standing third in line before Jesus, who has loppers and is cutting people's hands off, not one but both; those standing behind Jesus are bandaged. I wonder how I might continue to do what I've always done without my hands! Surprisingly, no one in the dream seems alarmed.

As she awoke to transcribe the dream, John 15:2 came to her: *every branch that does bear fruit he prunes so that it will be even more fruitful.* She then understood that "sometimes we need to prune back what seems to be flowering to preserve energy for new blossoming, that what might have been experienced as a devastating loss could actually introduce something hopeful and creative."

Contemporary seekers and guides have also noted how the interplay of Scripture and dreams can impact both physical and emotional wellbeing. Linda also shared the dream of a spiritual directee who envisioned King Saul shooting arrows into his lower back. After sharing with him the Biblical story of Saul's pursuit of David,[75] she asked about the physicality of her directee's dream and if he were having back problems? The dreamer confessed to experiencing dropping in his right foot. A subsequent doctor's visit revealed he has kidney cancer; Louise continues as his spiritual and dream companion during this ongoing journey.

Cynthia draws on a variety of disciplines and traditions to inform her work as a somatic and spiritual healer. Once plagued by continuing PTSD dreams, her prayerful offering of Psalm 23 became a dream amelioration rite that aided in her healing.

> Truthfully, I turned to the twenty-third Psalm, my paternal grandmother's favorite, out of desperation. Since each night felt like the 'Valley of the Shadow of Death,' I just hoped for some needed peace of mind while I awaited sleep with its onslaught of dreaded dreams. Slowly and silently I recited each phrase before bed, pausing to pray and determine what each meant to me. I prayed not to heal myself nor to be healed; I didn't know nor could I anticipate what the outcome might be. As It happened, 'praying' the Psalm shifted the emotional experience of my dreams. While the dreams' basic content remained the same, their intensity gradually lessened. Uncoupling from their over-whelming Effect. I became an 'observer' to my dreams' unfolding, sensing the support of a 'wise presence' by my side.

Cynthia clearly recognizes that the prayerful amelioration of her

PTSD dreams was graced: *the feeling-content is so dramatic, so paralyzing that one doesn't just rationally figure out something that will help.* Among treatment modalities, Cynthia now guides others in the practice of praying Psalm Twenty-three when they come seeking healing from trauma and their own PTSD dreams.

Just as ancient dream practices were used to interpret Scripture, methods of Scriptural interpretation can inform and sanctify contemporary dream work. Several years ago I noticed parallels between the stages of projective group dream process[76] and a four-level approach to Scriptural exegesis common to Christianity, Islam and Judaism.[77] Having developed a practice of contemplatively led projective group dream work expressed through the vocabulary of scriptural interpretation, I've been privileged to facilitate this process in both Jewish and multifaith settings. Over the last five years it has often yielded rich insights and deep spiritual experience. Framed within the same schema employed by centuries of religious exegetes it affirms, in a very real sense, that one's dreams help compose the innermost Scripture of one's life.[78]

V. Send Me a Dream

Responsa from Heaven[79]

Dream Incubation is a delicate issue for the monotheistic traditions, as it would be heretical for any pious Jew, Christian or Muslim to imply that s/he could compel the One, Incomparable God to do anything. We can find but allusions to dream incubation rites in the Hebrew Bible in the practices of the Judge Samuel[80] and King Solomon.[81] However, each of the three traditions developed formulae for seeking divine guidance through dreams. The Jewish practice of posing dream questions, known in Hebrew as *She•eilat Ḥalom*, varies with rites including: fasting, weeping and/or refraining from marital relations; the cleansing of one's person, clothing and sleep setting; and counsel on which side one should sleep, and whether one should sleep atop an entreaty note?[82]

St. Jerome's fourth century rewriting of Biblical law through conscious mistranslation, added dream observation to scripturally prohibited forms of sorcery[83]; at St Augustine's behest, the Council of Carthage forbid dream incubation at churches and martyrs' tombs in 418 CE.[84] Despite such clerical opposition, the popular practice of dream incubation persisted. Reports of the devout and the sick sleeping in churches and receiving dream guidance and healing range from eighth century Cambridge, England to late nineteenth century Zante on the Isle of Rhodes.[85]

The Muslim practice of *Istikhara* (Arabic: "to wish what is beneficial") involves worship, ritual and sleep. A person first prays:

> My Lord, I ask you to inform me what is beneficial and make me strong. For you are powerful, but I am not. You know but I do not. You know all secrets. My Lord, if my task...is beneficial for my religion, my life and my

afterlife, make it easier and make it my destiny. If my task... is bad for my religion, my life or my afterlife, make me lose my desire, send me away and do not make it my destiny. Ordain for me what is good, wherever it be and then make me happy with it.

One then goes to sleep. If one sees white and green colors, great religious figures or something desirable in one's dream the task is deemed beneficial and is to be performed contentedly. If one sees black, blue and red colors, unwelcome persons or disgusting things, the task is not considered beneficial and should be foresworn.[86]

As one might expect, Scripture plays a significant role in these rites, particularly in She•eilat Ḥalom and Istikhara. Popular Biblical selections invoked when Jews have proposed dream questions include: David's invocation of God before the gathered community[87]; the aforementioned God's promise to speak to visionaries other than Moses through dreams[88]; Jacob's Ladder Dream[89;] and Ezekiel's vision of God's Chariot Throne.[90] Responses to incubated dreams have also been expressed through Scriptural citation. Rabbi Jacob of Marvege (d. 1230) who decided selected matters of Torah law by posing dream questions would at times be answered "in the name of the Great, Powerful and Awesome God." (Deut. 10:17)[92]

While the Qur'an itself doesn't mention Istikhara, several ahadith, including Sadih al-Bukhari, report that the Prophet taught it to his companions, including details of the *Istikhara* prayer.[93] Additionally, some variations of the *Istikhara* do include reciting the first Sura of the Qur'an, *al-Fatiḥa*, as well as verse 68 of the twenty-eighth Sura, *al-Qasas*, and verse 33 of the thirty-third Sura, *al-Ahzaab.*[94]

You Light My Lamp...

In May 2016, Sophia Said[95] gave a keynote presentation, which she called "Our Common Humanity," at the 2016 Haden Institute Summer Dream Conference in Hendersonville, North Carolina. She spoke of her own family's *Istikhara* practice, which includes washing, offering a ten-minute prayer, setting one's intention for the dream, then going to sleep. She noted that her mother would never offer final approval on suitable marriage partners for her children without performing *Istikhara*. Sophia's own daughter only came to decide in which one of two colleges she should enroll after Sofia encouraged her to submit a dream question using this rite. When asked, Sofia replied that she and other Muslims might perform *Istikhara* when confused by the meaning of a Qur'anic passage. If the confusion is not clarified during the first night's dream, the dream question would be resubmitted on successive nights until it was.

Marcia, a pastor and spiritual guide from Indiana, offers the following counsel to those who seek her guidance:

> 'I love you . . . Fear not, I am with you,' from Isaiah 43:4-5, is one that I often teach as a Breath Prayer,[96] letting them know they are not alone inviting God to send a

dream or when facing any difficult dreams/messages from the Divine One in their dreams. This reminds them that all dreams are given with great love for their healing and wholeness... and to trust. This has brought deeper, experiential trust in the Divine One's unconditional love.

This past summer, while teaching a "Judaism and Dreams" seminar, I learned that Scriptural dream narratives can shed light on one's life while also helping to incubate illuminating personal dreams. I invited participants to conduct individual, imaginal interviews with a character or image[97] found in the Genesis 32 vision of Jacob wrestling the Angel. Albert,[98] whose own mobility has been compromised, described his identification with the wounded Jacob. He wondered aloud if his own walking impairment might not be a curse but an "angel" challenging him to become a better person. All of us paused in silent awe at the depth of Albert's insight and his courage to share it with us.

The next morning Albert told me he had a dream that night: a handsome, successful, aggressive former work colleague, whom he hadn't seen in decades, asked Albert to watch his eight-year old son. Albert agreed, thinking he'd take the boy shopping at the renowned toy store, FAO Schwarz. Upon telling a current synagogue friend of his plan, Albert was aghast to learn this warm-hearted man thought Albert might be acting from ulterior motives. Albert feared that he might lose this friend's respect as well that of their shared congregational family.

Despite any misgivings Albert went ahead and watched the boy. When the work colleague returned a couple of days later, he offered to drive Albert home; "home" turned out to be Albert's synagogue's Friday night Sabbath collation. There Albert was seated at a table for four with his work colleague (not a synagogue member) and the colleague's recently arrived seventeen year old son; the fourth seat remained empty.

Upon reviewing the dream it became clear that all its characters were male; their differing ages, from the little child to himself, represented the span of a man's life. Each character's age correlated either to a turning point in Albert's degenerating mobility or a recent, debilitating bereavement; some of those numbers also intimated new beginnings. His "synagogue friend's" reaction paralleled some friends and family hesitance at Albert's decision to take a three-night trip and then to attend our multi-day seminar by himself. He understood this as a warning that he remain sensitive to his loved ones' concerns for his safety. The dream also highlighted the playfulness of youth (the eight-year-old and FAO Schwarz) and the energy of the aggressive colleague—not the warm-hearted friend—that drove Albert to the place he experiences as home.

Our discussion made it increasingly clear that Albert's dream had, in part, been incubated by his encounter with Jacob's visions over the last two days. When asked about his mobility, he realized that he had gotten around just fine in the dream. When asked who or what might be the missing fourth at his synagogue collation table, Albert, a widower, replied, "female companionship," Jacob's putative reason for leaving Canaan for

Mesopotamia.[99] Looking back upon the dream he discerned that, like Jacob, he was being called to summon his resolve, if not a bit of audaciousness, to move forward, recapture some youthful joy and arrive at a state of being that feels like home. He was also being cautioned not to be reckless nor ignore the justified concerns of loved ones. In his words he was being reminded "to keep living as long as I'm alive." Like our Father Jacob, Albert realized that there is still much to experience and savor despite or, in some ways, even due to his wounding.

VI. Renewal and Sanctification

As seen above, the integration of Scripture and dreamwork can offer fresh, exciting opportunities for spiritual awakening, psychological integration and emotional healing. The confluence of the two can offer new sources of guidance while deepening one's personal identification with the sacred texts, prompting a new appreciation for the wisdom traditions from which they grew. The Scriptures become imbued with further meaning through our lives' narratives and dreams while the latter become "sacred" when contextualized and viewed through the lens of Scripture, the records of humanity's ongoing encounters with the Holy over the millennia.

It is true that all the respondents cited above are in some way religiously affiliated. One could argue that of course they will experience, report and understand their dreams within the context of their traditions. However, one can tell by the responses that most have experienced significant shifts in their religiosity, some to greater observance, and all to a more inward identification with the traditions' profound power and with the Sacred as personally manifest in their lives.

And the non-religious? Brother Don Bisson, a Marist Brother, Jungian teacher and spiritual guide told me in a personal interview that he takes special note when non-Christian symbols appear in his dreams or in those of Christians whom he guides.[100] He feels the unconscious is calling "pay attention" more emphatically than if a Christian image had appeared; the exploration of these "foreign" symbols and their meanings open new realms of insight and guidance. To the increasing numbers unmoored from religion, particularly among the young, most religious symbols and allusions seem "foreign." However, they are not totally unknown due family ties, cultural context and the media. They may show up in a dream, sparking curiosity. Entrée to spiritual engagement could be found by asking: *why do you think your unconscious sent you this symbol, these words, this allusion at this time; would you like to explore what they mean in context, and what might these mean for you?*

Nearly a hundred years ago, Rabbi Abraham I. Kook[101] wrote: "Let the ancient be renewed and the new be made holy." To this call for a culture re-sacralized, let us add our twenty-first century "Amen." Through an integration of Scripture and dream work may we transpose ancient practice and teaching into compelling modern keys. In turn, may these provide us with some redemptive avenues, amid the "Flatland" of our increasingly secular society, to deepen and see as holy the ever new and changing realities that compose our lives.

ENDNOTES

1

 BT Berakhot 55a. The scriptural proof text offered for the third type of petition offered by Rav Yehudah, a third century CE Babylonian sage, cites King Hezekiah imploring God, saying: *va-taḥalimeini v'haḥayeini* . Since the Hebrew root *ḥ-l-m* can denote both healing and dreams, one could interpret this phrase as: *You heal me through dreams....*

2

 Hoffman, J. "A New Vision for Dreams of the Dying" *NY Times,* February 2, 2016.

3

 Cohen, F. "Inside the Actors' Dream Studio" *NY Times,* Dec. 29, 2016.

4

 Bulkeley, K. *The Wilderness of Dreams.* SUNY Press, 1994. p 213

5

 Bulkeley, p 209

6

 Nordquist, R. "root metaphor" (March 6, 2017) Retrieved from thoughtco.com/root-metaphor-1692067

7

 Bulkely, p 152

8

 pewresearch.org/fact-tank/2017/09/06/more-americans-now-say-theyre-spiritual-but-not-religious/

9

 The practice of the *Istikhara* is derived from *Hadith Sahih al-Bukhari,* Volume 2, Book 21, Number 263. Retrieved from http://islamicacademy.org/html/Dua/How_to_do_Istakhara.htm

10

 Edgar, I & Henig, D. "Istikhara: The Guidance and Practice of Islamic Dream Incubation through Ethnographic Comparison," *History and Anthropology,* 2010. Retrieved from www.researchgate.net/publication/249027033

11

    Murphy, K. "Take a Look Inside My Dream," New York Times, July 9, 2010

12

    While not exhaustive, the list includes: Covitz, J. *Visions in the Night*. Shambhala, 1990, Harris, M. *Studies in Jewish Dream Interpretation*. Jason Aronson, 1993, Frankiel, T & Greenfield, J. *Entering the Temple of Dreams*. Jewish Lights, 2000, Ochs, V. *The Jewish Dream Book*. Jewish Lights, 2003, Shainberg, C. *The Kabbalah of Dreams*. Inner Traditions, 2005, Kamenetz, R. *The History of Last Night's Dream*. HarperOne, 2008 and most recently Frankiel, T. *She Rises While It Is Still Night*. Gaon Web, 2017

13

    In Celtic tradition, a "thin place" is where the veil separating heaven and earth is nearly transparent, where the spiritual world and the natural world intersect. When applied intra-personally to dream work it may also connote moments when the conscious and unconscious touch. See Wills, M H, "Pressing into Thin Places" in beliefnet.com/inspiration/christian-inspiration/pressing-into-thinplaces.

14

    Retrieved from www.hadeninstitute.com/dream-work-training

15

    As used here, the term "Flatland" first appears in Abbott, E A. *Flatland: A Romance in Many Dimensions*. Seeley & Company, 1884. Retrieved from https://ned.ipac.caltech.edu/level5/Abbott/paper.pdf

16

    Tertullian, *De Anima* 47.2 cited in Stroumsa, G.G. "Dreams and Visions in Early Christian Discourse" in Shulman, D and Stroumsa, G.G. (eds), Dream Cultures. Oxford University Press, 1999) p.191

17

    A *Hadith* is a report of the words, actions or habits of the Prophet Muhammad. While the *Qur'an* is a unitary work, the collections of *Ahadith* (pl.) derive from many sources and have canonical status second to the *Qur'an*. Sunni Islam accords the highest status among *Ahadith* collections to *Sahih al-Bukhari* and *Sahih Muslim*.

18

Sahih al-Bukhari, vol. 9, book 87:119 cited in Hermansen, M. "Dreams and Dreaming in Islam" in Bulkely, K, (ed.) *Dreams* (New York: Palgrave, 2001) p. 75.

19

Zohar I: 183a-b

20

One among the myriad examples of this phenomenon can be found in Tishken, J.E. "Whose Nazareth Baptist Church? Prophecy, Power, and Schism in South Africa," in *Nova Religio: The Journal of Alternative and Emergent Religions,* Vol. 9 No. 4, May 2006; pp. 79-97

21

https://www.jewishhistory.org/sabbatai-zevi/

22

https://www.u-s-history.com/pages/h3747.html

23

Edgar, I.R. "The Dreams of Islamic State." *Perspectives on Terrorism* · September 2015. Retrieved from https://www.researchgate.net/publication/281202852_The_Dreams_of_Islamic_State?

24

See Maimonides, *Guide to the Perplexed* 2:36-7; Robert Moss, "St Jerome Bewitches Dreams and Dreamwork" in http://www.beliefnet.com/columnists/dreamgates/2011/08/st-jeromebewitches-dreams-and-dreamwork.html, and: selections from *Ahadith Sahih Al-Bukhari* and *Sahih Al-Islam* retrieved from http://www.myislamicdream.com/

25

See https://psi-encyclopedia.spr.ac.uk/articles/dreams-and-esp

26

Jung, C G, "The Meaning of Psychology for Modern Man" 1933. Retrieved from www.ahistoryofthepresentananthology.blogspot.com

27

Natural Spirituality, Revised Edition. (Chiron Publications,2016)

28

Telephone interview with Joyce Rockwood Hudson, January 16, 2018.

29

Gen. 25: 19 – 26

30

See commentary of Abraham Ibn Ezra (d. 1164) on Gen. 25: 19-

31

   Ezra 7:10

32

   Tigay J. "An Early Technique of Aggadic Exegesis" in *Tadmor*, H & Weinfeld, M (eds.) *History, Historiography and Interpretation: Studies in Biblical and Cuneiform Literature* (Jerusalem, Magnes Press, 1984) pp 169-70. Also see Spiegel, S. "On Medieval Hebrew Poetry," in Finkelstein, L. (ed.) *The Jews: Their History, Culture and Religion.* Jewish Publication Society, 1949. pp. 854-856.

33

   ibid.

34

   See Fishbane, M. (1973). "The Qumran Pesher and Traits of Ancient Hermeneutics," *1*(A). p. 101-5. Retrieved from jstor.org/stable/23515557
For the structural parallels between Pesher and ancient dreamwork see Finkel, A. (1963). "The Pesher of Dreams and Scripture." *Revue de Qumran,* 4(3). p. 370. Retrieved from jstor.org/stable/24600881.

35

   Leviticus Rabbah 29:4.

36

   See "The Nag Hammadi Codices and Gnostic Christianity" (2017)   in biblicalarchaeology.org/daily/biblical-topics/postbiblical-period/the-nag-hammadi-codices/
Also Robinson, S. "Second Treatise of the Great Seth" in *Claremont Coptic Encyclopedia* Retrieved from ccdl.libraries.claremont.edu/cdm/ref/collection/cce/id/1726

37

   Matthew 1:18-23.

38

   The Hebrew of which is *Yehoshua*, Joshua.

39

   Modern scholars attribute it to a thirteenth century CE Yemenite author, Rabbi David ben Amran Adani of Aden. See "MIDRASH HAGADOL" in jewishvirtuallibrary.org/midrash-ha-gadol

40

   Schechter S. (ed.) *Midrash Hagadol Bereshit.* p. XXV, retrieved from Lieberman, S. *op. cit,* p. 70.

41
Lieberman, S. *Hellenism in Jewish Palestine.* The Jewish Theological Seminary Press, 1950. pp. 68-77.

42

The key to the **ATBaSh** cypher is created by writing the Hebrew *Aleph-Bet* in its correct order on one line and its reverse on the line below. Thus *Aleph*, the first letter, corresponds to *Tav*, the last *(AT)*, *Bet*, the second, for *Shin*, the penultimate *(BaSh)* and so on, forming mutually substituting pairs for Hebrew's 22 letters.

A Biblical example of ATBaSH revolves around the king of an unidentifiable realm, *Sheshakh*, mentioned in Jeremiah 25:26. The kingdom's name appears again in Jeremiah 51:41 in a synonymous parallelism with Babel. **Sheshakh,** composed of a double *Shin*, Hebrew's penultimate letter, and its eleventh, **Khaf**, is interpreted as a cryptogram for **Babel**, which doubles Hebrew's second letter, **Bet**, and ends in its twelfth letter, **Lamed**.

43

such as the Seven Cows and Seven Ears of Corn representing Seven Years in Pharaoh's Dreams Gen. 41:1-32.

44

An example of Gematria claims the 318 warriors who accompanied Abram to free his nephew Lot (Gen. 14:14) were not a whole company but Abram's lone servant, whose name Eliezer bears the numerical value of 318! Eliezer -- E (1 א) + L (30 ל) + I (10 י) + Eh (70 ע) + Z (7ז) + R (200 ר) = 318   *BT Nedarim* 32a; Genesis Rabbah 43:2.

For a brief overview of Gematria and the numerical value of Hebrew Letters see Ratzabi, H. "What Is Gematria" in Myjewishlearning.com/article/gematria/.

45

The term *Midrash,* as can be readily surmised, is derived from the same verb found in the above cited phrase *lidrosh et Torat YHWH*—to inquire of the Eternal's Torah (Ezra 7:10). See fn. #28.

46

It was taught in the School of Rabbi Ishmael: *Behold, My word is like fire-declares the Lord-and like a hammer that shatters rock"* (*Jer. 23:29*). Just as this hammer produces many sparks [when striking the rock], so a single verse has several meanings -- **BT Sanhedrin 34a**

God's blessing to mankind 'to be fruitful and multiply' (Gen.1 :22, 28) ...express in manifold ways what we understand in but one, and to understand in manifold ways what we read as obscurely uttered in but one way -- Ryan, J K (ed. & trans.). **The Confessions of St. Augustine.** Image books,1960, p. 360.Augustine himself offered five different interpretations to Gen. 1:1.

It is He (Allah) who revealed to you the Book. Some of its verses are definitive; they are the foundation of the Book, and others are unspecific. -- **Qur'an 3:7**

47

"*Tawil*" retrieved from http://www.oxfordislamicstudies.com/article/opr/t125/e2358. Also "Esoteric Interpretation of the Quran" retrieved from https://www.revolvy.com/topic/Esoteric%20interpretation%20of%20the%20Quran&item_type=topic

48

Shah, M.A. et. al. "Meaning of Quranic Abbreviations," *Academic Research International.* Vol 2 #3, May 2012. Retrieved from http://www.savap.org.pk/journals/ARInt./Vol.2(3)/2012(2.3-86).pdf

49

See "The Miracle of the Quran" in http://quranislam.org/main_topics/miracle_of_the_quran_(P1313).html

50

Tirmidhi Hadith No. 4023 Retrieved from https://pakobserver.net/interpreting-holy-quran/

51

O'Bryan, T. "The Daughters of Zelophehad: A Dream-Story of Justice and Truth" (unpublished) Submitted in fulfillment of the Final Essay Requirement, Haden Institute Dream Leaders Training Program, Hendersonville, NC

For further information on Sub-personality Psychology and the "synthesis of Self" see Wakefield, C. *Negotiating the Inner Peace Treaty.* Balboa Press, 2012.

52

Maḥlah (Hebrew), "One who mollifies or appeases."

53

Noa, "One who wanders forth."

54

Ḥoglah, "Partridge," a favorable omen for accumulating property.

55
Milkah, "Royalty, Queen" indicating abundance, court etiquette and the rule of law.

56
Tirzah, "Pleasure, Desire"

57
Hollis, J. *Tracking the Gods: The Place of Myth in Modern Life.* Inner City Books, 1995.

58
See fn. 26. For a brilliant interpretation of Jesus' "Parable of the Sower and the Seed" (Matthew 13) using similar dreamwork techniques to those found in Theresa's above cited essay, listen to Joyce Rockwood Hudson, "Dreams, Parables and the Kingdom" (audiocassette) 2004 Haden Institute Summer Dream Conference www.hadeninstitute.com

59
Naḥum 2:2: *Write the vision and explain (inscribe) it upon the tablets that it might be easily read*

60
Miller, P.C. "'A Dubious Twilight': Reflections on Dreams in Patristic Literature" in *Church History*, Vol. 55:2, June, 1986, pp. 156-159. Retrieved from jstor.org/stable/3167417

61
Philips, A.A.B. et. al. *Dream Interpretation According to the Qur'an and Sunnah.* A S Noordeen, 2001. p. 49.

62
Sahih Muslim, vol:4, pp.1225 #5635 & 1226 #5639 retrieved from http://www.myislamicdream.com/prophet_muhammad.html

63
Tertullian. "The Passion of the Holy Martyrs: Perpetua and Felicitas," ch 4. Retrieved from http://www.earlychristianwritings.com/text/tertullian24.html

64
Four angelic "Holy Creatures" bear aloft God's Chariot Throne in Ezekiel 1. A Jewish prayer invokes the four Archangels, Michael, Gabriel, Uriel and Raphael to guard one's bed and body as the soul ascends on its nocturnal dream journey. This formulas seems adapted from an ancient Babylonian bedtime incantation: *Shamash before me, behind me Sin, Nergal at my right, Ninib at my left* See Trachtenberg, J. *Jewish Magid and Superstition* (1939), p. 156.

Retrieved from http://www.sacred-texts.com/jud/jms/jms13.htm
A later Christian petition, the "Black Patemoster," will identify these
four with the Gospel Writers: Matthew, Mark, Luke and John. See Opie
and P. Opie, *The Oxford Dictionary of Nursery Rhymes* (Oxford: Oxford
University Press, 1951, 2nd ed., 1997), pp. 357–60.

65

Pardes (Hebrew) at that time was identified both as a place of
Heavenly delight and also as the realm of God and the angels. JT
Ḥagigah 2:1, BT *Ḥagigah* 14b.

66

Isaiah 6:3

67

Daniel 7:9

68

Tertullian. "The Passion of the Holy Martyrs: Perpetua and Felicitas,"
ch 4.

69

BT Berakhot 57b

70

BT. Berakhot 55b, attributed to one of three late Talmudic figures of
the fourth-fifth century CE, Ameimar, Mar Zutra, or Rav Ashi. For a full
treatment of this prayer see Addison, H. A. "I Have Dreamed a Dream"
in Birnbaum, D and Cohen, MS, ed. *Birkat Kohanim: The Priestly
Benediction*. Mesorah Matrix Press, 2016. pp. 341-364.

71

Num. 6:22-27.

72

The personal narratives and practices that appear in this essay were
shared with me through responses to a questionnaire I sent to several
hundred Haden Institute alumni and other participants in North
American dream groups during November, 2017.

73

Isaiah 55:1 *Let all who thirst come and drink water...*; Psalms 42:7
Deep calls to deep...

74

A pseudonym.

75

I Samuel 26:1-7.

76

Ulman, M & Zimmerman, N. *Working With Dreams* (ISBN-10:
9781138095649) and Haden, R L. *Unopened Letters from God*. Haden

Institute Press, 2010.

77
Based on St Augustine's notion that Scripture has four levels of meaning, the eighth century schema of the Venerable Bede includes: the **Literal** or plain sense of the text; the **Tropological** or figurative connotations, the **Allegorical** or philosophical allusions; and the **Anagogical,** from which one could infer the secrets of life everlasting. Stein, RH. *An Introduction to the Parables of Jesus*. Philadelphia, Westminster Press, 1981, p. 47.

Later in the eighth century, Caliph Jafar al-Sadik's methodology includes **'ibāra,** the literal expression, **ishāra,** allusion, **laṭā'if**, the subtleties and **ḥaqā'iq,** the deepest realities. *Spiritual Gems: The Mystical Qur'an Commentary* ascribed to Ja'far al-Sadiq as contained in Sulami's *Haqa'iq al-Tafsir* (Louisville: Fons Vitae, 2011), trans. Farhana Mayer, p. 1.

This fourfold approach only appears among Jewish circles in Spain in a late thirteenth century Torah commentary and is known as *PaRDeS* a variation of the acronym's letters: *Peshat* (Literal), *D'rash* ("Inquiry" Homoletic), *Remez* (Allusions),. *Sod* (Secret). See www.jewishencyclopedia.com/articles/3263-bible-exegesis

78
For a full presentation of this practice see, Addison, H. A. "In the Presence of Three" in *Presence: An International journal of Spiritual Direction* vol. 22:2 pp 46-51.

79
*She•eilot u-Teshuvot min ha-Shamayim (*Hebrew) is the name of Rabbi Jacob of Marvege's book. Written in 1203 CE, it contains twenty-two legal decisions based on his dream questions.

80
I Samuel 3

81
I Kings 3:4-15

82
For a short treatment of this subject see Idel, M "Dream Techniques in Jewish Mysticism." Retrieved from www.jhom.com/topics/dreams/techniques.html

Also see Ochs, V. *The Jewish Dream Book*. Jewish Lights, 2003.
83

http://www.beliefnet.com/columnists/dreamgates/2011/08/st-jerome-bewitches-dreams-and-dreamwork.html *op. cit.*
84

Shulman, D & Stroumsa, G G, (eds.) *Dream Cultures*. Oxford University Press, 1999. p. 194.
85

Hamilton, M, op. cit. pp. 113, 210   Retrieved from. http://hdl.handle.net/2027/nyp.33433070255421.
86

Aydar, H "Istikhara and Dreams: an Attempt to Predict the Future through Dreams" in Bulkeley, K. et. al. (eds.),
Dreaming in Christianity and Islam: Culture, Conflict and Creativity. Rutgers university Press, 2009. p. 123.
87

I Chronicles 29:11-12.
88

Num. 12:6.
89

Gen. 28:12.
90

Ezekiel 1:1.
91

Shalom, B. *The Mishnah of Dreams* (Hebrew) B'nei B'rak, Israel, 2005 p. 156.
92

"Jacob of Marvège." From *Encyclopaedia Judaica.*
Retrieved from http://www.encyclopedia.com, October 17, 2018.
93

Aydar, H. *op. cit* pp. 126-7.
94

"Istikhara – Seeking the Best from Allah." Retrieved from https://quranacademy.io/blog/istikhara/
95

Sophia Said is a Sufi Muslim who serves as Program Director of The Interfaith Center, the Institute for Theological Studies at St Margaret's Episcopal Church, Little Rock, AK.
96

Breath Prayer, the continuing, usually silent, repetition of a sacred word or verse to the rhythm of one's breath, is practiced in many traditions:

Buxbaum, Y. *Jewish Spiritual Practices*. Jason Aronson, 1990. ch. 21; On Christian practice see "Breath Prayer" https://gravitycenter.com/practice/breath-prayer/

On Muslim practice see"A Sufi Breathwork Meditation" http://www.techofheart.co/2011/02/sufibreathwork-meditation.html

[97]   Hoss, R. "Imagery Work (6 'Magic' Questions)" Retrieved from www.dreamscience.org/articles/image_activation_dreamwork.htm.

[98]   A pseudonym.

[99]   Gen. 28:1-9.

[100]   October 26, 2017. For Br Don's background, retreat offerings and seventy cassette series see http://donbisson.com/

[101]   Abraham Isaac Kook (d.1935) First Chief Rabbi of Pre-State Israel.

Re-Discovering the Afterlife

Simcha Paull Raphael

When dealing with dying, grief, loss and the inevitability of human mortality, people frequently ask, "Is there a life after death?" and, as to be expected, Jews more specifically inquire: "Does Judaism believe in an afterlife?" Today this second question frequently creates a quandary for Jews and non-Jews alike. The reality is that the whole topic of life after death in Judaism is perplexing and problematic.

Some years ago, a rabbi was lecturing a group of nurses on "Bio-Medical Ethics: The Jewish Approach." When asked by a member of the audience, "Does Judaism believe in an afterlife?" forthrightly the rabbi replied: "Judaism celebrates life and the living. It dwells on life here rather than on the hereafter as other religious faiths do. Life is precious, the here and the now."[1] This response, characteristic of modern Judaism's attitude towards the afterlife, is the singularly most problematic Jewish belief about life after death today. Why? Because it's simply not true!

Yes, Judaism does value life, here and now, over and above a future death and eternal life.[2] As Abraham Joshua Heschel, so eloquently expressed: "the cry for a life beyond the grave is presumptuous if it is not accompanied by a cry for eternal life prior to death."[3] Yes, it is accurate to maintain that Judaism has a life-affirming, this-worldly orientation which proclaims the sanctity and significance of physical plane life. After all, it is only within the context of physical, embodied life one can fulfill the divine commandments, *mitzvot,* sanctify reality and heal both society and the planet through acts of *tikkun olam* – "mending of the world." But this does not imply there is no Jewish belief in an afterlife! Over the course of millennia, Judaism evolved a multi-faceted philosophy of post-mortem survival, comparable to other great religions of the world. In short—Judaism has always believed in life after death.

The Pre-Modern Jewish Legacy on the Afterlife

To illustrate how pervasive afterlife teachings have been in premodern Judaism consider the following vignettes of Jewish literary history:

While most people have heard of Dante's The Divine Comedy,[4] almost completely unknown is a thirteenth century poetic chronicle of the afterlife written by Dante's contemporary and fellow Italian, Immanuel HaRomi ("the Roman" d.1328). Based upon ancient Rabbinic traditions, *"Ha-Tofet ve-ha-Eden"* ("Hell and Paradise") is as visionary and imagistic as anything produced by Dante. One of many legendary creations of the medieval period it describes with ornate detail the divine judgement experienced at the time of death, and the Jewish afterlife realms of heaven and hell—known as Gan Eden—the Garden of Eden, and *Gehennah*—or purgatory.[5]

In 1626, a later Italian Jew, Rabbi Aaron Berachia ben Moses of Modena authored a text entitled *Ma•avor Yabok,* literally "Crossing the River *Yabok.*" (In Genesis 32 Jacob crossed over the River *Yabok* and this is the metaphor used in the title of this text). *Ma•avor Yabok* is a compilation of writings on death, dying and the philosophy of the afterlife. Based upon sixteenth century Lurianic Kabbalah's philosophy of the soul, this text is replete with descriptions of the soul's experiences at the time of death, and beyond.[6] More than any other Hebrew book, *Ma•avor Yabok* may be considered as a "Jewish Book of the Dead." Produced originally for the of Mantua Ḥevra Kadisha, or Burial Society, this text was rapidly accepted in both Ashkenazic and Sephardic Jewish communities and has become the standard Burial Society manual for Jews in Southern, Central and Eastern Europe.[7]

Rabbi Menasseh ben Israel[8] was a scholar, commercial entrepreneur and political statesman. Originally a Marrano who re-embraced Judaism when he migrated from Spain to Amsterdam in the early 1600s, Ben Israel was the first rabbi of the Amsterdam Jewish community and negotiated with Oliver Cromwell permission for Jews to re-enter England.[9] His introduction to *Nishmat Ḥayyim,* "The Soul of Life," relates, how a *"Mal'akh,"* angel or spirit guide, appeared to him at his bedside while he was lying awake one night. This "visionary being" then dictated, or channeled, a treatise on "*din gilgul neshamot,*" literally "the law of the transmigration of souls"—reincarnation. *Nishmat Ḥayyim* is an eclectic text which presents a survey of Jewish beliefs on topics such as: immortality of the soul; the nature of the astral body; the death-moment itself; post-mortem judgement; the afterlife wanderings of the soul; and other conceptions of the hereafter found in Rabbinic or kabbalistic sources.

So, What Happened?

As these examples suggest, it is not that Judaism lacks a belief in the afterlife. However, when impacted by modernity, Judaism lost touch with these age-old teachings. As Jews left behind the traditional ghetto lifestyle of pre-modern Europe, traditional teachings have lost their hold on people's lives, and there has been increasing assimilation and a rapid diminution of commitment to the study and practice of Judaism. In the twentieth century, as the center of Jewish life shifted from Europe to North America, and from a Hebrew and Yiddish linguistic environment to an English-speaking one, knowledge of and interest in pre-modern Jewish teachings on the afterlife became lost. While spirits, ghosts and the afterlife all found their way into Yiddish fiction and drama, Judaism as a living religion seemed to lose touch with ideas about postmortem survival.[10]

To understand why modern Judaism lost touch with the whole notion of life after death we need to examine some historical factors from within Judaism itself.

Biblical Judaism's Inherent Ambivalence towards the Afterlife

Ancient Israel's inconsistent beliefs concerning the afterlife are revealed in 1 Samuel 28. There, King Saul travels to the Witch of *Ein-Dor*, requesting her to evoke the spirit of the deceased Prophet Samuel, which she does. To enlist her aid, however, Saul had disguised himself because he had previously "expelled all the mediums and wizards from the land" (1 Sam. 28:3). Thus, two contradictory attitudes exist simultaneously in this tale: one may successfully engage in oracular communication with the dead, yet; necromancy and spiritualistic practices were officially condemned.

Early Biblical religion maintains a distance from the realm of the deceased by associating communion with the dead and forbidden idolatrous practices. Thus, condemnation of both mediums and child sacrifice appear side-by-side:

> Let no one be found among you who sacrifices his son or daughter in the fire, who practices divination or sorcery, interprets omens, engages in witchcraft, or casts spells, or who is a medium or spirits or who consults the dead (Deut. 18:10-11).

This ancient taboo has insidiously affected Jewish thought for thousands of years, leaving modern Judaism with a tainted, negative attitude towards life after death.

Individual and Collective Eschatology

Scholars make a distinction between individual and collective eschatology. Collective eschatology is concerned with the future of humanity and the cosmic order at the end of time; individual eschatology focuses specifically upon the destiny of each unique human being after death. Biblical Judaism focuses on collective rather than individual eschatology, on redemption at the end-of-days, messianic renewal, establishment of a divine kingdom on earth, last judgement and eventually, in Daniel 12, resurrection of the dead. In Rabbinic tradition the term *Olam Haba*, the World to Come, is often used when referencing a future, post-mortem life. But it is often unclear whether this World to Come is inaugurated immediately after an individual's death[11] or in the distant future, at the end of time and history when the world will be redeemed.[12]

After the Babylonian Exile, beginning in the sixth century BCE, the conception of an individual post-mortem survival slowly emerges, and in early and later Rabbinic literature there are teachings on the immortality of the soul. Even more, from the twelfth century CE onwards, as cited above, an increasingly sophisticated series of teachings on the afterlife journey of the soul are produced in the mystical and mythical literature of medieval Judaism.

The Influence of Moses Maimonides

Although he affirms the existence of an immortal soul, when speaking of *Olam Haba*, the World to Come, Moses Maimonides (d. 1204), the most famous Jewish scholar of the medieval period, describes it as an other-worldly realm, totally beyond human comprehension. "As to the blissful state of the soul in the World to Come, there is no way on earth in which we can comprehend or know it."[13] With this statement, Maimonides, like other Aristotelian rationalists of the medieval age, successfully wedges a gap between the spiritual and human realms, thereby convincing many people that contemplating the question of life after death is a task beyond human ability.

For close to eight hundred years after Maimonides, this belief has persisted within Judaism. The German-Jewish theologian Leo Baeck (d. 1956), states quite explicitly:

> We need but recall the pitying derision with which Maimonides dismissed as antiquated child's play all these fantasies and sensuous conceptions of the world beyond. Basic to Judaism, was the imageless spiritual conception of immortality, which permits no representation, hardly even a verbal one.[14]

A generation later Maurice Lamm (d. 2018) reiterates Maimonides' point of view, saying that, despite the Jewish belief in immortality, there are few details available on the afterlife. Why? Because "flesh-and-blood man cannot have any precise conception of the pure, spiritual bliss of the world beyond."[15] Sadly, this uncritical acceptance of Maimonides' philosophical rationalism ignores the mystical and mythic streams of Judaism wherein are found striking textual depictions of the afterlife realms.

Modernity and Death of the Afterlife

The Enlightenment

Belief in a life after death can be found in cultures across the globe and throughout the history of civilization. Archaeological discoveries dating as far back as 50,000 BCE, indicate that in the early stone age people were buried with food, tools, and other implements, "sent on their journey to the eternal hunting ground, into a realm where a divinity perhaps had its residence."[16] It was a mutual relationship; the living provided physical nourishment for the deceased; in turn, they offered blessings and assistance with the ongoing demands of physical life.[17] Textual studies also reveal widespread beliefs in an eternal realm of the dead in both the ancient and historical religions of the world.

In the modern era these once-traditional creeds have eroded. Influenced by Rene Descartes and Immanuel Kant, the scientific worldview of the Enlightenment emphasized the value of objective, observable dimensions of human experience. Thus, Western culture has given decreasing credence to all human experiences deemed "non-empirical" or "non-rational." The growth of early twentieth century scientific rationalism, logical positivism and psychoanalysis further eliminated God, angels, souls, mystical visions and the idea of individual survival after death from the agenda of intellectual inquiry.

In a scientific, rationalist universe, death is seen as the final cessation of life. Since consciousness is regarded as an epiphenomenon of the brain, there can be no awareness separate from the body. When the body dies, a person dies and that is the end. Once the brain waves cease functioning, life is over. No soul. No afterlife. No heaven. Dead is dead. It is this view of life and death which has become the predominant intellectual point-of-view in the twentieth century.

One individual who had a monumental impact in promulgating the materialist, rationalist attitude towards the afterlife was Sigmund Freud. As a product of nineteenth century European thought, Freud's own philosophical worldview precluded any belief in God, a soul or an afterlife. Freud was an atheist Jew who regarded religion as a "universal obsessional neurosis" which reflected a regression to infantile forms of behavior. Just as a young child yearns for the protection of a father, similarly, in times of vulnerability and helplessness adults respond by yearning for a supra-human figure, a God who can guarantee security and protection against the hostile forces of life. For Freud, the very idea of God is a distorted human creation and thus religion will be rightfully superseded by rationalism, empirical science and by psychoanalysis itself.

In *Totem and Taboo,* Freud examines early humanity's response to death, and offers his reflections on the evolution of ideas of the hereafter. In response to human mortality, which s/he couldn't fully understand, the so-called primitive "invented" the idea of spirits and post-mortem survival:

> Man could no longer keep death at a distance, for he had tasted it in his pain about the dead; but he was nevertheless unwilling to acknowledge it, for he could not conceive of himself as dead. So, he devised a compromise; he conceded the fact of his own death as well, but denied it the significance of annihilation...It was beside the dead body of someone he loved that he invented spirits...His persisting memory of the dead became the basis for assuming other forms of existence and give him the conception of a life continuing after apparent death.[18]

In "Thoughts for the Times on War and Death," Freud goes on further to explain:

> It was only later that religions succeeded in representing this after-life as the more desirable, the truly valid one, and in reducing the life which is ended by death to a mere preparation. After this, it was no more than consistent to extend life backwards into the past, to form the notion of earlier existences, of the transmigration of souls and of reincarnation, all with the

purpose of depriving death of its meaning as the termination of life.[19]

For Freud, to believe in an afterlife or even to show any concern with ideas about heaven and the survival of the soul is a denial of the reality of death, a defense against the inherent fear of annihilation and extinction. These ideas on the afterlife influenced an entire generation of psychoanalysts, psychiatrists, and other helping professionals, as well as philosophers and social scientists. As a result, until very recently, the whole topic of post-mortem survival has been ignored or regarded with great suspicion in psychology, philosophy and even theology. There is no doubt the modern era's rationalist, secularizing forces have impacted the Jewish world. Before Freud, the German-Jewish philosopher, Hermann Cohen (d. 1918), the leader among Neo-Kantian Jewish thinkers, was embarrassed by the Jewish doctrine of life after death.[20] Cohen reinterpreted traditional Jewish conceptions of immortality, maintaining individuals alone do not survive after death, though their legacies do as part of the evolving history of humanity. "Only in the infinite development of the human race towards the ideal spirit of holiness can the individual soul actualize its immortality."[21]

This belief, often referred to as "social immortality," has persisted for over a century, and has become an increasingly widespread modern Jewish response. In 1989, when asked by a Newsweek journalist about Jewish views of afterlife, Rabbi Terry Bard, Director of Pastoral Services at Boston's Beth Israel

Hospital explained that after the individual dies—dead is dead—"What lives on are the children and a legacy of good works."[22]

Given the materialist, rationalist orientation of the past one hundred years, it is no wonder that the issue of life after death is problematic for modern Jews. But this is part of a larger spiritual alienation in which questions of faith, God, religious experience and the inner life are perplexing to an entire generation of Jews influenced by the intellectual climate of the more recent past.

Where Judaism and Christianity Differ

When examining the history of Jewish-Christian relations, there is no doubt that Christianity's belief in eternal life impacted Jews negatively. In 1442, the Council of Florence proclaimed: "none of those outside the Catholic Church, not Jews, nor heretics, nor schismatics, can participate in eternal life, but will go into the eternal fire..."[23] Sadly, this teaching's legacy lingers despite the Second Vatican Council and ongoing contemporary Church efforts to eliminate anti-Semitism and other forms of racism. If the prevailing cultural assumption had been that non-Christians could not enter heaven, many modern Jews decided to opt out of the system, abandoning belief in both heaven and hell, and in a life after death.

We see this very overtly in the anecdote mentioned early in this essay about the nurse who asked the rabbi if Judaism had a belief in the afterlife. The rabbi maintained that Judaism "dwells on life here rather than on the hereafter as other religious faiths do." The underlying assumption expressed here is "Christians believe in all that stuff about heaven, hell and eternal life. But we Jews don't!" Given the relative unfamiliarity of traditional Jewish teachings on the afterlife and, thanks to Dante and others, the West's association of the hereafter with Christian imagery and dogma, it is little wonder this belief has been promulgated. Not surprisingly, a 2015 Pew Research study reveals that 85% of American Christians believe in Heaven and 70% believe in Hell; those numbers plummet among American Jews to 40% and 22%, respectively.[24]

The Holocaust

Undeniably, the Holocaust has been a powerful force operating upon the psyche of twentieth and even twenty-first century Jews. The overwhelming nature of the murder perpetuated against Jews, by the Nazis, has made it difficult for modern Jews to really reflect on the whole issue of life after death. After Auschwitz, the Jewish response was to focus energy on life and re-birth, not on the hereafter. The mandate of the Jewish people was functional and practical: re-settle refugees, build a Jewish homeland, and guarantee the ongoing survival of Jewish life around the world. Could the task at hand have been accomplished if Judaism emphasized a philosophical preoccupation with the state of the souls of six million dead? After the liberation of the concentration camps, post-World War II Judaism simply could not integrate the Jewish philosophy of the immortal soul with the reality of the Holocaust. So, it was best ignored, left to the private sphere but not the public sphere of religious life, except for *Yizkor*, Holy Day Memorial services when the six million martyrs were remembered. Although the Israeli *Knesset* formally established *Yom Ha-Shoah*, Holocaust Memorial Day, in 1951, decades would pass before it became widely observed by American Jewry.[25]

The spirit of the fifties, sixties and seventies necessitated building a socially responsive and intellectually viable Judaism. Within the context of a post-World War II, North American Judaism, there had not been any room for a concern with spirituality and disembodied souls in the hereafter. It may well be that for many Jews, raised in the shadow of the Holocaust, there was simply no need for a philosophy of the afterlife.

What's Changed?

Modernity's promise of "Progress," that science would fulfill all human needs, has not materialized. Previously undreamed-of advances in knowledge, travel and communications, among the twentieth century's crowning achievements, also made possible Auschwitz and the threat of nuclear annihilation. Despite profound technological innovations—satellites, computers, the internet, smartphones etc.—the quality of human life in the Western world is often plagued with challenges to physical security. Drug wars and addiction continue; families break up at alarming rates; poverty, hunger and fatal diseases are spreading not disappearing, terrorism remains a perpetual threat around the planet and, of course; despite the climate science deniers, we are waking up to the damage, to the toxicity we are inflicting on the Earth and its creatures.

With all this and more going on, an increasing number of people find themselves deeply questing for personal meaning. What's it really all about? Many no longer question: "Is God dead?" but rather, "How can I, as an individual, personally access the Sacred in my own life, and enhance the quality of life for myself and the people around me?" More than seventy years after World War II we are living in an age of paradoxical transition, characterized by declining denominational affiliation and by spiritual thirst. People are longing for functional resources which offer meaning, a connection with the transcendent, and an ability to experience the deep layers of the human psyche, wherein genuine healing can be found.

Thanatology – the Interdisciplinary Study of Death and Dying

Whereas sex was the cultural taboo in Victorian times, it was replaced in the twentieth century by the topic of death. Geoffrey Gorer taught that by the mid-twentieth century death had become the pornography of society, a taboo area about which people were profoundly afraid to speak.[26] Thankfully, Dr. Elizabeth Kübler-Ross' pioneering work with the dying served to unlock the cultural taboo on death. As a University of Chicago psychiatrist in the mid-1960s, Kübler-Ross dedicated her time to interviewing terminal patients to understand what it was like for those approaching death. Her simple willingness to listen to dying people inaugurated a growing cultural movement concerned with improving the quality of life for the dying and bereaved and their families.[27]

Today there is a much greater honesty and openness in the face of death. Dying individuals are given more opportunity to speak openly about their feelings; conscious efforts are made to meet the social, emotional and spiritual needs of the dying, along with their medical and physical ones. We also understand more clearly that the bereaved need to express their grief, sometimes repeatedly, as growing numbers of resources and helping professionals are available for support.

Even more than this, new developments in biotechnology are forcing people to re-think questions about the meaning of life and death itself. "Near death experiences," the visionary reports of people declared clinically dead and then brought back to life, have forced medical doctors and scientists to reopen the whole question about life after death, and re-think the materialistic definition of death. In place of the materialistic view that biological death is the end of life, a spiritual view of death and life, is emerging. Increasingly, a new paradigm is being articulated which gives due recognition to the perennial wisdom of the ages, encoded in the esoteric traditions of the world. This paradigm reopens the possibility that death is not the end of life but merely a transition to a different state of existence.

A Renewed Jewish Vision of the Afterlife

Elisabeth Kübler-Ross herself recounts a story suggesting that seeds for the rebirth of the Jewish approach to the afterlife may have emerged out of the Holocaust itself. A relief worker at the Maidanek concentration camp in 1945, Kübler-Ross was overwhelmed but fascinated by the mystery of the human encounter with death. There, amid empty barracks marked by graffiti with hundreds of initials carved into the five-tiered wooden bunks, she noticed countless drawings of butterflies! Perhaps days or only hours before dying in the gas chambers, adults and children left behind their final message— butterflies—the symbol of hope, rebirth, the symbol of the eternal human soul.[28]

The Holocaust obliterated Eastern Europe's traditional Jewish life, murdering spiritual leaders who had direct access to Judaism's mystical teachings about the soul, and its afterlife pilgrimage. However, the tragedy left by the Holocaust inspired young Elisabeth Kübler-Ross, catalyzing her life work investigating the mysteries of dying and death. The aftermath of her "death and dying revolution" has generated thousands of new publications documenting medical, psychological, sociological, anthropological, and spiritual perspectives on death and dying.

In the early 1970s, Kübler-Ross noted a surprising dearth of modern Jewish death literature:

I have always wondered why the Jews as a people have not written more on death and dying. Who, better than they, could contribute to understanding of the need to face the reality of our own finiteness?[29]

Thankfully, the Holocaust's psychic shackles concerning death, dying and mourning have begun to loosen these last decades. We are witnessing a continuing integration of traditional Jewish wisdom on mortality, bereavement and the hereafter with newly emerging perspectives on the psychology of death and dying. A cursory examination reveals that Amazon.com alone lists over 45 titles on this subject, all published since 1991.

As we conclude the second decade of the twenty-first century, circumstances necessitate an even further re-claiming of Judaism's death traditions' wisdom. People are living ever longer, many well into their nineties.[30] As a result, there is an increased concern with both the quality of life, and—even more—the quality of death! The number of elderly Jews is rapidly increasing, as the baby boom generation not only deals with parents who are aging and dying but is staring its own mortality in the face as well. Debilitating illnesses, including Alzheimer's, and cancer, continue to affect the lives of countless families. The US suicide rate is at a thirty-year high,[31] and there have been more than twenty-five school shootings since Columbine in 1999.[32] As a society, we desperately need all the information and resources available to enable us to deal more effectively with the reality of human mortality.

In recent times, however, there has been a progressive yearning for spirituality and spiritual renewal. While denominational affiliation falls in the U.S, the percentage of Americans who label themselves "Spiritual but not Religious" has grown to 27% of the population.[33] Many alienated Jews are turning back to their roots. Even previously committed Jewish men and women are looking beyond the legalistic, rational dimensions of Judaism, for an internal experience of transformation. Many people, young and old alike, are searching to unearth the ancient wisdom of the Jewish past and make it viable for daily life in this age. As a result of this questing, there is a burgeoning interest in the mystical, mythical and apocalyptic traditions of Judaism.[34] Against this background, there is little doubt that Judaism, in the fullness of its ancient wisdom, has a contribution to make to the new ways of understanding the experiences of dying and death. Seven decades after Auschwitz it is time to further redeem the ancient Jewish tradition on the afterlife journey of the soul, and to make those teachings available in a language and style appropriate for contemporary Jewish life, in the metaphor of the psychology of consciousness.

ENDNOTES

1

   This quote appeared in 1981 in a newspaper article about a rabbi who had given a lecture on the Jewish approach to Bio-Medical Ethics. When asked by a young nurse, "Does Judaism believe in an afterlife?" he responded as quoted here. Jean Herschaft, "Patient Should Not Be

Told of Terminal Illness: Rabbi," The Jewish Post and Opinion (New York), 13 March 1981, p. 12.

2

There is a Rabbinic teaching that proclaims: "Better is one hour of bliss in the World to Come than the whole of life in this world." However, this statement is immediately followed by the claim that "Better is one hour of repentance and good works in this world than the whole life of the World to Come (*Mishnah Avot* 4: 17). The juxtaposition of these two ideas in the same place, serves to emphasize that the world beyond does not have a primary value in the Jewish schema of things, over and above embodied, physical plane life.

3

Heschel, A J. "Death As Homecoming" in Jack Riemer, (ed.), *Jewish Reflections on Death*. Schocken Books, 1974., p. 73.

4

Alighieri, D. *The Inferno*. Ciardi, J. (trans). New American Library, 1954. _____. *The Paradiso*. Ciardi, J. (trans). New American Library, 1961.

_____. *The Purgatario*. Ciardi, J. (trans). New American Library, 1961.

5

Yardin, D. (ed.) *Maḥbarot Immanuel HaRomi*, 2 Volumes. Mosad Bialik, 1954. Vol. II, pp. 511-554.

6

Aaron Berechia ben Moshe Mi-Modina, *Ma•avor Yabok*. Yishpah Press, 1967.

7

Marcus, J R. *Communal Sick-Care in the German* Ghetto. Hebrew Union College Press, 1947, pp. 229-230.

8

Menasseh ben Israel, *Nishmat Hayyim*. Sinai Offset, n.d.; originally published Amsterdam, 1651.

9

For biographical information see: Roth,C. *A Life of Mensaaeh Ben Israel*. Jewish Publication Society, 1934.

10

For examples see Ansky ,S. *The Dybbuk and Other Writings*. Roskies, D G. (ed.), Werman, G. (trans.) Yale University Press, 2002. Singer, I B. (trans.) "Sabbath in *Gehenna*" in *The Death of Methuselah* and Other Stories. Faffar, Straus and Giroux, 1971, 1988. pp. 212-219; Ruth Wisse, R (ed.) "Bontshe Shvayg" in The I.L. Peretz Reader. Schocken Books, 1990. pp.146-151.

11

    Sifre Leviticus 18:4.

12

    BT Ketubot 111b.

13

    Maimonides, M. Mishneh Torah, Vol. I: The Book of Knowledge, Hyamson, M. (trans. and ed.) Boys Town Publishers, 1965. p. 91a.

14

    Baeck, L. The Essence of Judaism. Grubenwieser, V. and Pearl, L. (trans.) Schocken Books, 1948; 1976. p. 185.

15

    Lamm, M. The Jewish Way in Death and Mourning. Jonathan David Publishers, 1969. p. 225.

16

    A. Rust, "Der primitive Mensch" in Propylden Weltgeschichte. Mann, G. and Heuss, T. (eds.), Berlin, 1961, Vol. I, p. 194, quoted by Kung, H. Eternal Life? Quinn, E. (trans.) Doubleday and Co., 1974). p. 51.

17

    Wilson, I. The After Death Experience, William Morrow and Co., Inc., 1987 pp. 7-26.

18

    Freud, "Totem and Taboo," Standard Edition of the Complete Psychological Works of Sigmund Freud. Strachey, J. (trans. and ed.) Hogarth Press, 1953-1974. 13:1-161, 1913; quoted by Schur, p. 298.

19

    Freud, "Thoughts for the Times on War and Death" Standard Edition 14:273-302, 1915.

20

    Allan Arkush, "Immortality" in Cohen, A A. and Mendes-Flohr (eds.) Contemporary Jewish Religious Thought. Charles Scribner's Sons, 1987, pp. 479-482.

21

    Cohen,H. Religion of Reason out of the Sources of Judaism. Oxford university Press, 1971, p. 308; quoted by Arkush, p. 481.

22

    Woodward, K L. "Heaven," Newsweek, (March 27, 1989) pp. 52ff.

23

Quoted by Kung, p. 130.

24

Murphy, C. "Most Americans believe in heaven...and hell" retrieved from *www.pewresearch.org/fact-tank/2015/11/10/most americans-believe-in-heaven-and-hell/*

25

For an overview of the history and observance of *Yom Hashoah* see "*Yom HaShoah* – Holocaust Memorial Day"*https://www.jewishvirtual library.org/yom-ha-shoah-holocaustmemorial-day*

26

Gorer, G. *Death, Grief and Mourning.* Anchor Books, 1967.

27

Kübler-Ross, E *On Death and Dying.* Macmillan Co., 1970. p. 23.

28

This story is related in Riemer, J. *Jewish Reflections on Death and Dying.* Schocken Books, 1974. p. 1, and in Gill, D. *Quest - The Life of Elisabeth Kübler-Ross.* Ballantine Books, 1980. p. 131.

29

Riemer, p. 2

30

Kaplan, K. "Is 90 the new 85? More Americans are in their 90s, Census reports" Los Angeles Times, November 17, 2011 Retrieved from http://articles.latimes.com/2011/nov/17/news/la-heb-oldestold-90-census-20111117.

31

Tavernise, S. "U.S. Suicide Rate Surges to a 30-Year High" *NY Times* April 22, 2016 Retrieved from https://www.nytimes.com/2016/04/22/health/us-suicide-rate-surgesto-a-30-year-high.html.

32

https://www.usatoday.com/story/news/nation/2018/02/15/fox-news-anchor-shepard-smith-emotionally-lists-all-25-fatal-schoolshootings-since-columbine/340108002/.

33

www.Pewresearch.org/fact-tank/2017/09/06/more-americans-now-saythey're-spiritual-but-not-religious/.

34

For a fuller account of this phenomenon see Raphael, S. P. *Jewish Views of the Afterlife.* 2nd ed. Rowman and Littlefield Publishers, Inc., 2009. pp. 31-35.

The Soul Lives On

Converts to Judaism and Past Lives

Charlotte Sutker

Resurrection and Reincarnation

Many people, Jews and non-Jews alike, do not know that Judaism holds a belief in reincarnation. In Hebrew it is called *Gilgul Ha-Nefesh* (lit. "The Revolving" or Transmigration of the Soul), which means a soul leaves one body and returns to life in another. In the last several years many books have been published that address this long held kabbalistic (Jewish Mystical) concept. This may surprise many Jews who do not think of reincarnation as a part of Judaism. As Simcha Paull Raphael, whose work appears in the previous essay, states in *Jewish Views of the Afterlife* (1996):

> ...the rationalistic biases that impelled twentieth century Jews to disregard ancient traditions on the afterlife like-wise concealed from awareness the legacy of teachings

on reincarnation. As a result, many contemporary Jews, as well as non-Jews, are often astonished to discover that this concept is given expression in Judaism. Yes, kabbalists do believe in reincarnation! And after the twelfth century, reincarnation is as kosher to Judaism as is Mogen David wine.[1]

Before reincarnation is explored, it is necessary to distinguish it from resurrection. Resurrection is the Jewish belief that when the Messiah comes, all dead people will be resurrected, specifically in Israel. This is one reason why cremation is not part of Jewish burial practices.[2] Somehow, it had been considered more feasible to have a completely disintegrated body be reconstructed than the ashes of a cremated person reshaped, before rolling through the earth and popping up in Israel. While still opposing voluntary cremation, the forced immolation of millions of Jewish bodies during the Holocaust has led contemporary Orthodox believers to acknowledge God's unfettered ability to reconstruct their ashes as well.

Neil Gillman in *The Death of Death* (2003) traces the evolution of the concepts of resurrection and reincarnation in Judaism. Historically, the concept of resurrection has been part of Judaism longer than the concept of reincarnation and has deeper roots in Jewish theology than reincarnation. For example, resurrection is mentioned five times in one paragraph of the Amidah, the standing prayer of devotion recited in lieu of the sacrifices that had been offered in the Holy Temple:

You are eternally mighty, *YHWH* (Eternal). You revive the dead; great is Your power to save.

(You make the wind to blow and the rain to fall.)

You sustain the living with compassion; You revive the dead with abundant mercy. You support the falling, heal the ailing, free the captive; and maintain faith with those who sleep in the dust. Whose power can compare with Yours, who is comparable to You O Sovereign, Who brings death and restores life and causes salvation to sprout!

You are faithful to restore life to the dead. Praised are You, *YHWH*, Who restores life to the dead.[3]

Gillman states, "The centrality of this passage to Jewish consciousness cannot be overestimated. To this day, it is recited at least three times daily, every single day of the year, in the traditional worship service."[4]

Gillman notes that the *Amidah* as we know it today was probably written over time.[5]

By introducing this doctrine into the central portion of the liturgy which rabbinic law mandated Jews to recite daily, our liturgist has accomplished another notable purpose. He has accorded it canonical status...From this date on and for centuries thereafter, every worshipping Jew would proclaim daily that God revives the dead; in the modern era, when Jews ceased believing in this doctrine, the liturgy had to be changed."[6]

Further from Gillman:

> Rabbi Simai taught that there is not a single weekly Torah portion that does not refer to the doctrine of resurrection—if only we had the ability to see it there. When the Sadducees challenged Rabban Gamaliel to prove resurrection is in the Torah, he cited passages from each of the three units that comprise Scripture: The Pentateuch, the Prophets and the Writings.[7]

Gillman states that the Talmudists had two beliefs about the afterlife. One indicated that at some point after death, God would raise the body from the grave. The second taught that, at death, the body disintegrates and returns to dust, but the soul leaves the body and lives eternally.[9] However, "For its part, the doctrine of the immortality of the soul also appears in a Talmudic/liturgical text, but it is accorded nowhere as central as position as the doctrine of resurrection."[9]

The morning prayers, *Birkhot ha-Shaḥar*, (lit. "Blessings of the Dawn") clearly praise God for the giving and taking of the soul from the body and the returning of the soul to the body at a later time. The following is a part of *Birkhot ha-Shaḥar*, which "include[s] this passage from the Talmud *(BT B'rakhot 60b):*

My God, the soul that You have given me is pure. You created it, You fashioned it, You breathed it into me, You safeguard it within me, and You will eventually take it from me and return it to me in time to come. As long as the soul is within me, I thank you *YHWH*, my God and God of my ancestors, Master of all things, Lord of all souls. Praised are You *YHWH*, Who restores souls to dead bodies.[10]

Another reference to resurrection is in the morning prayer, *Modeh Ani* (I am grateful), that is said upon awakening, with sleep as a metaphor for death, and awakening as a metaphor for resurrection. "I am grateful to You, living enduring King, for restoring my soul to me in compassion. You are faithful beyond measure."[11]

Gillman explains that it is Greek influence that brought into Judaism the concept of the soul entering the body at birth and leaving at death. Jewish belief is that the soul does this not because it is an entity separate from the body, but because God decided that it should be so. God bestows immortality on the soul.[12] Developmentally, if the concept of the living soul exists, it was not too much of a leap to think that the soul lives on and returns to live again in another body, perhaps more than once.

Maimonides, a twelfth century Spanish physician and philosopher living in Egypt, was instrumental in promoting the belief, citing biblical verses that allude to reincarnation, such as Daniel 12:13, and the practice of the levirate marriage.[13] He was influenced by the Greek philosophy of the time and brought this belief into a Jewish context. The belief in reincarnation was not popular and was one of the reasons that he was shunned by some rabbis. Gillman writes,

> From this flows the classical Maimonidean conclusion that authentic Judaism demands an authentic belief structure. Maimonides disagreed with the frequently voiced claim that Judaism is simply a religion of deeds, not of beliefs; that what counts is how we behave as Jews and that our beliefs are of secondary importance. For how is it even possible to know what God commands us to do without an underlying philosophy?[14]

Maimonides' *Mishneh Torah* (lit. "Re-iteration of Torah") was not well received by all Jews, partly because he wanted "to uproot the idolatrous notion that God has a body..."[15] In the section of the *Mishneh Torah* entitled *Hilkhot Teshuvah* (*The Laws of Repentance*), Maimonides differentiates between the Greek belief that eternity belongs to the soul and the Jewish belief that eternity belongs to the soul and the body (resurrection). Maimonides' explanation for the fact that resurrection is not mentioned in the Torah is that the people of those times lived close to nature and it seemed unnatural to have a dead person come alive. When a camel died, it did not live again, when a tree died it did not live again, so how could a person?

Maimonides' writings created such a stir within the Jewish community that they provoked heated discussions centuries after his death. In the modern era, his words find greater receptivity. Maimonides is widely revered, as he should be, for the breadth and depth of his insights, even among those who now consider bodily resurrection to be a quaint idea.[16]

While there had been previous Jewish mystical movements, the first text to outline kabbalistic philosophy including reincarnation, is *Sefer ha-Bahir (The Book of Brilliance)*, written in southern France at the end of the twelfth century.

> The issue is not the grand resurrection to come. The fact that God will resurrect the dead is assumed. What is of primary concern to the mystics, however, and what remains their most distinctive contribution to the development of the afterlife doctrines in Judaism, is their portrayal of the fate of the soul in the period of metempsychosis, the transmigration of souls, or to use a popular term, reincarnation. In Hebrew, the term is gilgul, or literally, 'revolving.'[17]

Gillman states that, as opposed to resurrection, the concept of reincarnation is not found in Talmudic literature. Reincarnation as a concept had been opposed by some major Jewish philosophers, including Saadia Gaon (d. 942 CE), and ignored by others. Promoted by the medieval Kabbalists,[18] reincarnation began to capture the Jewish imagination; through the influence of the Safed Kabbalists, particularly *The Ari* ("Holy Lion"), Rabbi

Isaac Luria (d. 1572), it became embedded in Jewish practice.

The prayer accompanying the bedtime *Sh'ma* ("Hear O Israel...") speaks explicitly of reincarnation. Here are both a traditional translation from the ArtScroll *Siddur* and a more contemporary rendering by Rabbi Zalman Schachter-Shalomi:

> Master of the Universe, I hereby forgive anyone who angered or antagonized me or who sinned against me—whether against my body, my property, my honor, or against anything of mine; whether he did so accidentally, willfully, carelessly, or purposely; whether through speech, deed, thought, or notion; whether in this transmigration or another transmigration—I forgive every Jew. May no one be punished because of me. [19]

> You, My Eternal Friend, Witness that I forgive anyone who hurt or upset me or who offended me—damaging my body, my property, my reputation or people that I love; whether by accident or willfully, carelessly or purposely; with words, deeds, thoughts, or attitudes; in this lifetime or another incarnation—I forgive every person; May no one be punished because of me...[20]

For the mystics, the soul was what life and death was all about. Before one was born, throughout life, and after one died, the soul was the essential self.

What psycho-spiritual question does the idea of reincarnation

Seeking Redemption in an Unredeemed World

address? Based on transcribed lectures and tapes by the contemporary scholar, Rabbi Ezriel Tauber, Yaakov Astor states in *Soul Searching*:

> The purpose of reincarnation is generally twofold: either to make up for a failure in a previous life or to create a new, higher state of perfection not previously attained. Resurrection is thus a time of reward; reincarnation a time of repair. Resurrection is a time of reaping; reincarnation a time of sowing[21]

At first, only sinners were thought to need to reincarnate to correct what they did wrong in their previous lifetime. Later, reincarnation became more democratic and was believed to be needed by everyone no matter how well a life had been lived. As Simcha Raphael asserts:

> Regardless of how reincarnation was understood and whether justice or mercy was emphasized, *gilgul* had as 'its singular purpose...the purification of the soul and the opportunity, in a new trial, to improve its deeds.[22]

Modern, anecdotal, compelling accounts of reincarnation can be found in the books by Brian Weiss.[23] Weiss, a Jewish psychiatrist with an international medical reputation, has documented thousands of cases of people who, with his guidance, have completed past life regressions through hypnosis and have reported on having been alive previously.

Perhaps the book that is most directly relevant to this study is *Beyond the Ashes* by Yonassan Gershom. Gershom has counselled and heard the story of hundreds of Jews, Gentiles, and Jews by Choice who all have reincarnation memories of living in the years leading up to and during the Holocaust and dying in the Holocaust era. His book contains not only anecdotal reports of people's stories that he heard from all over the world, but also an overview of Jewish beliefs in the afterlife and reincarnation. Gershom writes:

> Over the centuries a number of beliefs about life after death have evolved within Judaism, and these continue to exist side-by-side, with each individual Jew free to choose from among them. These beliefs fall into four main categories: (1) survival through one's descendants; (2) physical resurrection; (3) an immortal soul in Heaven; and (4) reincarnation. The categories are not mutually exclusive, and many Jews believe in a combined version.[24]

A commonly known Hebrew phrase within the Jewish world is *l'dor va-dor*, from generation to generation. This phrase is usually thought to mean, from parent to child, or from grandparent to parent to child. However, the aforementioned *Sefer ha-Bahir states:* What is the meaning of (the phrase) "generation to generation?" Rabbi Papas said, "A generation goes, and a generation comes. (Ecclesiastes 1:4)." Rabbi Akiba said, "The generation came"—it already came." [25] Gershom explains, "This is a very important passage, because it tells us that the Sefer Bahir reads generations as incarnations: that is, that the generation which 'goes' is the same one that 'comes.'"[26]

As mentioned earlier, Rabbi Isaac Luria lived in sixteenth century Safed. A charismatic personality with a devoted following, Luria was a profoundly innovative Kabbalist, whose impact is felt even to this day.[27] He firmly believed in reincarnation; however, he thought that a Jewish soul returned in every incarnation to a person who was Jewish. Gershom has not found this to be true:

> ...I have been told that these people cannot 'really' be Jews in Gentiles' bodies, because that 'just doesn't happen.' One *Chabad* Hasid told me, 'Right after the Holocaust somebody asked the *Rebbe* if a Jew could come back as a non-Jew. The *Rebbe* said, 'No; once a Jew, always a Jew.'[28]

However, even postings on contemporary *Chabad* websites seem to challenge this view. Brian Weiss also found that Gentiles had reincarnated in previous lifetimes as a Jew.[29]

In addition, Schachter-Shalomi, himself rooted in *Chabad,* asserted at the January 2007 conference of OHALAH, the Association of Rabbis and Cantors for Jewish Renewal, that some converts have lived previous lifetimes as Jews.

After the Holocaust it is also important to find out if we

are dealing with a recycled soul who in a former life was a Jew. We take a great deal of responsibility for our converts, not only for this incarnation but for previous and subsequent ones.

My Research: Jews by Choice and Reincarnation

In this study, respondents from around the world who were born non-Jewish related their experiences of sensing that they had been Jewish in a previous lifetime. While this study draws no conclusions about the existence of past lives or the validity of such experiences it does reveal the significant impact of such awareness on self-perception, underlying motivation, and spiritual journeys of contemporary Jews by Choice. At least on the level of belief and self-identification, Gershom's quote from the *Rebbe* is refuted by this study. The books mentioned are but a few of the many that deal with reincarnation and Judaism. From the classically text-based studies by Gillman and Raphael to the anecdotal accounts relayed by Gershom, Weiss, and Spitz, there are many approaches to exploring the concept of reincarnation.

Since the nineteenth century, the development of Reform, Conservative, and Reconstructionist Judaism have ignored, discounted or openly repudiated any literal belief in reincarnation. Born in response to the Enlightenment amid the scientific era, those branches of Judaism wanted to bring Judaism into the "modern world;" the belief in reincarnation was based on folklore, too superstitious, and couldn't be proved. However, various branches of Orthodoxy and newer liberal branches, such as Jewish Renewal, acknowledge reincarnation and its place in the theology of Judaism. There is no central registry for Jews by Choice, yet each branch of Judaism has noticed that in the past twenty years significant numbers of people are choosing Judaism.

My research was done between 2005 and 2007 with 83 responses from Jews by Choice from around the world: Canada, the United States, Europe, Israel, and South America. Fifty-four percent believed that they had been Jewish in a previous lifetime. Almost all believed that they had lived during the Holocaust. Many believed that they had returned in a non-Jewish body to be safe in this lifetime. Some did not believe that safety was a factor when they returned to life in a non-Jewish body, but they didn't know why they were born in a non-Jewish body.

Overview of Respondents' Experiences

Total Number of Respondents (7 responded who had not completed a conversion process)	90
Number of Respondents who were Jews by Choice	83
Number of Respondents who Sensed that They had been Jewish in a Previous Lifetime	52 (57%)
Number of Jews by Choice that Sensed that They had been Jewish in a Previous Lifetime	45 (54%)

How Respondents *Experienced* Being Jewish
in a Previous Lifetime
(Respondents could choose more than one category.)

Lighting *Shabbat* Candles	Jewish Ritual was Familiar	Knew Info about Judaism without Studying
5	13	18
Concentration Camp Memories and Experiences	Feeling of Coming Home	Jewish Food was Familiar
2	32	6

Of the fifty-four percent of Jews by Choice who believed they had been Jewish in a previous lifetime, they had a "sense" that this was so. In this study, a *sense* does not imply that the subjects actually were Jewish in a previous life or that reincarnation is a scientifically verified fact. It does means that they have come to recognize and believe this identification through various experiences including dreams, daydreams, intuition, memories or memory fragments, meditation, past life regression, hypnosis, body sensations, or they have knowledge of facts or rituals related to Judaism that they did not acquire in this lifetime.

Here are some of the stories that respondents related about their sense of being Jewish in another lifetime. The stories below are from seven participants whom I interviewed individually, in addition to responding to the questionnaire. These respondents talked about their relationship to God, their beliefs about and their relationship to the Jewish community.

When I asked Dan to speak about his Jewish past life memories, he spoke about being in the Holocaust. This is a past life memory many of the respondents had; however, Dan did not think that all of his past lives had been Jewish.

> I had these persistent dreams of being in the Holocaust, of being taken and the sense of persecution. I had other ones in times of revolutionary war, or of walking, of being in fields. I would go bike riding. In this lifetime, I've had a lot of solitary time in the country and I could close my eyes and it felt like I was back a long time ago, in a body that wasn't mine in a field somewhere, just having that sense of enjoying this little moment while I can because I knew something ominous was coming.

> I always had this sense of ominousness. It left as I started to read more and broaden my perspective of spiritual walks and spiritual paths.

Dan had a near-death experience and this has influenced his relationship to God and his belief in reincarnation. Judaism's emphasis on *Tikkun Olam*, Repair of the World, or social action is important to him:

I guess my relationship to Spirit, God and the Great Divine has definitely been influenced in my belief in past lives and my experience of drowning and crossing over and coming back because I know that is a reality and that there is so much more out there. Obviously, that is part of my foundation of how I approach Spirit and the Divine. I think my belief that I was Jewish in a past life is one of the reasons why I have connected so closely to a Jewish identity and have moved in quite smoothly. In fact, it is kind of strange. I can't imagine my life not being Jewish. I often find that I enter into discussions about Spirit and different things very easily with people. It is often around the awareness that I was Jewish in a past life and I often talk about that. I am surprised at how many times that comes up in conversation or can work itself into a conversation.

Below is Dan's recounting of his near-death experience when he almost drowned at age eight. It made a lasting impression on him, bringing him in touch with the spiritual world.

I had a crossing over experience, which as a child I interpreted as a dream or an image. It was an amazing feeling of incredible relaxation that just overcame me from inside. The bubbles were tickling my nose as they were streaming up in front of my face. I sank down to the bottom of the pool. I remember lying down on the bottom of the pool and looking up and seeing the sunlight shafting through the water, and just closing my eyes and then being pulled through a major tunnel, lots of lights, superfast, faster than anything I have ever experienced.

I then fell into this whitish, yellow light, sort of a free for all, and just floating and suddenly I was in this place that was incredibly warm and safe and beautiful. I was just sitting there. Then I heard this voice, this very loud voice. It was kind of like the ocean crashing, thunderous waves and so forth, but it wasn't frightening at all. The voice just said, 'This is not your time.' And I was like 'What!' And then these two energy beams, or these two entities formed and suddenly the light became a tunnel and one of them came towards me and it said, 'You have to go back.' I remember very clearly going, 'No, I don't want to go back. I want to stay here. This is great. I don't want to go back there.' And the energy went through my heart and pierced me... Then this voice said, 'You will be protected, and we will be reunited...'

The next thing I'm being pulled back through this very dark, black, cold place and then thumped, literally I felt like I was being slammed back into my body. I came to and I was in the hotel room and there were people around me and I was coughing and splattering.· My mom was freaking out and there was lots of activity. I didn't understand what had happened. All I knew was that I felt fat and I felt ugly and I felt stuck and I didn't want to be here...

After that, I had this awareness of spiritual energy and of entities. I would walk into places and I could see and feel the spiritual or psychic energy that was in the room, not only from this generation, but from past generations too. I could see spirits sometimes and get audio messages or clairvoyant messages and different things. Watches would stop on me, electromagnetic stuff, weird things. That followed me throughout most of my teen years and into my early adulthood. But from that point on I had no fear of death at all. I also had no fear of other things.

Sam is in his senior years. This time in his life brings him to think about death from a more immediate and intimate perspective. It is not an abstract concept, but a reality that he faces. And reincarnation is a topic he thinks about and that influences how he lives his life now. He also speaks about bringing reincarnation and the soul journey into his work where he helps mentally ill people, some of whom are suicidal.

I find more and more I talk in terms of 'in this lifetime.' It is a phrase that I use casually, but I really do believe that... Implying that there are others, and also suggesting that I don't have to do everything that I have to do in one lifetime. There is spaciousness for learning and growing. When I think of my death, I don't know. The question makes me think that there is more that I could do because I certainly do believe in reincarnation. There is more that I could do in this lifetime in a broader context... I'm sensing that is an area where I need to do more work.

I really would like the sense that the hasidic talk about—that death should be as easy as pulling a hair from a cup of milk. And so, I would like to be easier about the fear of my own death... What pops up is that if I can be attached to God's plan and the long history of creation, including multiple lifetimes and the upward movement of the soul through all sorts of curious developmental processes, which often don't make much sense as we look at them, but if I can do that, I can be more peaceful as I go through the day and look at my own life expectancy.

Sam also has memories of being in the Holocaust and thinks that what his soul wants him to do now is experience more joy. He shares the type of inner dialogue he has with his soul.

More of just doing things just for the sheer joy of it, that is what I am being called to do more of, and I think my soul wants that. And maybe the poor old soul that went through the Holocaust is saying, 'Come on, what is the deal here? You are not going out and celebrating more. What is wrong with you?'...I was locked up and couldn't have any of it... Well, it ties in for me in that, one thinking about the previous body that the soul occupied would have had very restricted opportunities for joy. And the other is that I do have that in my heart and it does want to be expressed and it wants to be expressed now while this body is still available to express it in, with the people that I know, with the other bodies that are here with me, with the other souls that are here with me, which is all

one soul I think, but are here with me in this lifetime.
That would be a wonderful thing. And a wonderful thing
in a really worthwhile thing to do with the time that this
body has before it wears out.

Vivian was born in South America and describes how her family and friends spoke about spirits often. Her mother belonged to a group that met to speak directly to the spirits of loved ones who had died. For her, reincarnation was assumed. When she started to get images and memories of the Holocaust, she was not alarmed. However, it is because of these images that she became afraid of dying—not death or being dead—just the dying process.

We call them Spiritualists. They talk to spirits. They are
not really a religion. They believe that souls come back
all the time and that sort of thing... I think the first piece
that I need to clarify is that my thoughts and my feelings
are different, one from the other. While in my head I
have no fear of death, sometimes I am just terrified... I
feel big disassociation between what I think and what I
feel. I don't know if that is normal, or common.
Sometimes, at night, I am afraid that my heart will seize.
Sometimes, I think maybe if I saw more experiences of
people dying, I will be less afraid emotionally, but at the
same time, I am just terrified.... In my head I know things
go on. In my head, I am not afraid.

I had beautiful dreams about dying. I had one about two

or three years ago, a beautiful dream about going... up there and seeing what happened when people were talking about the sufferings they had during the Holocaust. It would come up and they'd just begin saying what had happened to them. Some partition on the top opened and you could see the tears of the Shekhinah coming down. Everything was very colourful. There was a lot of orange, as I recall. I know something goes on. I know in my head. Maybe I remember it. I don't know, but I am sometimes just terrified...

Ellen talks about multiple lives and that perhaps her soul was Jewish before. She talks also about her family's tradition of sitting with the dead. This is an important part of her Judaism and also her work in a hospital.

My life as a Jew doesn't feel newly minted. I don't know if it is because my soul was Jewish before or if Jewishness is so deep and so ancient that it connects to the soul, wherever that soul has been before. And I'll give you an example that I think helps make it concrete. I was talking to my mom recently, telling her about shomrim (those who guard and sit with the dead before they are buried). And she said, 'Oh we did that when I was a little girl... We always did that. When somebody died in the community we would be called, not on the phone, just called.... We would take turns sitting through the night and watching. There was usually two or three usually sitting together.'

That is something that really appealed to my sense of being a Jew, but I wondered if it is just my sense of being a soul. I can more easily accept the possibility of my soul having been here before. The specificity of being Jewish, I don't know. I guess part of that is because I think that our intellect instructs Jewishness sometimes. I don't know that our soul is so bound to any one faith. I think the soul is hoping to be helped in a practice, but I don't know that it, in itself, is anything other than a soul and we give it Jewish flavour, shape, or container – or a Christian container or a Catholic container. They all feel like containers to me. And soul is the light within that container, though not necessarily defined by the specific influence.

The more that I think about it, or feel about it, the more I feel that the soul is something that transcends any one particular religion. And perhaps I was in that container before . . . . And I guess part of what I feel is that the soul that I might have now in the Jewish container, although it is practicing and maybe it is the dominant container, but I know a way of looking at it is, 'Why?' Maybe my soul has spent some time in an oak barrel and how it has been put into a very beautiful crystal carafe. Who knows? I don't see it as static. I think that each container has influence and shapes it. They are not separate things. Containers shape and flavour the soul. And the soul flavours and shapes the container it is in. It is an interesting dynamic....

While Ellen has some ambivalence about the term "reincarnation," she has had experiences that indicate to her that people do come back and that they have several lives. She makes sense of it by theorizing that the soul comes back, perhaps not as a complete identity, but more as "little strings of self," as "filaments" or pieces of the person. No matter the constructs, Ellen believes and experiences the soul, in part or whole, as returning for another life.

I have room for reincarnation in my imagination. I wouldn't say that I absolutely believe. In thinking of people that I know, and thinking particularly of children, it is really clear to me that there are souls that have come back. Even my youngest son is really convinced that he has come back. He feels that he was here and had to go back to Heaven and then came back again. He has that sense of having not been ready the first time... One of my sons was a twin. They were twins and I miscarried in a very early stage. I miscarried one of the twins after a few months, early on, so I was quite familiar with what was going on. My youngest son is convinced that he was that twin, but he needed to learn more. He calls it Heaven. He says that he went back to God and had more things to learn so that he could be a better brother for his brother because he knew that brother would need help...

He is not the first person to conceive of that thought. He knows that his brother was a twin and just assumes that he was that twin and that he needed to go back to

Heaven to learn more from God so that he could help his brother... He came up with this. I had thought of it, but in another context. Quite recently, he said that he knew that he had to help his brother, but he needed to learn more first. Even more with children than adults, I feel that sometimes there is stuff in them that feels so layered and maybe the layers are other existences, so it feels like a stretch to say I believe in reincarnation, but I certainly believe in these layers...

With his brother, I think I often have said that he is my precious teacher and meaning it in my Buddhist way, that he is the person that challenges me and therefore teaches me. There is something about his soul that is not just showing up now. He said, 'I just wish I could remember more.' He wished he could remember the details of what happened elsewhere. He feels that he has things that he needs to do, but he doesn't remember all the instructions, all the details.

I think that is how a lot of us feel... In the same way I became Jewish and connected with death and connected with taharah and it happened all at once. When we talk about a restless soul, I think maybe because there is a task assigned to this soul. We don't necessarily get clear instructions and we have to be awake and figure it out. In that sense, it doesn't feel like it was just this time around where I needed to know this. It is hard to express it because the language is cumbersome, but I can believe *that maybe I was really good with death before or maybe I was really bad with death before... now I am certain that death will be okay.*

I don't want to leave people I love, but it won't be horrible. I don't want to lose, God forbid, any of my children whom I love, but I will survive that because I know that it is not horrible. It will be devastating because this part of me is so attached to life. I hope that that is true. I really feel that. I really believe that now... I like the notion of fragments and little strings of soul. That makes sense to me in an easier way, rather than an entire soul starting all over again. I don't see it that way. I see it more of a mosaic, of little pieces, being reconstructed and sent back.

Irene speaks very clearly about her relationship with God and how it has enabled her to heal her heart. She is grateful for the gifts that God has given her. Mostly she talks about the challenge, that we must try to be like God, showing kindness and giving love.

Regarding my relationship with God, it is just this feeling of strong connection. I felt that when I became a Jew that I felt I was going home. That it was basically a formality. Once I did that, there was this sense of finally coming home to the place where I was supposed to be... For me the word is déjà vu, more than anything. Perhaps, that is saying the same sort of thing. I have been here before. I remember the first time I came to the synagogue, I was twelve years old, and it was really quite overwhelming. I felt that this was a good place to be, where I needed to be, where I was supposed to be. Of course, I never came back until much later... I think the confidence that I have in my relationship to God has actually enabled me to do a lot more heart healing. Whereas before, I was always trying to get into God's good books because I was afraid of going to Hell. Now, this is a relationship that is bilateral. It is not unilateral where I am talking at God and God answers. It feels like a relationship where you communicate. In strong relationships, you can communicate with silence. It doesn't really matter. In that sense, since I have gone to the mikveh, I have probably felt a lot clearer of conscience.

Irene uses a poetic metaphor taken from a children's storybook series to explain her understanding of reincarnation.

I guess one of the reasons why I love reading from The Lion, the Witch and the Wardrobe is that the children don't go into Narnia once, but they go into Narnia multiple times. To me, each time they go into Narnia, it is a different adventure, a different set of circumstances. But at the same time, they still remain who they are. I guess I see that as the soul. You don't get multiple souls. You have one soul, but the soul has multiple journeys.

Seeking Redemption in an Unredeemed World

Ned strongly believes in reincarnation and had this belief before he became Jewish. Here are his words.

I had a strong sense reincarnation even before I knew I was Jewish. I was a monotheist for as long as I can remember. I knew that everything was unfolding for the good and that everything was evolving upward to a greater good. I love my life right now. I am happy to be living it and I guess my sense is that my next life is going to be even better, even if I am not reincarnated into the Age of the Mashiaḥ, the Messianic Age, even if I die tomorrow and I am reincarnated a year from now. That next life is going to be even greater. There is going to be more sh'leimut, wholeness.

Ned had dreams that he interpreted as windows into previous lifetimes. He interprets them as informing him on how to live his life this time around. He speaks about them as *Tikkunim*, karmic lessons pointing toward repair.

You know that we say Kaddish, the prayer for the dead, for eleven months and so that there is this idea of purification in Gehennah (Hebrew for Purgatory) that we go through, of having to face our own karma... the suffering that we have caused others will be visited upon us... There is the Jewish thought of Tikkun Olam. I had a horrible dream one time. In the dream, I was in bed sick. And somebody came in and asked for my command and it was something to do with the gas chambers. I was in a level of authority and said, 'Okay.' That segment of the dream was seconds, a flash. I don't know what that means. Obviously, I reserved a tiny bit of doubt because there is so much in your dream space... My sense was that maybe I had made the crematoriums... But somebody came to me asking about how it works, or to let me know that they are up and running... It was quite horrible actually... it wasn't so much that they were asking, it was like I couldn't do anything about it. I was silent, and they were giving me the respect, 'Just so you know, it is happening like you wanted it to.' Then I was like, 'I don't want it.' I was silent. It was just a second. When we dream, it is part of our soul. I'm still me. That feeling of, 'Stop it. No,' that could be who I am now. Interjecting me now with me then...

I haven't really told anybody. It is not something to be proud of. 'I think in the past life I might have made gas chambers...' Who knows if I was Jewish? So, my sense is that there has been a long journey and that there has been a Jewish thing. What I have learned through my dreams is that I turned back from it... I think that by being Jewish, having a Jewish family, is part of that Tikkun... In our first session I shared a dream about something that was a lot more vivid and it corresponded with a piece of history that I learned about. It was about a program where Jews committed suicide and I escaped from the suicide. And then I learned that those people that did escape tried to convert to Christianity and were *murdered.*

Marsha states that she is both terrified of dying and not afraid to die. She has a scientific mind that wants proof that there is reincarnation, and yet she had a dream that she believes is a window into a previous lifetime. This dream she takes as truth. This war between her experience, which she believes in, and her rational mind, keeps her from unequivocally stating that she believes in reincarnation. As she says, if she believed in reincarnation, then she wouldn't be so afraid of death. And she wants to believe. She thinks that if she is a reincarnated Jew, then she would be a more authentic and legitimate Jew. She is the only respondent that stated this hope and belief. Marsha had some thoughts about death and the soul journeying.

> *I have always had dual feelings about death. I'm terrified of it and I have been so thankful that it is there because if we didn't die there would be very little motivation to do anything, or at least for me. In my life I feel very connected to mortality in the sense of finite existence. I see it as a motivating factor. I have got this much time... When people say they are not afraid to die, I am always impressed because I think I'm afraid to die... It goes to the idea that if I wasn't a Jew in the past, and if this is another journey, it would be exciting, but for me not knowing and being in a place of not knowing, it is uncomfortable... I think about when I was going through the process of converting and went to the mikveh. One of the things that the mikveh symbolized to me was rebirth.*

The rabbis asked me, 'What are some of the things that you would bring to Judaism?' What came to me was, 'At some point I would probably see myself being involved in the death and dying side in terms of a society, to attend the soul.'... That surprised me when it came out of my mouth.

Again, death has always been important, even when I was a child...When I closed my eyes, I had the image about that theory of how the world was like a clay vessel that exploded. We all have a little piece of that vessel inside of us and our job is to put it all back together. That is how I feel about my husband and me. It has the feeling of something before, coming to the present. I find myself hesitant to use the word reincarnation. I would say, 'something before' or 'the hint.'...The soul moving on, I think that is what I crave. That is why I have been drawn to religion, period. For me, it is more about the mystical side and I firmly believe that links to death. The idea that something lives on, I think that is where I want to go. Almost every part of me wants to go there, and then there is the rational part of me that says, 'Where's the incontrovertible proof?'... I love the Song of Songs: 'For love is as strong as death.'

The following anecdotes are from respondents who only wrote in the questionnaire about their sense that they were Jewish in a previous lifetime:

- *From the time I was young, I had Holocaust nightmares that escalated during my pregnancy (age 19-20). In 1989, I had a frightening past-life regression that led me to believe that I had died in the Holocaust. My first memory is studying about World War II in high school, reading about the concentration camps, and having to leave the classroom because I was so nauseous from reading the accounts.*

- *Since I was about four or five years old, I have known that I lived before. It had something to do with Jews, Germans, and gas. During the past-life regression (using a CD from the therapist Brian Weiss, MD), I saw this beautiful woman, Tzipporah, right before she married. She was stunning with long curly black hair and an incredible smile. I saw her making love with her husband after their marriage, and then not long after walking into the gas chamber comforting a small child.*

- *I was born in 1950 in the shadow of the Holocaust. Always, as far back as I can remember, I have believed that I died in the Holocaust. My adopted parents weren't Jewish and where we lived, I don't believe there were any Jews. As a child I devoured all kinds of books and movies about the Holocaust. As I grew up, I had dreams and meditations where I saw myself as a man in the concentration camps. I was a scientist and given the responsibility of growing a garden on top of one of the one-story buildings. It wasn't a terrible time for me as I enjoyed the work. I have had visual* and body memories of being shot by a man in a Nazi uniform and dying. I felt very grateful to him as I knew it would have been much more painful to die in other ways. I believe that a good friend of mine, in this lifetime, is that man. Since I converted, I have done several 'Focusing' sessions where several lifetimes came up where I was a Jew.

- Once I began my studies, Hebrew came to me like an old friend and languages do not usually come easily to me.

- I have a sense of urgency about having to make a certain food for a holiday—a food completely out of my usual repertoire. I have a sense of rhythm about the Jewish calendar that feels entirely familiar; a certain time/place feels inordinately familiar to me. These feelings have a certainty that is unusual. There is a sense of fit that I feel. It wasn't a conversion so much as a waiting for the time to be right to return.

- My father and I walk to school and work together every day. One day, I told him about a dream I had where I was in a concentration camp, and while escaping I was shot and killed. My father stopped walking and turned to me and told me that he, too, had a dream last night and that he was the prison guard who shot and killed me.

Conclusions

The Jews by Choice in this study who believe that they are reincarnated Jews have a spiritual yearning to bring God into their lives and a communal yearning to (re)assume their roles as Jews. How they have journeyed to Judaism, how they attach to the Jewish community, and how they bring God into their lives is important information for rabbis and the Jewish community to know. Fifty-four percent, or over one-half, of my respondents a decade ago sensed they were Jewish in a previous lifetime. Discussions with friends and colleagues who now serve as liberal rabbis in Europe indicate that my findings are at least as relevant today, if not more so, for those living upon the lands where World War II was fought and the Holocaust was perpetrated. These findings have serious implications for both the individual convert and the Jewish community.

While no longer the norm, many Jews by Choice sadly continue to experience rejection or shaming from both born Jews and non-Jews.[30] Just this past *Shabbat,* while I was conducting the *Shabbat* meal *b'rachot* (blessings), a non-Jewish guest stated that since I was not born Jewish, I wasn't Jewish. I looked her straight in the eye and stated, "I am Jewish and have been for forty years." There was a pause in the conversation and then the talk started up again. I mention this as it is a recurring issue. At this stage of my life, comments such as, "You're not really Jewish," or "What do you know?" usually come from people who do not know me, my commitment or my involvement, including leadership roles, within the Jewish community. It is my experience that once Jews by Choice demonstrate their willingness to participate in Jewish observance and study and to work in some capacity within the Jewish community, the comments generally stop, at least from the born Jews who know them. However, everyone needs education on the validity and place within the Jewish community that Jews by Choice hold.

In this regard, what does it mean to the Jewish world that some converts to Judaism believe that they were Jewish in a previous lifetime? To quote Valerie Thaler: "Yet even as they might fully accept proselytes as co-religionists, American Jews often feel that Jews by Choice cannot fully share the bond of Jewish ethnicity, peoplehood or history – at least not immediately."[31] Other studies have shown that these concerns mirror those of Jews by Choice themselves, who often feel more immediately comfortable with their Judaism than with Jewishness. Perhaps my findings might point the way to help those Jews by Choice, who sense they were previously Jewish, more easily confirm their current places among *Am Yisrael,* the Jewish People.

They might also help some who doubt the authenticity of such Jews by Choice to accept that these proselytes (Hebrew: *gerim*) feel so strong a connection to our people that it seems to transcend this lifetime. To them, their formal acceptance of Judaism can at times seem less like an act of conversion and more like an act of *teshuvah,* return.

One final point. Can these reincarnation experiences be taken at face value and believed? While others might disagree, I personally say yes. While I have not conducted extensive research, I have informally spoken to many born Jews who recount stories of experiencing previous lives as Jews. Interestingly, even non-observant Ashkenazi Jews,[32] who scoff at the idea of reincarnation, recoil from the idea of naming a child after a living relative while continuing to name their children after deceased kin. Why? Because of an often unstated but enduring belief that the elderly relative and her/his newborn namesake share at least a spark of the same soul. Certainly, more research is needed here, particularly as new discoveries unfold concerning meta-genetics, near-death experiences and the neuroscience of consciousness. Such continued reflection can prove beneficial not only to Jews by Choice, but to the rabbis and spiritual directors who mentor and offer them spiritual guidance, to the laity who support and welcome them, and most importantly, to the Jewish community as a whole.

ENDNOTES

1
   Raphael, S. P. *Jewish Views of the Afterlife.* 2nd ed. Rowman and Littlefield Publishers, Inc., 2009.p. 314.
2
   Another reason is that we are made in the image of God and therefore, we must not destroy our body, and harm, by implication, God's body. Additionally, "Burning" (*S'reifah*), traditionally bears punitive connotations as one of four types of capital sentences by which ancient Jewish courts executed criminals.

[3]

The Seif Edition, *ArtScroll Translated Linear Siddur, Sabbath and Festivals*. Mesorah Publications, 1998. pp. 35-36.

[4]

Gillman, N, *The Death of Death: Resurrection and Immortality in Jewish Thought*. Jewish Lights Publishing, 2000; p. 123.

[5]

Gillman, p.124.

[6]

Gillman, p.126.

[7]

Gillman, p.129.

[8]

Gillman, p.134.

[9]

Gillman, p. 135.

[10]

ibid.

[11]

Harlow, J. (ed.) *Sim Shalom Siddur: A Prayerbook for Shabbat, Festivals, and Weekdays;* The Rabbinical Assembly, 1997. p. 3.

[12]

Gillman, p. 136

[13]

Retrieved from https://www.jewishvirtuallibrary.org/reincarnationand-judaism

[14]

Gillman, p. 145.

[15]

Gillman, p. 146.

[16]

Gillman p 172

[17]

Gillman p. 177

[18]

ibid.

[19]

"whether in this transmigration or another transmigration. This term *gilgul* refers to the doctrine of (in Hebrew) *gilgul neshamot*, transmigration of souls, one of the most mystical doctrines in kabbalistic literature. In very simple terms it refers to the reincarnation of certain souls for a second period of physical life on earth." *The Complete ArtScroll Siddur.* Mesorah Publications,1984, pp. 196 & 288.

[20]
    Rabbi Zalman Schachter-Shalomi's rendering of the bedtime *Sh'ma* prayer first appeared in *New Menorah.* Fall 1997;

[21]
    Astor, Y. *Soul Searching.* Targum Press, 2003. p. 318.

[22]
    Raphael, p. 318.

[23]
    Brian Weiss' books include: *Many Lives, Many Masters* (1996); *Only Love is Real* (1997); *Same Soul, Many Bodies* (2004); *Messages from the Masters* (2008); *Miracles Happen* (with Amy Weiss, 2012); and *Through Time into Healing* (with Raymond Moody, 2012).

[24]
    Gershom, Y. *Beyond the Ashes.* A.R.E Pr Publishing,1992. p. 49.

[25]
    Sefer ha-Bahir #121.

[26]
    Gershom, p. 71.

[27] For further information on Luria and the Lurianic Kabbalah see Drob, S. "The Lurianic Kabbalah," Retrieved from *http://www.newkabbalah.com/newkabbalah.htm*

[28]
Gershom, p. 94.
    "The Rebbe" refers to the Seventh Grand Rabbi of Chabad-Lubavitch
    Hasidism, Rabbi Menachem Mendel Schneerson (d. 1994)
For brief sketches of hasidic Judaism and what delineates *Chabad/Lubavitcher* Hasidism see "The Hasidic Movement: A History," retrieved from
https://www.myjewishlearning.com/article/hasidicmovement-a-history/
and "What is Chabad Hasidism..." retrieved from
https://www.quora.com/What-is-Chabad-Hasidism-and-how-is-itdifferent-from-other-Jewish-movements

[29]
    On whether Jews can reincarnate as non-Jews see "The Nefesh of the Ger [Convert, Stranger]" Retrieved from
https://www.chabad.org/kabbalah/article_cdo/aid/1161280/jewish/The

-Nefesh-of-the-Ger-111.htm

30

For a particularly heart-wrenching tale see Bodenner, C. "What If the Religion You Choose Doesn't Want You?" Retrieved from https://www.theatlantic.com/notes/2016/04/what-if-the-religion-youchoose-doesnt-want-you/477909/

31

Thaler, V. S. "Jewish Attitudes Towards Proselytes"
Retrieved from
https://www.myjewishlearning.com/article/jewishattitudes-toward-proselytes/

32

Ashkenazi Jews are of Eastern, Central of Western European descent. *Sephardi* Jews descend from Jewish communities on the Iberian Peninsula; following the 1492 and 1497 expulsions, they spread to North Africa, Anatolia, the Netherlands, the Levant, Southeastern and Southern Europe, as well as the Americas. *Mizraḥi* Jews include descendants of Babylonian Jews and Mountain Jews from modern Iraq and Syria east to India and Pakistan. While Yemenite Jews are sometimes included among the *Mizraḥi,* their history differs from those of Babylonian descent.

גאולה

GE·ULAH/REDEMPTION

The Shofar and the White House

Festival, Midrash and Eco-Social Justice

Arthur Waskow

The Beginning of Transformation

If one looks in the Torah for a festival called Rosh Hashanah one will search in vain. The feast that occurs during the first day of *Tishrei*, then the seventh month of the year, is alternately known as *Zikhron T'ruah* (Lev. 23:24) or *Yom T'ruah* (Num. 29:1), the "Remembrance" or the "Day" to read forth the Sounding of the Shofar, the Ram's Horn. Rabbinic texts refer to this festival as *Yom Ha-Din* and *Yom Ha-Zikaron*, the Day of Justice and Judgment, the Day of Remembrance. Later liturgical sources, associating the Holy Day with the birthing of the World, proclaim *Ha-Yom Harat Olam*, "Today the world was (is) born."[1]

The term *Rosh Hashanah* appears but once in the Hebrew Bible (Ezekiel 40:1) and it's unclear there whether it refers to the first of *Tishrei* or the tenth, which is observed as *Yom Kippur*. While the festival's Hebrew name usually is translated as "Beginning of the Year" it can also mean the "Beginning of Transformation."[2] At least twice in Jewish history the observance of Rosh Hashanah marked social, political and religious transformations in the face of crisis.

The first occurred in the mid-fifth century BCE. Even though the Second Temple had been built in 516 BCE, the walls of Jerusalem were in ruin and the Judean community was in a state of social and religious ennui. Nehemiah, cupbearer to the Persian King Artaxerxes, was granted royal authority to repair both the walls and the socio-religious fabric of Jerusalem. In the face of fierce external opposition Nehemiah oversaw the rebuilding of the walls, which took fifty-two days. The process of religious and social reform was ritually marked on the first of Tishrei as Ezra the Scribe publicly read the Torah to the people. Moved by recognition of their past shortcomings those assembled were on the verge of despair. Ezra then proclaimed to them:

> *Go your way, eat of the fat, drink the sweet, and send portions to those for whom nothing has been prepared: for this day is holy unto our God: don't be forlorn; for the joy of the YHWH is your strength* (Nehemiah 8:10).

Modern scholars trace our current observance of Rosh Hashanah, with its themes of repentance and rejoicing amid holy convocation, to this transformative event.[3]

After the Second Temple was destroyed in 70 CE, Rabban

Yoḥanan ben Zakkai sought to reconstruct Judaism, substituting prayer and sacred study for the shattered sacrificial cult. Until that time the shofar was only blown in Jerusalem and the Temple precincts when Rosh Hashanah fell on the Sabbath. Rabban Yoḥanan skillfully circumvented the opposition of colleagues and blew the shofar in Yavneh, seat of his rabbinic academy, the next time Rosh Hashanah occurred on Shabbat.[4] On that Rosh Hashanah, Rabban Yoḥanan heralded the survival and regeneration of Judaism in the face of political and spiritual catastrophe. His shofar blowing effectually announced that the House of Study and Prayer *(Beit ha-Midrash)* was the *de jure* successor to the destroyed Holy Temple *(Beit ha-Mikdash).*[5]

Rosh Hashanah 5758

Rosh Hashanah 5758 fell on September 20-22, 2017. During the months preceding the festival, America, peoples of the world and the planet itself came under assault by the Trump administration.[6] If Rosh Hashanah is a day of judgment and justice, a day to remember the birthing of the world and our commitment to its healing, we at The Shalom Center[7] framed our response based on the sacred practices of the festival. Our goal, like that of Nehemiah, Ezra and Rabban Yoḥanan, was that this Rosh Hashanah also marks a beginning of transformation in the face of crisis.

Such liturgical and ritual resistance based on *midrash,*[8] the contemporary interpretation and application of traditional prayers and texts, is not new to us. In their origins, most of the

Jewish Holy Days are rooted not just in history but in the rhythms of the Earth, God's creation and sacred arena for connecting with humanity. Thus, the Jewish festivals, which carry this powerfully explicit message, have already provided us with extraordinary resources to fashion *midrashim* (pl.) for speaking truth to power – and to the disempowered.

In the year 5757[9] on *Tu biSh'vat* (January 23, 1997), the midwinter full moon festival celebrating the regrowth of trees, we at The Shalom Center challenged the corporate destruction of ancient redwood trees in California. On *Hoshana Rabbah* 5759 (October 11, 1998), the seventh day of the autumnal harvest festival of Sukkot, when we chant prayers for the healing of the Earth from locusts and other plagues, was a fitting time to challenge General Electric's dumping of poisonous PCBs (polychlorinated biphenyl) into the Hudson River.

During the summer of 2010 when British Petroleum killed its own workers and poisoned large parts of the Gulf of Mexico, we gathered on the steps of the US Capitol during *Tisha b'Av* 5770 (July 20, 2010), the midsummer Jewish day of grief and fasting to mourn the destruction of ancient Temples in Jerusalem. We gathered to focus, instead, on the danger of the continuing destruction of Temple Earth by chanting in English a modern version of the Book of Lamentations.[10] The primal power of the festivals combined with their direct relevance to our world today, has drawn Jews, Catholic nuns, Buddhist monks, secular environmentalists, and others to action rooted not in secular politics, but in the Spirit.

Since Rosh Hashanah is traditionally understood as the anniversary of the Creation of Humanity, Society and the World, we focused on prayers and scriptural readings which bring that metaphor into bold relief. These included: A) a prayer to precede and accompany the lighting of the festival candles on the first night of Rosh Hashanah; B) a *"Sh'ma* for the 21st Century,"* bringing modern science into the traditional affirmations of interconnection among the One, human action, and the Earth; C) a way of praying with trees and hearing their prayers; D) an alternative scriptural reading; and E) an approach to hearing the outcry of the shofar amid the congregation.

Between the Fires: A Prayer for lighting Candles of Commitment

At the very beginning of Rosh Hashanah eve, all gathered are welcome to share in a moment of silent reflection and then recite together:

We are the generation that stands between the fires: Behind us
the flame and smoke that rose
From Auschwitz and from Hiroshima
From the burning forests of the Amazon,
From the hottest years human history has brought upon us.
Melted ice fields, Flooded cities, Scorching droughts.
Before us the nightmare of a Flood of Fire,
The heat and smoke that could consume all Earth.

The Shofar and the White House   259

It is our task to make from fire not an all-consuming blaze,
Not fire and fury,
But the light in which we see each other fully.
All of us different All of us bearing One Spark.
We light these fires to see more clearly
That the Earth and all who live as part of it
Are not for burning.
We light these fires to see more clearly
The rainbow in our many-colored faces.

In unison, everyone present can then recite this variation of the traditional candle blessing.

Barukh attah YHWH[11]—Yahhh—Eloheinu ruaḥ ha-olam,
asher kid'shanu b'mitzvot vi-tzivanu l'hadlik ner
shel Yom Tov, Yom Harat Olam.

Blessed are You, Inter-breathing Spirit of the world, Source of all creation, Who calls us into holiness through making connections with each other, and Who connects us by kindling the lights of this festival, the Day of the Birthing of the World.[12]

All are then invited to light candles reflecting the light and joy of the New Year, the Anniversary of Creation. Ritually, this kindling marks our commitment to utilize fire not to burn the Earth, but as the radiance that allows us to see each other more fully amid our divinely created, many-colored faces.

Sh'ma for the 21st Century

The Sh'ma Yisrael, Hear O Israel (Deut. 6:4-9) and its attendant paragraphs (Deut. 11:13-21 and Num. 15: 37-41) constitute one of two foci of the Jewish morning and evening service. The paragraph that follows the Sh'ma, Judaism's traditional affirmation of the Unity underlying all being, asserts a connection between human action and the flourishing or destruction of Earth's abundance. The final selection speaks of the weaving that must occur at our corners and boundaries.

The interpretive (read *midrashic*) translation below brings our present scientific understanding to bear on these affirmations, which speaks pointedly to this time of human induced climate change and increased exclusionary tribalism separating peoples.

At the appropriate point in the service the gathered community chants together:

Sh'ma Yisra•el: Yahhh Eloheinu, Yahhhh Eḥad.
(lit. Hear O Israel: YHWH is Our God, YHWH is One.)

Then, going around the room, individuals are invited to read a paragraph each.

Sh'sh'sh'ma Yisra•el—

Hush'sh'sh and Listen, You Godwrestlers[13] —Pause from your
wrestling and hush'sh'sh to hear—
YyyyHhhhWwwwHhhh/ Yahhhhhh.
Hear in the stillness the still silent voice;
The silent breathing that intertwines life;
YyyyHhhhWwwwHhhh / Yahhhh Eloheinu
Breath of life is our God, What unites all the varied forces
creating all worlds into one-ness.
Each breath unique, And all unified;

Listen, You Godwrestlers—No one people alone owns this
Unify-force;
YyyyHhhhWwwwHhhh / Yahh is One.

If you hush and then listen, yes hush and then listen to the
teachings of *YHWH/ Yah,* the One Breath of Life, that the world
is One—
If you hear in the stillness the still silent voice,
silent breathing that intertwines life;
If we Breathe in the quiet, Inter-breath with all Life—Still Small
Voice of us all—We will feel the
Connections;
We will make the connections;
The rain will fall rightly
The grains will grow rightly;
The rivers will run; The heavens will smile;
The forests will flourish; The good earth will fruitfully feed us,
And all life weaves the future in fullness.

Earthlings / good Earth.

But if we break the One Breath into pieces, erect into idols
these pieces of Truth,
If we choose these mere pieces to worship: gods of race or of
nation; gods of wealth and of power; gods of greed and
addiction—Big Oil or Big Coal—
If we Do and we Make and Produce without Pausing to Be;

If we heat One Breath with our burnings, then the Breath will
flare into scorching,
Great ice fields will melt and great storms will erupt; Floods will
drown our homes and our cities.
The rain will not fall—or will turn to sharp acid—
The rivers won't run—or flood homes and cities;
The corn will parch in the field;
The poor will find little to eat,
The heavens themselves will take arms against us:
the ozone will fail us,
the oil that we burn will scorch our whole planet.
The Breath, Holy Wind, Holy Spirit will become Hurricanes of
Disaster.
and from the good earth that the Breath of Life gives us, We
will vanish; Yes, perish.

What must we do?
At the gates of our cities, where our own culture ends, and
another begins,

Where we might halt in fear—
"Here we speak the same language
"But out there is barbaric, they may kill without
speaking—"
Then pause in the gateway to write on its walls And to chant in
its passage:
"Each gate is unique in the world that is One."

On the edges of each Self
take care to weave fringes, threads of connection.
So we end not with sharpness, A fence or a wall,
But with sacred mixing of cloth and of air—
A fringe that is fuzzy, part ours and part God's:
They bind us together, Make One from our one-ness.
Good fringes/ good neighbors.

Deep mirrors/ true seeing.
Time loving/ right action.

The Infinite/ One.

Connect what we see with our eyes To what we do with our
hands.
If we see that a day is coming
That will burn like a furnace—Turn for our healing to a sun of
justice,

To its wings of wind and its rays of light To empower all
peoples.

Then the rains will fall
Time by time, time by time;
The rivers will run; The heavens will smile,

The grass will grow; The forests will flourish,
The good earth will fruitfully feed us,
And all life weaves the future in fullness.

Honor the web that all of us weave—
Breathe together the Breath of all Life.

Before continuing, the community simply breathes quietly for
several minutes, staying aware that each breath comes from all
breath.

Praying with Trees

From time immemorial, trees have been integral to and often
revered within the calculus of Heaven and Earth. The Garden of
Eden story (Genesis 3) is replete with images of the Tree of
Knowledge and the Tree of Life, while Deuteronomy draws an
analogy between humans and trees (Deut. 20:19).

Later scripture envisions the trees enthusiastically joining all of nature to praise God by clapping their hands (Isaiah 55:12) and singing for joy (Psalms 96:12). Kabbalah's most frequent configuration of the ten *Sefirot,* manifestations of the divine, is the *Eitz Ḥayyim,* the Tree of Life, while the Spanish Kabbalist Joseph Gikatilla (d. 1310 CE) taught: *For all God's Names that are mentioned in the Torah are included in the Tetragrammaton, YHWH, which resembles a tree trunk. Each of the other Names—those I have compared to roots and branches* . . .[14]

Early in *I And Thou,* Martin Buber writes about how one can enter a reciprocal I-Thou encounter with a tree.[15] He does not, however, speak of praying with nor of listening to the trees' song as mentioned in Psalms.

At a time when those in power pay little to no heed to nature's cry, the practice described here can open our ears and hearts during the anniversary of creation. If one is worshipping in a small community with easy access to the outdoors this practice can serve as the *Amidah,* the "Standing" prayer, which is the second focus of the morning and evening service.[16]

If one is worshipping alone or as a member of a large metropolitan congregation where a mass exodus is impractical, one might try this in solitude or with a gathered small group.

Opening Meditation (leader or lone worshipper)

*We are about to enter the **Amidah,** where we take our own stance in the Breath of Life, murmuring prayer with our own* *breathing. Though we often call the Amidah "silent," as long as we are alive, there is no silence, as we are always breathing. The trees are breathing with us. Indeed, the exchange of CO_2 and Oxygen between trees and grasses on the one hand and humans and other animals on the other is what keeps life alive on Planet Earth, and it is precisely that Inter-breathing that is now in crisis through global scorching. For this breathing Amidah, we invite you to stand near a tree and breathe together. Hear the tree's Amidah. Listen to what the tree is praying.*

Those participating disperse to stand by, listen to, and pray with the trees. This portion of the ritual can conclude by the participants coming back while singing *Eitz Ḥayim* by Hanna Tiferet Siegel:

She is a tree of life

More precious than gold

Hold Her in your heart

And you will understand

Eitz ḥayim hi

Her roots are deep and wise

Her branches full of light

And all Her pathways are peace[17]

This practice was first introduced in advance of Rosh Hashanah during the 2017 *Ruach Ha'Aretz* Jewish Renewal Spiritual

Retreat at Stony Point, New York. The following reflections were among those shared in response to the ritual:

- *The tree I befriended had prickly pine needles, and I could hear it saying to me, 'You who breathe me in and out, I am breathing out to you—a prickly scent just like my prickly needles—a prickly scent to say to you, 'Wake up!' A scent of more than sleep. 'Wake up. Wake up. Wake up. Wake up. Breathe with me. I may be in danger but my prickly needles, my prickly scent, I'm sending to awaken you.'*

- *I heard my son's voice, 'Mommy!' whispering from the tree, and I felt the wind rustling the canopy of branches. And then part of me remembered how some trees are hurt because crowds of tourists walk over their ground, on their roots, they're hurt. So I ask the trees' forgiveness.*

- *Hearing that image of the Yod Hey Waw Hey (YHWH) in the tree and in the human, what came to me was God's Name as a Tree, the Tree of Life: The Yod—tiny, a seed in the ground. The Hey—curvy, the roots growing out of that seed. The straight tall Vav, the trunk. The other curvy Hey, the leaves, the foliage, and in the foliage, hanging, ready to fall into the earth is the next generation, another seed, another Yod. So the real Name, the full Name, is: Yod Hey Waw Hey Yod. And on and on: Yod Heh WaW Hey Yod . . . A spiral. Always returning, always becoming.*

An Alternative Scriptural Reading

Traditionally, the Torah reading on the first day of Rosh Hashanah, Genesis 21, tells of the expulsion of Hagar and Ishmael from Abraham's family. Instead, there could be substituted the following, drawing on the tradition that Rosh Hashanah is the anniversary of the Creation of Humanity:

GENESIS 2:5-17, 3:16-19

[adapted from The Five Books of Moses,

trans. Everett Fox (New York, Schocken, 2000)]

5 No bush of the field was yet on earth, no plant of the field had yet sprung up, for *YHWH* [the Name of God that can only be "pronounced" by breathing with no vowels, thus "Yahhh, Breath of Life"] Creator God, had not made it rain upon earth, and there was no human earthling/*adam* to till the earthy humus/*adamah*— 6 but a surge would well up from the ground and water all the face of the soil; 7 And *YHWH/* Breath of Life/ Yahhhh Creator God formed the *adam* [human earthling] from the *adamah* [humus-earth] and blew into her/his nostrils the breath of life; and the human-earthling became a living being. 8 *YHWH*, God, planted a garden in Eden/ Land-of-Delight, in the east, and there he placed the human whom he had formed. 9 *YHWH*, God, caused to spring up from the soil every type of tree, desirable to look at and good to eat, and

the Tree of Life in the midst of the garden and the Tree of the Knowing of Good and Evil.

15. *YHWH*, God, took the human and set him in the garden of Eden, to work it and to watch it. 16. *YHWH*, God, commanded concerning the human, saying: From every (other) tree of the garden you may eat, yes, eat, 17 but from the Tree of the Knowing of Good and Evil — you are not to eat from it, for on the day that you eat from it, you must die, yes, die.

[But the human race rejected this warning to restrain itself from gobbling up all the abundance they could see, and the consequence of their lack of self-control was this:]

Genesis 3

16 To the woman he said: I will multiply, multiply your pain (from) your pregnancy, with pains shall you bear children. Toward your husband will be your lust, yet he will rule over you. 17 To Adam he said: Because you have hearkened to the voice of your wife and have eaten from the tree about which I commanded you, saying: You are not to eat from it! Damned be the soil on your account, with painstaking-labor shall you eat from it, ail the days of your life. 18 Thorn and sting-shrub let it spring up for you, when you (seek to) eat the plants of the field! 19 By the sweat of your brow shall you eat bread, until you return to the soil, for from it you were taken. For you are dust, and to dust shall you

return.

Blowing of the Shofar

When we blow the shofar on Rosh Hashanah, there are three "stanzas" of the blowing: *Malkhuyot, Zikhronot,* and *Shofarot.* The first, *Malkhuyot,* Majesty, is about justice, which must be kept in balance with compassion. The second, *Zikhronot,* is about "Re-membering" not in the sense of evoking the past, but as the opposite of "dis-membering." That is, it is putting back together pieces of truth and life that have been cut apart from each other. It is about compassionate reconnection. The third, *Shofarot,* is about Transformation, which absorbs both compassion and justice and integrates them both into a new level of society.

In each stanza, there are four distinct notes of the shofar. "*Tekiah*" means "Awake!" to the crisis that we face. "*Sh'varim,* Broken," evokes the shattering of our habitual patterns and our broken-heartedness at their loss. "*T'ruah*" is the sobbing of sorrow as we realize the pain of those who are suffering in the disruption. "*Tekiah gedolah*" is the long, long breath of life in a new dimension—once again, Transformation.

Communities of prayer could draw on these meanings of the shofar to address transforming events that we have experienced. For Majestic Justice, they could be asked to describe the moments in which they found themselves through acting justly. After the stanza of Remembering, worshipers could be invited to recount their own stories of unexpected compassion. And for *Shofarot*, when the shofar is sounded in an exponential power of itself, they could share the times when they felt lifted beyond their ordinary lives, their conventional assumptions, to a place and time of Transformation.

The Shofar and the White House

Looking back over the past year we might judge four presidential actions as destructive to American and world society. Within the context of Rosh Hashanah, each event can be described as a shofar-blast blown by the world itself. These mirror the four shofar sounds: *Tekiah, Sh'varim, T'ruah, Tekiah gedolah.*

- The first shofar blast was sounded at Charlottesville and became even more shrill when the White House commented on what happened there. It called on us, "Awake!" to the resurgence of violent white supremacism, white nationalism, Neo-Nazism no longer at the margins of American society but now with sympathizers and defenders and believers at the very peak of American power in the White House and the presidency itself.

More deeply, it called out the pain and despair of some "old Americans" who feel severed economically, culturally, and spiritually from a new transnational, multicultural world.

- A second shofar blast was sounded by the hurricane that shattered many parts of Texas. Far fewer Americans could also hear the same shofar crying out from Asia, in the floods that killed thousands in Nepal, India, and Bangladesh. These storms called on us, "Awake!" to the truth of global scorching caused by the corporate greed of Big Coal, Big Oil, Big "Unnatural" Gas, now vigorously made the "Law of Greed is God" by the White House.

Here it is the Earth itself that those who rule our society try to exclude and subjugate—pretending that all the Earth is not an ecosystem and that what we do to rip and tear its inter-wovenness does not come back to harm us.

- Third, the shofar blast of threats of nuclear "war" thrown back and forth by the governments of the United States and the People's Republic of Korea, along with a Hydrogen Bomb and long-distance missiles tested successfully by the PRK government, echoed by war-like threats of "fire and fury" from the US government— together with the announcement that the White House will seek Congressional authorization of a trillion-dollar budget to "upgrade" and "strengthen" the US arsenal of thousands of H-Bombs.

This is the shofar blast of The Bomb reawakened, after almost thirty years of comfortable neglect as we thought the genocidal danger had been parked in a musty barn, unvisited. The trillion dollars proposed for advanced nuclear weapons could instead be spent on removing a trillion tons of CO_2 from our planet's atmosphere. Then, our children and grandchildren could derive joy and sustenance from the same life-giving climate that sustained our parents and grandparents, combined with a level of economic social justice unknown to our forebears.

- Fourth: The Shofar blast of efforts to wreck the lives of Dreamers and other immigrants, documented or not. We hear the wailing of heartbreak and sorrow in worsening deportation sweeps of these last few months, and in the cancelation of the DACA exemptions from deportation of the Dreamers who came as little children to the United States. These actions not only cruelly shatter immigrant families, but are also inexorably moving toward wounding the civil liberties and freedoms of many others.

In all four of these Traumas, there is the possibility of Transformation:

- Transformation by bringing together the different segments of working class and lower middle class Americans of every race and gender and ethnicity in a joyful amalgam, a New New Deal of sharing.
- Transformation by affirming our interconnectedness with all of our planet's life-forms, and taking action to heal and restore a livable climate.

Seeking Redemption in an Unredeemed World

- Transformation by moving swiftly to carry out the Treaty to abolish all nuclear weapons that was recently adopted by the United Nations, freeing us all from the threat of nuclear holocaust. And we could take legal, political, and economic steps to try and welcome North Korea into the comity of nations, even though we decry its government.

- Transformation by reworking our entire approach to immigration. We could not only welcome into citizenship all migrants in our midst, but with a new "Marshall Plan" we could revitalize the economies and polities of Mexico and Central America. Then their citizens would not feel flight from poverty, violence, and despair is their only choice.

In short, to each dimension of these echoing outcries of the Shofar we could respond not with more repression, but with Transformative Inclusion — Love.

Raise Your Voice Like a Shofar

The examples cited above model how we might respond to the present multidimensional crisis and, sadly, to those that will arise during this yet to be redeemed era of world history. As people of faith, we can accomplish two profound changes: framing these crises in categories that reflect the prophetic visions of our inherited spiritual traditions, and transforming our forms of prayer and celebration to respond to these crises through spiritual practice.

The Shofar and the White House   275

The symbols, texts, and practices addressed in this essay honor Rosh Hashanah as a celebratory, yet prayerful time observed primarily through home ritual, congregational worship and gatherings of communal prayer groups.

Other festival observances, like the *Tu BiSh'vat, Hoshana Rabbah* and *Tisha B'Av* rites cited above in Section II, better lend themselves to carrying communal rituals into public space. By practicing actual sacerdotal elements of the festivals as nonviolent public protest, possibly including nonviolent civil disobedience, we hope to mobilize the deep spiritual energies of human society to address the planetary crises of our generation. Our hope—that the spiritual wellsprings of our Holy Days can call forth the profound social changes so necessary for Earth and its human "Earth-lings." Martin Luther King Jr. said fifty years ago that we face "the fierce urgency of now."[18] Now the urgency seems even fiercer.

Jewish tradition teaches that God's own self will blow the Great Shofar to herald the coming of Messiah and the days of healing, peace, and justice. One ancient rabbi proclaimed: *May Messiah come, indeed, indeed—And may I not live to suffer through the turmoil that will accompany that Coming!*[19]

We have yet to see whether the turmoil and suffering we are living through betokens the Messianic Transformation, what the Buddhist teacher Joanna Macy calls The Great Turning[20] toward what Martin Luther King Jr. called the Beloved Community.[21] In the meantime, we can hope and pray and carry on the sacred work.

Each Holy Day comes with its own observances and imperatives. Rosh Hashanah calls us to emulate the Great Shofar, to show that we are joining in the great outcry of Transformation, an outcry we need to sound and act upon throughout the year. Let us meet the prophet Isaiah's challenge: *With full throated cry raise your voice like a Shofar—don't hold back![22]*

ENDNOTES

[1]
For a full treatment of the evolution and names of Rosh Hashanah see Jacobs, Louis. "Rosh Ha-Shanah." *Encyclopaedia Judaica.* Ed. Michael Berenbaum and Fred Skolnik. Vol. 17. 2nd ed. Detroit: Macmillan Reference USA, 2007. 463–466.

[2]
The Hebrew root **sh-n-h**, means to change or transform, the same letters that form the word for year, **Shanah.**

[3]
Elon Gilad, "How an Obscure Holiday Created by Ezra the Scribe Became Rosh Hashanah" Retrieved from: https://www.haaretz.com/jewish/holidays/roshhashanah/.premium-1.744821

[4]
Baraita, Rosh Hashanah 29b.

[5]
For a fuller treatment of his historical impact see Schechter, S. & Bacher, W. "Johanan B. Zakkai" in http://www.jewishencyclopedia.com/articles/8724-johanan-b-zakkai

[6]
See https://www.nytimes.com/2016/05/27/us/politics/donaldtrump-

global-warming-energy-policy.html,
http://www.npr.org/2017/04/13/523804487/trump-reverses-courseon-variety-of-key-economic-issues,
https://www.washingtonpost.com/politics/trump-and-race-decadesof-fueling-divisions/2017/08/16/

7

The Shalom Center, A Prophetic Voice in Jewish, Multi-religious and American Life https://theshalomcenter.org/

8

For a brief overview of Midrash and its importance see https://www.myjewishlearning.com/article/midrash-101/

9

According to the Hebrew calendar.

10

See *"Eicha* for the Earth" by Rabbi Tamara Cohen. *https://theshalomcenter.org/node/1733*

11

The Tetragrammaton, spelled either in Hebrew or in English transliteration (*YHWH*) contains no hard consonants, since the Hebrew letter *vav* (ו) was originally pronounced as a "W."

12

Thus, when vocalized with no vowels *YHWH,* and also its contraction *Yah* (as in *Hallelu-***Yah**), is the sound of Breathing Spirit. This then replaces the monarchical appellations referring to God as *Adonai* (usually translated "Lord") and *Melekh* (King).

The conclusion of this blessing highlights Rosh Hashanah as the Anniversary of Creation, *Yom Harat Olam,* whereas the traditional formulation, *Yom Ha-Zikaron,* stresses the festival as a Day of Remembrance.

13

Gen. 32:28 offers an etymology for the name Israel: Then the man said, "Your name will no longer be Jacob, but **Isra**el, because you have wrestled (***sarita***) with God and with humans and have prevailed." The translation of Israel as "Godwrestler" is both literally accurate and carries a more inclusive connotation ("whoever repudiates Idolatry is accounted a Jew [a member of Israel] *BT Megillah 13a).*

14

Gikatilla, J. *Sha'are Orah,* Gate 1: Sphere 10. see *Gates of Light.*

Weinstein, A. (trans.) Altamira Press, 1994, p. 13.

15

Buber, M. *I And Thou,* Kaufmann, W (trans.) Charles Scribner's Sons, 1970, p 57-59.

16

For a short description of the *Amidah* see https://www.myjewishlearning.com/article/the-amidah/.

17

Or Shalom: Songs of the Heart by Shir Hadash http://digital.library.upenn.edu/webbin/freedman/lookupartist?what=8844.

18

Martin Luther King, "Beyond Vietnam: A Time to Break Silence." (April 4, 1967: Riverside Church, New York) Retrieved from *http://www.hartford-hwp.com/archives/45a/058.html*

19

BT Sanhedrin 98b.

20

http://www.joannamacyfilm.org.

21

http://www.wearethebelovedcommunity.org/bcquotes.html.

22

Isaiah 58:1.

Imagining a Jewish Theology of Liberation

An Invitation

Mordechai Liebling

To be truly radical is to make hope possible
rather than despair convincing.

- Raymond Williams[1]

Let me state the goal of this essay from its outset. I write these words to hopefully initiate a conversation leading to the creation of a contemporary Jewish Liberation Theology, a theology that: inspires, strengthens and guides us in building a society that has a sustainable relationship with our living Earth, known as *Adamah* in Hebrew, *Gaia* in Greek; and that equally values every human being so that each would feel comfortable changing places with any other, knowing that neither would lose any opportunities.[2]

It is reasonable to ask why there needs to be a new Jewish theology of liberation; isn't that what the Exodus story is about? Aren't the prophets of the Hebrew Bible the quintessential fighters for justice? Isn't the whole purpose of the Torah to bring about a just society? The answer to all those questions is yes—and. God, as imaged in the Hebrew Bible, is not identical with God as understood by the medieval Jewish philosophers, Kabbalists or Hasidic masters and is certainly not identical with liberal Jewish understandings of the Divine today.

Within Judaism the prophetic tradition is the beacon of justice. However, the biblical tradition of prophecy was not a collective reflection, but the message of a personal God channeled through a charismatic person (with some exceptions, a man). It was God giving a clear message of what to do or not do. The prophets call the people to justice, to side with the poor, the widow, the orphan and the stranger. And . . . the last of the Hebrew prophets is Malachi who is generally thought to have been active in the fifth century BCE during the time of Ezra and Nehemiah, about 2,500 years ago.[3]

We can share in the faith of the prophets that working for justice is holy work that brings us closer to the Sacred, and we can call on the prophetic tradition for inspiration and values clarification. However, we, raised on the ideals of democracy, need to develop our own analysis of the actions needed today. Prophecy is neither democratic nor developed through dialogue. Collectively reflecting on how we might act justly in our own context will likely bring us to our own deeper understanding of God. That is not to say that there is no place for prophetic action. We still need individuals of courage and conscience speaking truth to power and calling us to our highest values. We also need large numbers of people willing to act in concert.

From my perspective, a contemporary Jewish theology of liberation will inspire people to act for a better world by offering a vision of how people can value themselves and each other, by reminding us to always look for the spark of divinity in our fellows and in all forms of life. Connecting us to Jewish history, tradition, values and ritual, it will provide a paradigm not of dominion and conquest but of "power with," of interconnection, love, cooperation with the Earth and one another and of strengthening our personal and collective relationship within the One.

A contemporary Jewish theology of liberation can provide us with spiritual sustenance to persevere over the "long haul" and to find hope amidst moments of despair. In truth, despair only colludes with those forces drawing power and profit from the inequities of our current system, immobilizing us during the current onslaught that threatens all forms of life. Instead let us attune hopefully to the Source of Life. Together let us bring forth a sacred narrative of a socially just, environmentally sustainable and spiritually fulfilling future, for the "stories" we tell and believe usually determine our deeds. The most important of cultural narratives is the "Big Story," the metanarrative that defines for its society what the sacred is. For those who would engage in the Jewish Liberation Theology dialogue, there can be no more pressing cause than formulating and articulating that metanarrative for today. This is especially true when voices arrogating to themselves the mantle of "Religious Values," of being "Pro Life," often justify regressive and divisive policies, which threaten human dignity and the life of the planet. Cloaking their positions in piety and selected biblical verses, some are even willing to betray long held positions on personal morality if it gains them influence and access to power. As David Korten has written, "when we get sacred wrong, we easily become entangled in a web of self-destructive, even suicidal, deceptions."[4] Therefore, let's begin the disentanglement now.[5]

Formational Biography

Since theology, like all forms of study, reflects a particular perspective, mine is that of a white, heterosexual, cis-gendered man, son of refugee Jewish Holocaust survivors from Poland, an anchor baby (before the term was invented) from a working class/lower middle-class family. I'm a remarried widower, able-bodied, with four adult children of my own, one of whom has Down syndrome, plus an adult stepson. I grew up in poor and working class neighborhoods in Brooklyn of the 1950s and 1960s. Going from there, on scholarship, to an Ivy League university gave me a visceral understanding of class. I have been an activist for over fifty years beginning with organizing against the war in Vietnam and continuing today with organizing around environmental justice and anti-oppression work. Along the way, I became a rabbi. All of these in some way inform my theology, my point of view.

In keeping with the principle that all theology arises from biography, let me start with a story about my parents, Joel and Zelda. They met in 1941 during the Soviet occupation of Poland. She was a college student, he a dentist, living in the town of Chortkov. When the Germans invaded, they forced the Jews into a ghetto, began random killings, then rounded up people to create a labor camp. Amid the degradation and upheaval, Joel and Zelda kept up their romance.

One day in early spring of 1943, the *Lagerführer* (Camp Commandant) had machine guns trained on everyone still alive and told them to lie down. He then called out about dozen people whose labor was still valuable, among them my father. It was clear that everyone else was to be killed. Lying there was my mother, her sister and my father's sister. My father approached the *Lagerführer* and asked, "Can my wife get up?" He replied, "That was a sudden marriage," and told my mother to get up. Everyone else was killed. That evening my parents escaped the camp; they lived in hiding for a year until being liberated by the Soviets. My father wrestled the rest of his life with the guilt of his sister's death and communicated the pain of that decision to me.

As the son of these two Holocaust survivors who both had lost their entire families, I could not believe in a supernatural, omnipotent, omniscient God. To this day I even hesitate to use the word "God" since it conjures traditional Jewish images and ideas culled from Christian societal norms far from what I believe and experience. As already demonstrated in this essay, I use the words Divine, Sacred, Mystery, Presence, One, *Shekhinah* (a Hebrew word in the feminine connoting the indwelling of the Divine), Life Force, Source of Life and Love interchangeably with "God."

Not surprisingly, I was estranged from Judaism from about age 14 until I was 30. I was a spiritual seeker sampling forms of Hinduism and Buddhism and an activist involved in combatting racism. One day, seemingly by chance, I came upon an essay by Dr. Mordecai M. Kaplan that changed my life. Rabbi Kaplan, founder of the Reconstructionist branch of Judaism, championed social justice while rejecting both the ideas of a "Chosen People" and of a supernatural God capable of choosing. He taught that God is a power that makes for salvation, and by salvation he meant freedom and justice.[6] Within a year I was studying to become a Reconstructionist rabbi.

Where was God in my parents' story? For me growing up, nowhere. Only with the wisdom of hindsight was I able to reframe that story and see it as the sacred act of heroism it was. My father risked his life to save my mother, the woman he loved. I exist because of that. Now, informed by Dr. Kaplan's theology and insights from my later teachers,[7] I can see my father's bravery as the Life Force flowing through him. He opened himself up to Love, to hope for the future. In that World of Darkness, he somehow believed that love would prevail; he went on to live another forty-five years as one of the most loving people I have ever met, celebrating life at every opportunity.

One more story: In my late twenties, I went backpacking with my friend, Ed, in Wyoming's Wind River Range, a spectacular section of the Rockies. We were off trail somewhere above 10,000 feet next to a clear, rushing sparkling stream tumbling down the mountainside. I expressed to Ed, a Christian who could trace his lineage back to colonial days, my feelings of separation from the land, from the earth, a child of Jewish refugees. He responded, "This is as much mine, as it is yours." I burst into tears.[8]

As the son of immigrants, I felt that this land, America, wasn't mine. On a deeper level, Judaism reshaped in two thousand years of Exile had become more a religion of time than of space.[9] In the absence of their own sovereign territory, Jews kept Judaism alive largely through set times for prayer and study, through sanctification of *Shabbat* and the Holy Days. In response to repeated forced exiles, the deeply Earth rooted Judaism of the Torah lost its connection to the land. While this connection was reclaimed in the Land of Israel by the Halutzim (early Zionist Pioneers), it lies mainly dormant in the largely urbanized Jewish Diaspora. This needs to change and, thankfully, is beginning to change.

Liberation Theology

In recent history, Liberation Theology has offered guidance on ways to be a religious activist for change. Drawing from a variety of liberation perspectives,[10] I suggest these are among the salient aspects of a theology of liberation:

- A commitment to acting for justice which precedes any articulation of philosophy or creed. Unlike centuries of doctrinal theology, the purpose of Liberation Theology is not to claim eternal truths or prove God's existence; its purpose is to bring about justice. It is reflection upon *praxis*, action, that leads to such a theology, not the other way around

- Any such theology must be embodied and contextual. While recognizing the interdependence of all life, it needs to be grounded in actual experience and rooted in particular times and places

- It is the oppressed whose status and treatment must be privileged. They must be the primary creators of the liberation narrative, birthed amid community through a dialogical process reflecting their perspective. One of its main goals: to increase self-respect and the sense of sacred self-worth among those subject to oppression.

Some of these assertions align easily with Jewish traditions concerning our relationship with God; others, at first glance, appear to be in tension. The idea of action preceding understanding reflects a rabbinic teaching that the Israelites

Seeking Redemption in an Unredeemed World

accepted the obligations of Torah before fully understanding them. This is the principle of *na•aseh v'nishmah*—first we will do and then we will understand.[11] This parallels Liberation Theology's tenet that our understanding of God comes from reflecting on the action(s) we take for justice. Note that the Hebrew *na•aseh v'nishmah* is formulated in the plural—both the action undertaken, and the understanding derived from further reflection are accomplished collectively. Common to Liberation Theology's reflective process is the study of relevant sacred texts that inform both the reflection and the next action step. All aspects of each action, its intention, means and consequences, must be fully considered to ensure a process of praxis worthy of its name.

A basic tenet of Liberation Theologies is that oppressed people receive preferential treatment. It is they, as the majority within their own group, who take the lead in developing the redemptive narrative born of their own experience. To many a Jewish ear this assertion of preference sounds closer to the Gospel's Beatitudes: Blessed are the poor...the meek... those who suffer (Matthew 5) than it does to the Torah's Holiness Code: ... *do not favor the poor nor defer to the rich; judge your people equitably* (Lev. 19:15). However, the Book of Proverbs reminds us: the heart knows its own bitterness and thus no outsider can *share in its celebration* (Proverbs 14:10). A rabbinic homily describes how Moses sent his father-in-law, Jethro, home from the Israelite camp prior to the giving of the Ten Commandments.[12] Despite his sage counsel and acknowledgement of God's liberating power, Jethro had been safe in Midian serving as its priest during Israel's enslavement in Egypt. Thus, he could not be a direct partner to the Covenant that emerged between God and Israel, whose redemptive narrative begins: *I, the Eternal your God, brought you out of Egypt, the Slave House* (Exodus 20:2).[13] Jethro's example reminds us that even the best intentioned, most loyal allies cannot presume to understand or articulate the direct experience of the oppressed or to formulate a theology born of their suffering.

While the North American Jewish community contains people of all races, classes, and gender identities, its majority is white, gender normative and middle class or wealthier. A significant number of poor or working class Jews belong to Orthodox or ultra-Orthodox communities, whose religious and social conservatism render them unlikely participants in developing any liberation theology.[14] Those who historically have formulated and identified with liberal Jewish theologies have most likely been Ashkenazi (of Western, Central or Eastern European descent), white, male, heterosexual, able bodied and of means (read: "the Empowered"). This raises some significant questions about the role of Jews who don't fall into those categories (i.e. Jews of Color, LGBTQ Jews, Jews of African and Asian descent) in developing a Jewish theology of liberation. To be in alignment with the principles of Liberation Theology don't they need to be prominent, if not taking the lead? How will the mainstream hear and respond to these Jews' own experiences of being marginalized within the North American Jewish community? Recognizing my current privileged status, this is, in large measure, why I present this essay as an invitation and outline rather than a formulation of Jewish Liberation Theology.

Of Antisemitism and Empowerment

No matter one's color, gender orientation or place of family origin, nearly all Jews are affected by antisemitism or "antiJewish Oppression," an interchangeable term: directly, if they experienced it themselves, or; indirectly through intergenerational trauma and/or learning about thousands of years of persecution. Jews internalize their oppression in the same manner as other oppressed groups.[15] At some deep level, Jews, especially those of Ashkenazi descent, fear for their survival, particularly in the face of resurgent neofascism here and around the world. Additionally, Jews still live within a culture of Christian hegemony, despite North America and Western Europe's growing trends towards secularization. Paul Kivel defines Christian hegemony as, "The everyday, systematic set of Christian values, individuals and institutions that dominate all aspects of US society. Nothing is unaffected."[16]

Jews have more work to do to understand how antisemitism and Christian hegemony have affected the ways we think about theology (including Liberation Theology), morality and our relationship to Earth. A Jewish theology of liberation must account for these two pervasive experiences if it is to help heal our wounds and promote creative Jewish survival, including a healthy remembering of the Holocaust. Such a remembrance needs to recognize that human barbarism has and continues to bring death and suffering to humanity and God's Creation throughout the world. It must continue to mark the ineffable horror of the Nazis exterminating one-third of world Jewry simply because they were Jews while reminding us of the most oft repeated commandment in the Torah: *Do not oppress the stranger, for you know the stranger's soul, having been strangers in the land of Egypt* (Exodus 23:9).[17]

One challenging component of any contemporary Jewish theology for justice and freedom is the issue of Israel/Palestine. The Exodus story was a key component for the early formulations of Liberation Theology, focusing on how God led the Israelites out of slavery and the revelation at Sinai. More recent voices reflecting on the ravages of colonialism, including those of Black Feminist (Womanist) theologians,[18] remind us that there is a second part to the story—the conquest of the land and the slaying of other nations, as recorded in the Book of Joshua. As Israel marks the seventieth anniversary of its independence, we as Jews need to come to grips with that part of our legacy as well.

In response to our history and immediate experience of oppression, our age-old ties to the land of Israel and the nationalist ethos of late nineteenth century Europe, Jews created the Zionist movement and eventually a state. That state, Israel, has been surrounded by hostile neighbors, including those who have launched wars and terror campaigns to destroy it. Israel has survived those wars, emerging today as a formidable military power in close alliance with the United States.

Our history of being oppressed, however, does not justify Jewish oppression of others. As of 2017 approximately 2.16 million Palestinians, composing 78.5% of the West Bank's population, live under conditions which the Israeli High Court of Justice itself has deemed as "occupation."[19] They have limited self-rule and face ongoing encroachment by Israeli settlements, while Israel maintains the authority over internal and external security.[20] In the spring of 2018, over one hundred demonstrators were killed by the Israeli army and over a thousand were injured at the Gaza-Israel border, yet Israel will only allow investigations by its own military. A Jewish theology of liberation and justice must advocate equally for justice, security and freedom for Jews and Palestinians; one can, and need not come at the expense of the other.

Our Contemporary Milieu

As indicated above, theology is born of biography; it is equally born of historical context. We are living in a rapidly changing, highly commodified society that is using up the Earth's resources at a rate far beyond replacement.[21] We are hurdling into the disasters of human-made climate change that are likely to lead to wide scale death for many life forms, possibly including *homo sapiens*.[22] Rapid technological change may well cause massive structural unemployment.[23] The current opioid epidemic—opioid overdose is the largest cause of death for people under fifty—is but one symptom of a collapsing society.[24] In addition, America still seems incapable of overcoming its racist heritage; any examination of statistical well-being will find people of color at the bottom.[25] Perhaps the greatest danger is the wealth and income gap that keeps growing.[26] Could democracy in the United States collapse? One could argue that it is currently threatened even before we face the great challenges that lie ahead.

Some might ask: if Liberation Theology is to reflect the experience of and increase self-respect among the oppressed, for whom would we write a contemporary Jewish Liberation Theology? Despite a measurable rise in antisemitic incidents,[27] we Jews still enjoy significant social and economic status in North America. However, in a world where everything is commodified, should we not address the stress, the toll on the spiritual and emotional wellbeing of all people's souls, including the privileged? If we aspire to fulfill Latter Isaiah's charge to be a "Light unto the Nations" (Isaiah 49:6) we must also take a more universal perspective. Amid our industrial growth, neoliberal, capitalist society where the division between the haves and have nots grows ever wider and the wellbeing of the planet grows ever more tenuous, large-scale public action has already begun in parts of the faith community.[28] As concerned Jews and activists, we need to further join in this great work, to engage in praxis -- action, reflection, action -- as we develop Judaism's own contemporary contributions to the theologies of liberation. A tradition that first proclaimed the One as Creator of us all and whose guiding tenet is *Tikkun Olam,* Repair of the

World, surely has a role to play in the development of new Liberation Theology.

Theological Fractals

From Plato through Descartes and beyond, Western culture has principally embraced a dualistic view of the world. In turn, classical Christianity has preached a pronounced dualism of body and spirit, good and evil, heaven and hell. Such thinking has often led to hegemonic binary thinking. Claiming all virtue and prerogatives for oneself while projecting only instrumental value, if not evil, upon the other can lead to religious justifications of oppression and extremism. It has also engendered cutthroat competition, domination, racism, oppressive patriarchy and an unbridled exploitation of the earth's resources.[29]

In recent decades, many Westerners have become more familiar with the non-dualistic views of existence embedded in Taoism, Hinduism and Buddhism.[30] The contemporary Buddhist teacher, Thich Nhat Hanh, refers to the inter-connection of all that is, as "Inter-being," and sees it as the foundation of any informed, contemporary theology.[31] From the latest discoveries in physics, biology and environmental science to the millennia old wisdom of indigenous peoples, we learn that nothing exists in isolation; everything is part of a system.[32] The system that we are a part of had its origins 14 billion years ago in the Big Bang. Everything is energy, composed of atomic particles that originated in the stars; to echo an old Joni Mitchell song, "we are stardust."[33] The Life Force manifest in and through evolution has brought us to "this moment. Consciousness or awareness has been gradually been made manifest through the evolution of life. Though human beings seem to be the furthest along in self-awareness, we should not assert that our species is the purpose or center of existence. The great lie of Western Civilization is that we are essentially separate beings. It is not possible for humans to live outside of community with others, be that other humans or the creatures with whom we share this planet. Perhaps foremost among my experiences of the Divine, I see God as the connective tissue of the universe.[34]

Rabbi Arthur Green, among others, has begun to articulate a non-dual Judaism grounded in the teachings of Jewish mysticism.[35] This panentheistic understanding of reality asserts that Divinity envelops, infuses and pervades all that is. The entire system of inter-being is a manifestation of the Divine and thus each new evolutionary development is yet another expression of the Source of Life. Evolution moves towards more complex life forms and greater awareness—the complexity and awareness are evident both in our bodies and social structures. Human beings participate in furthering evolution through imagination, creativity and cultivating awareness. We are probably the first life form that can take responsibility for consciously participating in evolution. As manifestations of the Source of Life, what is our responsibility to fourteen billion years of evolution that brought us here?

The first story about humans in Genesis is that of Adam and

Eve. After they eat the forbidden fruit God asks, "Ayekah—Where are you" (Gen. 3:9)? Classically, God was considered all-seeing and all-knowing. Thus "Ayekah" must be an existential rather than a spatial question, a call to responsibility. Judaism's foundational text first situates us in connection to all that is around us, for we are also formed from the earth; it then calls on us to take responsibility for our actions. From a panentheistic perspective, this call to responsibility is bound into the very fabric of Being. A bedrock principle of Judaism is that each human being is created in the image of God—b'tzelem Elohim—and thus deserving of equal dignity; indeed, a case has been made, grounded in Jewish texts, that all creatures are created in God's image.[36] Respect for the inherent dignity of each person, each creature, and all that is, remains a sound basis for working for justice.

Scholars have long pointed out that within the Torah there are two names for the Divine, each denoting a different set of aspects. We are first introduced to Elohim, the God of Creation, of the way things are, the God of Being. Later in the text, the Eternal, YHWH, the God of History, appears to Moses. This is the God that calls for us to bring about a world of justice, the world as it ought to be, of linear time, the God of Becoming. Rabbi Michael Lerner wrote that the genius of Judaism was incorporating both spirituality and ethics, Being and Becoming.[37] Despite Classical Judaism's embrace of dualism, it never went so far as to advocate a strict dichotomy between body and spirit.

If Divinity both envelops the world and exists in this world, of necessity, theology must be embodied, grounded in the lives of people, in their bodies, in their conduct, relationships and in their history. In response to the exhortation *You shall be holy people unto Me* (Exodus 22:31), the acerbic hasidic master, Mendel of Kotzk (d. 1859), reminded us that God has enough angels in heaven. The Holy One calls us to embodied sanctity here on Earth.[38]

Our ongoing, actual life is dependent on the Earth—food, air, water, our relationships to others—everyone we interact with to get the material and emotional necessities of life. In Genesis, humans are called *adam*, because we come from humus, *adamah*, the Earth. Rabbi Ellen Bernstein has carefully looked at the creation story in Genesis to illustrate how the original Jewish teachings understood our connection to all of life.[39] Our requirement to care for the Earth is evident in many biblical laws.

The rise of industrial society sanctioned the exploitation and resultant pollution of our natural environment. No other species systematically destroys its habitat. Theology must call us back to having a sustainable relationship with the world in which we exist, because the alternative is mass destruction.

The contemporary Jewish environmental movement is re-examining the Torah and bringing to the fore its rootedness in agricultural traditions. I am a lifelong urban dweller yet an important part of my spiritual life, of my experience of the

Source of Life, is in the natural world. I firmly believe that only an embodied theology will lead us to cultivate spiritual practices that connect us more deeply with the Earth. This can be a source of strength, guidance and well-being.

My teacher, Rabbi Jack Cohen,[40] taught that the miracle of Sinai was that a community created a covenant to establish a society based on the pursuit of justice. A community dedicated to Divine service is a community dedicated to making sure that everyone is taken care of and that there is a regular rebalancing of resources.[41] Unbridled Capitalism is a system that depends on endless growth, competition and values the accumulation of wealth of individuals over the well-being of a community. As Thomas Piketty[42] and others have shown, it inevitably leads to great disparities of wealth. As we move into the era of robotics with the threat of high levels of structural unemployment, a theology of justice recognizing the dignity of each person should move us to reimagine an economic system based on cooperation and a fair distribution of resources.

Finally, there is a common misapprehension that nondualism is amoral, that it blurs distinctions by asserting that Essential Being transcends good and evil. The teachings and action of Thich Nhat Hanh and the current Dalai Lama are but two examples of ways in which non-dual religion can move individuals to paths of love, compassion, right relations and right action. As represented by Taoism's Yin-Yang symbol, nondualism calls us to realize that what we perceive as light and darkness is not delineated by a sharp line; instead, they are complementary and interwoven, like breathing in and breathing out. Thus, no individual, action, movement or institution is totally pure, so devoid of shadow, that it is free from all self-serving motives or harmful impact. Nor, except for extreme sociopathy, is anything so bereft of light that it contains no inherent radiant spark which awaits recognition, amplification and redemption.[43]

Thus, nondualism calls us to approach others and ourselves with humility, compassion and curiosity. It takes us out of male-female, black-white, straight-queer, win-lose dichotomies that often justify injustice and oppression. Since the energy of domination, competition, patriarchy, racism and unbridled exploitation has long been dominant in Western civilization, nondualism calls us towards a rebalancing that would emphasize: "power with," cooperation, the enfranchisement and leadership of women and people of color and the preservation, indeed the restoration of the Earth. After all, healthy living systems move towards rebalance; the unhealthy wither and die.

Heart

Ultimately for a theology to have any import it must move our hearts. In many ways I still embrace the notion of my younger hippie days, that God is love and when we so guide our actions we are most in harmony with Spirit. It takes ongoing spiritual practice to cultivate the compassion and gratitude necessary to strengthen our hearts, guide our actions and calm our fears. We are happier when we feel loving towards the world; all too often that's something we sadly forget.

At the beginning of this essay, I expressed the hope that it might open a conversation leading to a new Jewish theology of liberation. I certainly don't have answers to all the questions such a discussion might raise; they can only be conceived and answered over time. In all humility, I have offered some initial thoughts based on a half-century of activism and dialogues with teachers, comrades and students. So, let's reflect together on a Jewish theology that will lead us to wise and compassionate action and inspire us to create communities of praxis through which we work together for the just, equitable and sustainable society of our highest aspirations. As the early Talmudic sage Hillel stated: If not now, when?[44]

ENDNOTES

1
Williams, R., *Resources of Hope: Culture, Democracy, Socialism.*
Recorded Books, Inc. 2016.
2
I want to thank the students in my class on Jewish Liberation Theology in Fall 2017 at the Reconstructionist Rabbinical College for being in dialogue with me about this.
3
A most thorough account of the prophetic tradition is found in: Heschel, A. J. *The Prophets.* Harper & Row, 1962.
4
Korten, D. Ecological Civilization and the New Enlightenment."
Tikkun, 32:4, 2017. pp. 17-24. doi:10.1215/08879982-4252947

5

The only explicitly Jewish title on this subject is Ellis, M. H. *Toward a Jewish Theology of Liberation*. Orbis Books, 1987.
Ellis does raise some important questions while providing certain useful critiques of immediate post-Holocaust Jewish theories. Since his writing doesn't apply the methodology of Liberation Theology to Jewish thought, our purposes differ. Therefore, I have respectfully chosen not to address his work in this essay.

6

Kaplan, M. M. *The Meaning of God in Modern Jewish Religion*. Wayne State University Press, 1994.

7

I would like to thank the teachers and thinkers whom I have liberally drawn from in developing these ideas, but who bear no responsibility for what I write: Ellen Bernstein, Arthur Green, Abraham Joshua Heschel, Mordecai M. Kaplan, Michael Lerner, Joanna Macy, Judith Plaskow, Jeff Roth, Zalman Schachter-Shalomi, Arthur Waskow, and Delores Williams. Let me also thank my friend, Howard Avruhm Addison, for his editing and help in "sourcing" this essay.

8

The irony of Ed's gracious but proprietary statement is not lost on me today, given that his forebears also immigrated to America from Europe, albeit a couple of centuries before mine.

9

Heschel, A. J. *The Sabbath: Its Meaning for Modern Man*. New York, NY: Farrar, Straus and Giroux, 2005.

10

I primarily draw on Latin American, Black, Womanist, Feminist and Eco-feminist theologies. A variety of sources on diverse expressions of Liberation Theology can be found at *http://liberationtheology.org/*

11

BT Shabbat 88a based on Exodus 24:7.

12

See Exodus 18: 24-27.

13

Retrieved from Ginzberg, L. *The Legends of the Jews Vol. III*. The Jewish Publication Society, 1968 (Fifth Impression) p 77 referring to Exodus 18:24-7

14

"A 'staggering' 61% of Jewish kids in New York City area are

Orthodox, new study finds" 13 June 2012
https://www.timesofisrael.com/new-study-reveals-ny-jewish-population-increasing-diversifying/

"On poverty in the Jewish community, about 19 percent of Jewish households are categorized as poor—defined by the survey as having an income under 150 percent of the federal poverty line. The number soars to 43 percent in Chasidic households." The results of a 2011 survey.

[15]
Alexander, J. C. (2013). *Trauma: A Social Theory*. Polity, 2013. Also, the field of epigenetics has now shown how trauma is passed on genetically from one generation to the next.

[16]
Kivel, P. *Living in the Shadow of the Cross: Understanding and Resisting the Power and Privilege of Christian Hegemony*. New Society Publishers, 2013. p 3.

[17]
BT Bava Metsia 59b. Ascribed to Rabbi Eliezer, the Torah "warns against the wronging of a ger (stranger) in thirty-six places; other say, in forty-six places."

[18]
Williams, D. S. *Black Theology in a New Key: Feminist Theology in a Different Voice*. Orbis Books, 1996.

[19]
HCJ 2056/04 Beit Sourik Village Council v. The Government of Israel. Retrieved from
http://elyon1.court.gov.il/Files_ENG/04/560/020/A28/04020560.A28.

The exact term used, "belligerent occupation," appears 22 times in the ruling.

[20]
CIA – The World Factbook: West Bank." Cia.gov. Retrieved *from en.wikipedia.org/wiki/Demographics_of_the_Palestinian_territories# cite_note-autogenerated1-8*

[21]
http://www.worldpopulationbalance.org/3_times_sustainable

[22]
https://www.theguardian.com/environment/2008/oct/29/

climatechane-endangeredhabitats

23

Campa, R, "Technological Growth and Unemployment: A Global Scenario Analysis." *Journal of Evolution and Technology* - Vol. 24 Issue 1 February, 2014 pp. 86-103.
Retrieved from *https://jetpress.org/v24/campa2.htm*

24

https://www.moveforwardpt.com/Resources/Detail/7-staggering-statistics-about-america-s-opioid-epi

25 *http://npc.umich.edu/publications/policy_briefs/brief16/ .*

26 *https://www.cbpp.org/research/poverty-and-inequality/a-guide-to-statistics-on-historical-trends-in-income-inequality.*

27

Abramson, A. "Anti-Semitic Attacks Rose Faster Last Year Than Any Time in Nearly 40 Years, ADL Says"
Retrieved from *http://time.com/5177193/anti-defamation-league-anti-semitismreport-2017/.*

28

The Reverend William Barber is calling for a moral vision and leading a multi-faith rebirth of the Poor People's Campaign. There are four large networks of faith-based community organizing groups, with estimates that as many as 20,000 churches, mosques and synagogues are involved.

29

This is not to say that Asian civilization has been totally free of such evils, but here we are concerned with developing a theology for North American Jews who share in both the blessings and the shortcomings of Western Culture.

30

Additionally, none of these Asian traditions have been totally immune to the curse of militant ethnic exclusivism as witnessed by the Myanmar Buddhist persecution and slaughter of the Muslim Rohingyas or the Hindu/Muslim violence in Kashmir.

31

Hanh, Thich Nhat, *Essential Writings of Thich Nhat Hanh.* Orbis, 2001.

32

Macy, J. *Mutual Causality in Buddhism and General Systems Theory.* State University of New York Press, 1991.

33

Lyric from "Woodstock," Mitchell, J. *Ladies of the Canyon*, Reprise:

March, 1970.

[34]
    Swimme, B. T. & Tucker, M. E. *The Journey of the Universe:* Yale University Press; Reprint Edition, 2014.

[35]
    Green, A. *Radical Judaism: Rethinking God and Tradition.* Yale University Press, 2010.
    Michaelson, J. *Everything is God: The Radical Path of Nondual Judaism.* Trumpeter, 2009.

Non-Duality is a continuing feature of Islamic Sufi mysticism. Cynthia Bougeault, an Episcopal priest, is a leading contemporary theologian of Christian Non-Duality.
See www.*garrisoninstitute.org/blog/cynthiabourgeault-christian-nonduality/*

[36]
    Seidenberg, D. A. *Kabbalah and Ecology.* Cambridge Univ. Press, 2016.

[37]
    Lerner, M. *Jewish Renewal: A Path to Healing and Transformation.* G.P. Putnam's Sons, 1994.

[38]
    Retrieved Friedman, A.Z., *Wellsprings of Torah: An Anthology of Biblical Commentaries.* Judaica Press, 1990, p 157.

[39]
    Bernstein, E. *The Splendor of Creation: A Biblical Ecology.* Cleveland: Pilgrim Press, 2005.

[40]
    Rabbi Dr. Jack Cohen (d. 2012) was an early disciple of Mordecai Kaplan. He served as Honorary Chairman at the Kaplan Center for Jewish Peoplehood and as director of the Hillel Foundation at the Hebrew University for 23 years.

[41]
    The laws of *Sh'mita* (seven-year cycle) and of the Jubilee Year (fifty-year cycle) call for debt forgiveness, the freeing of Hebrew slaves and eventually the rebalancing of land ownership.

[42]
    Piketty, T. (2014). *Capital in the Twenty-First Century.* Goldhammer, A (trans.) Belknap Press, 2014.

Kabbalah refers to this marginalized realm of the irredeemable as the *Sitra Achra,* "The Other Side." Kabbalistic imagery portrays sparks of divinity scattered throughout the world, (seemingly) encased by shells of worldly reality, awaiting redemption by us through intentionality and sacred action.

Psychologically, Carl Jung indicated that each of us possesses a "Shadow," the repository of unacknowledged and disowned aspects of ourselves. Much of the "Shadow" contains resources that can spark future creativity. Only a small proportion is irredeemable, but the "Shadow" grows ever darker and more dangerous if not acknowledged as part of oneself and consciously integrated.

For an accessible digest of Jung's psychology of the "Shadow" see *https://academyofideas.com/2015/12/carl-jung-and-the-shadow-thehidden-power-of-our-dark-side/*

44

Ethics of the Fathers 1:14.

Contributors

Howard Avruhm Addison serves as the Graduate Theological Foundation's Gershom Scholem Professor of Jewish Spirituality and directs its Jewish Spirituality Doctor of Ministry program. An Associate Professor for Instruction at Temple University, he earned his MA at Hunter College before pursuing post-graduate study in Philosophy at Fordham University. He was awarded his DMin by the Chicago Theological Seminary and completed his PhD at the Graduate Theological Foundation. Ordained by the Jewish Theological Seminary, he served in the active rabbinate for over forty years.

A founding teacher of North America's first Jewish Spiritual Direction training institute, *Lev Shomea* ("A Hearing Heart"), Rabbi Addison is certified as an Enneagram teacher (Palmer/Daniels), as a Dreamwork Leader (Haden Institute) and as a Shalem Institute Fellow in Contemplative Group Leadership. A member of the Haden Institute's faculty, Avruhm has lectured and presented workshops across North America, Israel and Australia; he also serves as a spiritual director and dream guide to seekers in the United States, Canada and South Africa. He is the author of *The Enneagram and Kabbalah:*

Reading Your Soul, Cast in God's Image; Show Me Your Way: The Complete Guide to Exploring Interfaith Spiritual Direction; and co-editor of *Jewish Spiritual Direction.* He can be reached at *Rabbia363@gmail.com.*

AUTHORS

Barbara Eve Breitman earned an MSW at the University of Pennsylvania and served for a decade as an Advanced Practice Instructor in its Graduate School of Social Work. She completed her DMin at the Graduate Theological Foundation and has taught at the Reconstructionist Rabbinical College (RRC) for twenty-three years as Assistant Professor of Pastoral Care. There she cofounded the Spiritual Direction program and has been its supervisor since the program's inception in 1999. Currently she is helping to launch RRC's *B'khol D'rakhekha Da·eihu* ("In All Your Ways Know God") Spiritual Direction training.

A founding teacher of *Lev Shomea*, the first institute to train spiritual directors in the Jewish tradition, she aided in developing Boston Hebrew College's *Ikvotecha* ("Your Footsteps") Spiritual Direction program for rabbinical students and helped create the Hebrew Union College-Jewish Institute of Religion's Spiritual Direction program in New York, including its *Bekhol Levavkha* ("With all Your Heart") two-year Spiritual Direction training. A Licensed Clinical Social Worker (LCSW), Dr. Breitman has been a psychotherapist in private practice for thirty years, after a decade working at Philadelphia's Jewish Family and Children Service. She is coeditor of *Jewish Spiritual Direction: An Innovative Guide from Traditional and Contemporary Sources* and a contributor to *A Mensch Among Men; Lifecycles vol. 2; Jewish Pastoral Care;* and *Chapters of the Heart.* Bobbi can be reached at *Bahirachava@aol.com.*

Julie Leavitt is a dancer, spiritual director and psychotherapist. Dr. Leavitt has served on the faculty of the *Lev Shomea* Institute for Training Spiritual Directors in the Jewish Tradition and currently offers spiritual direction to students at The Rabbinical School of Hebrew College in Boston, Massachusetts, as well as through her private practice. She is a visiting instructor at California's *Embodying Spirit, En-spiriting Body Institute,* directed by Rabbi Diane Elliot. She has served as an instructor of Dance/Movement therapy at Lesley University for thirty years. Julie has taught dance and body-centered Jewish spirituality at a variety of spiritual retreat centers, including *Elat Chayyim,* Isabella Freedman and other venues. She holds a Bachelor of Arts from Macalester College, a Master of Arts from Lesley University, and a Doctor of Ministry from the Graduate Theological Foundation.

Dr. Leavitt is a longtime student of Authentic Movement, an embodied spiritual/mystical/playful practice, which she learned from her distinguished teacher, Janet Adler. Julie's unique synthesis of Authentic Movement and Spiritual Direction is both described and visually portrayed in her doctoral project, *Embodied Jewish Spiritual Direction* (Graduate Theological

Foundation, 2014) for which she was awarded the Rabbi Samuel Cohen Prize in Jewish Studies. She can be reached at *injewel1@gmail.com*.

Herbert Levine was educated at Harvard and Princeton, earning his PhD in English and American Literature. His career has encompassed teaching, scholarship and organizational leadership. Dr. Levine currently teaches three groups of students through the Center for Contemporary Mussar, through the ALEPH Ordination Program, and as a Professor of Jewish Spirituality at the Graduate Theological Foundation. He is the author of *Words for Blessing the World: Poems in Hebrew and English* (Ben Yehuda Press, 2017), *Sing Unto God A New Song: A Contemporary Reading of Psalms* (Indiana University Press, 1995) and *Yeats's Daimonic Renewal* (UMI Press, 1983). Among his many articles, two on Whitman's "Song of Myself" have been reprinted in an anthology edited by Harold Bloom. Herb is a founding Board member of the Center for Contemporary Mussar.

Mordechai Liebling, Professor of Jewish Spirituality at the Graduate Theological Foundation, specializes in teaching the Ethics of Money and Food Justice. Ordained by the Reconstructionist Rabbinical College (RRC), he holds a BA from Cornell University and a MA from Brandeis University, having specialized in the history of American progressive movements.

The founding director of RRC's pioneering Social Justice Organizing Program, Rabbi Liebling has long recognized the unique power of spiritual leaders to inspire ethical choices and pursue justice through caring, not rage. A former community organizer, he served twelve years as Executive Director and later as Senior Consultant to the Jewish Reconstructionist Federation; in those capacities he was a member of the Conference of Presidents of Major Jewish Organizations. He formerly directed the Shefa Fund's "Torah of Money" initiative and was Executive Vice President of the Jewish Funds for Justice.

Mordechai currently serves on the Faith and Politics Institute and *T'ruah* boards and is President Emeritus of The Shalom Center. He has received awards from the Reconstructionist Rabbinical Association, the Interfaith Center for Corporate Responsibility and Mazon. An advocate of justice for people with disabilities, Rabbi Liebling's family was the subject of the award-winning documentary film *Praying With Lior.* You may contact Mordechai at *MLiebling@rrc.edu.*

James Michaels, DMin, is a Fellow of the Graduate Theological Foundation, where he serves as Rabbi A. Stanley Dreyfus Professor of Jewish Studies and Mentor in Jewish Pastoral Care. He recently retired as the Director of Pastoral Care at the Charles E. Smith Life Communities in Rockville, Maryland. Born in Auburn, New York, he received his Bachelor of Arts from Cornell University in 1968 and was ordained and received his Master of Arts in Hebrew Letters from the Hebrew Union College-Jewish Institute of Religion in New York in 1974.

Rabbi Michaels has served in pulpits in Whitestone, New York;

Wilkes-Barre, Pennsylvania; and Flint, Michigan. He received his Doctor of Ministry in pastoral counseling from the Graduate Theological Foundation in 2006, with a specialization in bereavement counseling. He became a board-certified chaplain in 2005 and was certified as a CPE supervisor in 2007. Jim co-edited *Flourishing in the Later Years: Jewish Perspectives on Long-Term Pastoral Care* (Mazo Publishers, 2012). He is married to Karen Markowitz Michaels, DPharm. You may contact Jim at *Rabbijim1718@verizon.net.*

Simcha Paull Raphael, PhD, is Founding Director of the DA'AT Institute for Death Awareness, Advocacy and Training. Originally from Montreal, Canada, he studied History and Philosophy of Religion at Sir George Williams University (BA, 1972) and Concordia University (MA, 1975). Reb Simcha received his doctorate in Psychology from the California Institute of Integral Studies (1986) and was ordained as a Rabbinic Pastor by Rabbi Zalman Schachter-Shalomi (1990). He is Adjunct Professor in Religion at LaSalle University, and serves on the faculty of the New York Open Center's Art of Dying Institute and the Graduate Theological Foundation's Jewish Spirituality Program. He works as a psychotherapist and spiritual director, affiliated with Mount Airy Counseling Center in Philadelphia, and is also a Fellow of the Rabbis Without Borders network.

For over three decades, Dr. Raphael's work has focused on death awareness education and bereavement counseling, and he has spoken at Orthodox, Conservative, Reform,

Reconstructionist, and Renewal synagogues, as well as churches and social service agencies in the United States, Canada, England, and Israel. He is author of numerous publications on death and afterlife, including the groundbreaking *Jewish Views of the Afterlife*. His website is *www.daatinstitute.net*.

Charlotte Sutker is a Registered Psychologist who incorporates Spiritual Direction in her private practice. She holds a Master of Arts degree and earned her DMin at the Graduate Theological Foundation. A member and Past President of Congregation Emanuel in Victoria, British Columbia, Canada, she initiated both its Simcha Gift Shop and Shalom Art Gallery. A coordinator of annual Jewish Women's retreats, she has taught *Ḥeshbon b'Nefesh* (lit. "Soul Accounting") classes and organized Women's *Mikveh* Immersions in the Pacific Ocean in preparation for the High Holy Days.

For over twenty years, Charlotte has lead *Tallit* (prayer-shawl) making workshops which have led to the crafting of over one hundred *tallitot* (pl.). Honored with the Ralph Berer Community Service Award, she was initiated into an international community of Jewish women as an *Eishet Ḥay·il* (Woman of Valor). In the Jewish Renewal world, she served on the inaugural ALEPH Ethics Committee for eleven years, the last four as its Chair.

A Jew by Choice and a practicing Jew for forty years, it was her own recollections of a past life during the Holocaust era that led her to research the issue of Jews by Choice and their sense of experiencing reincarnation. When she is not in the city, Charlotte is in the woods by the ocean at her beloved cabin, communing with God. You may reach her at *charlotte.sutker@gmail.com.*

Arthur Waskow, Professor of Jewish Social and Ecological Justice at the Graduate Theological Foundation, earned his PhD from the University of Wisconsin and received rabbinic ordination from Rabbi Zalman Schachter-Shalomi. He has served as a US Congressional legislative assistant and as a Fellow at both Washington DC's Institute for Policy Studies and Public Resource Center. During that time, he wrote seven books on US public policy and was elected as an antiwar, antiracist delegate from the District of Columbia to the 1968 Democratic National Convention.

Since writing the original *Freedom Seder* in 1969, Rabbi Waskow has been among the leaders of the Jewish Renewal Movement. He founded *The Shalom Center* in 1983 and has served as Director since its inception. His twenty-four books include: *Seasons of Our Joy; Godwrestling—Round 2; Down-to-Earth Judaism;* and, with his wife, Rabbi Phyllis Berman: *A Time for Every Purpose Under Heaven;* and *Freedom Journeys: Tales of Exodus and Wilderness across Millennia.*

In 2016, Arthur was named by *The Forward* as one of America's most inspiring rabbis. *T'ruah:* The Rabbinic Call for Human Rights, honored him with its first Lifetime Achievement Award as a Human Rights Hero. In 2017, he was awarded an Honorary

Doctorate of Humane Letters by the Reconstructionist Rabbinical College. He may be contacted through The Shalom Center Website, *theshalomcenter.org.*

Elyssa Wortzman, DMin, LLB, is a spiritual director, educator and artist located in Montreal and San Francisco working in the field of applied or practical spirituality. Recent publications on Dr. Wortzman's methodology and work include: "Process Theology, Aesthetics, Halakhah and Spiritual Development Through Art" in *Foundation Theology,* a series of the Graduate Theological Foundation, and "The Role of Mindful, Art-Making in Jewish Dialogical Spiritual Education" in *New International Studies on Religions and Dialogue in Education*, a new volume published by the Waxmann Verlag in Germany in their series entitled "Research on Religious and Spiritual Education," under the editorship of Martin Ubani. Elyssa recently spoke at the Spiritual Directors International Conference (Toronto) and conducted workshops at *Limmud* (San Francisco). She works as a consultant to educators and religious communities and is the Director of Education and Applied Spirituality at *Panui.* See *www.elyssawortzman.com.*

JEWISH SPIRITUALITY PROGRAM

Graduate Theological Foundation

The Jewish Spirituality program of the Graduate Theological Foundation (GTF) offers graduate level educational opportunities to those providing spiritual leadership both within the Jewish community and beyond. Rabbi Howard Avruhm Addison is Gershom Scholem Professor of Jewish Spirituality at the GTF and directs its Jewish Spirituality Doctor of Ministry program.

The GTF offers a Doctor of Ministry degree in Jewish Spirituality. The D.Min. acknowledges the students' proficiencies and experience, attesting to leadership and expertise in their chosen contemplative, pastoral or communal specializations. The curriculum, which will be tailored to fit students' specific needs, focuses on the refinement of applied skills and the pursuit of advanced professional and academic study. These educational goals are accomplished through thoughtful selection, skillful mentoring, and the flexibility of the GTF model.

The many areas of study include Jewish Pastoral Care, Jewish Meditation, Jewish Spiritual Direction, End-of-Life and Bereavement Care, and Jewish Social and Ecological Justice. Courses in Jewish Spirituality include, but are not limited to:

- *Journeys in Jewish Spirituality*
- *Afterlife and Eschatology in Judaism and World Religions*
- *Chapters of the Heart: The Power and Perils of Spiritual Autobiography*
- *Contemporary Psychological Approaches to Bereavement*
- *Death, Burial and Mourning in the Hebrew Bible*
- *Eco-Judaism: The Theology & Practice of Jewish Responses to Ecological Crises, Past & Present*
- *End-of-Life Counseling and Hospice Care*
- *Feminist Transformations of Judaism: A Twenty-first Century Perspective*
- *Jewish Rituals of Death and Dying*
- *Jewish Views of the Afterlife I: Immortality and Eschatology in Biblical and Rabbinic Tradition*
- *Jewish Views of the Afterlife II: Mythic and Mystical Teachings on the Post-Mortem Journey of the Soul*
- *Prayer as if the Earth Really Matters*
- *The Psalms and Jewish Spirituality*
- *Spiritual Guidance, Sexuality and the Divine Erotic*
- *Spirituality and Dreams*
- *The Spirituality of the Twelve Steps*
- *Tending the Divine Spark: A Contemporary Approach to Supervision*

For more information on the GTF, please visit the website at *www.gtfeducation.org*. For details on the Jewish Spirituality program, please visit the program's webpage at *www.gtfeducation.org/academics/jewish-spirituality*.